Homeland Security Scams

Homeland
Security
Scams

WITHDRAWN

James T. Bennett

Transaction Publishers
New Brunswick (U.S.A.) and London (U.K.)

Library of Congress Catalog Number: 2006044694
ISBN: 0-7658-0334-8
Printed in the United States of America

Library of Congress Cataloging-in-Publication Data

Bennett, James T.
    Homeland security scams / James T. Bennett.
        p.   cm.
    Includes bibliographical references and index.
    ISBN 0-7658-0334-8 (alk. paper)
        1. United States. Dept. of Homeland Security. 2. Internal security—
United States. 3. Civil rights—United States. 4. War on Terrorism, 2001-
I. Title.

HV6432.4.B45   2006
363.340973—dc22   2006044694

Contents

Acknowledgements

I am grateful to many for their assistance with and support of the research and editing of this book. The research would not have been possible without the generous financial support of the Sunmark Foundation and help from the Locke Institute. Research assistance was provided by Anthony Evans, Ninos Malek, and Brian R. Rooney. I also owe profuse thanks to my editor, Bill Kauffman, for I am indebted to him for significant contributions to this study.

James T. Bennett
George Mason University

Fairfax, Virginia

1

Introduction: Pork Has a New Name

"[P]rior to September 11th, if somebody had mentioned the term homeland security at one of our town-hall meetings, most people would have thought they were talking about a savings-and-loan association,"[1] remarked Rep. Bob Barr (R-GA) at a hastily scheduled June 20, 2002 congressional hearing on the proposed Department of Homeland Security.

Barr was very soon to be an ex-congressman. His skepticism over aspects of the Bush administration's war on terrorism earned him a party-line Republican primary opponent who sent one of the handful of independent-minded congressmen back home—or, more accurately, into consulting, which is what passes for "home" to most of our federal lawmakers.

Barr's point, though, is one that has been ignored in the "homeland security" frenzy of post-9/11 America. Just what is "homeland security"? What, an American may be excused for asking, is the "homeland"? The term, with its echo of "fatherland," has the unsavory odor of German fascism and Stalinist Russia. As the *Capital Times* of Madison, Wisconsin, cogently noted, "Americans have never used the word 'homeland' to describe their country"[2] and the many thousands of towns, villages, streets, states, and postage stamps of grounds therein. Homeland security—the very word—is, literally, un-American.

The leftist writer Douglas Valentine has charged that "Homeland security is a euphemism for internal security,"[3] and given the alternately spendthrift and repressive provisions of the Homeland Security Act, he is not wrong. But that is not the half of it.

For homeland security is developing into the largest boondoggle in the history of the U.S. government. Fed by the associated "war on terror," homeland security is being used as an excuse, as an irrefutable justification, for a vast expansion of government power and spending. This spending is often on matters far removed from anything that might be termed "defense" under even the most charitable definition.

Even those federal dollars going toward apparently legitimate anti-terror initiatives are disbursed in the most downright pork-barrel fashion. They flow into counties, programs, and departments that face no imaginable threat from bin Laden, bioterrorists, or the rest of the new rogue's gallery that is being used to justify this vast expansion of state power. "Homeland security" is not making us safer: just poorer, less free, and more dependent on the federal government.

While some have warned, not without cause, that "homeland security" is the American phrase for what the nations of the communist bloc used to call "internal security," it may be closer to the mark to say that homeland security is the most effective combination of words ever devised to disguise the pork barrel. Even more effectively than that hoary piece of cant "for the children," which is how vast stretches of the welfare and social services bureaucracies explain their mission, "homeland security" is—for now—a fail-safe way of forcing taxpayers to pony up for your favorite government program. Just try speaking in opposition to appropriations for homeland security: You'll be pegged as a bin Laden disciple, an al Qaeda plant, a fanatical and deeply unpatriotic hater of fire fighters. Across the heartland, fire chiefs and police chiefs and emergency medical crews—people who do good, vital work—have found themselves deluged by homeland security manna from Washington. Some have refused the bounty, protesting that it is quite unnecessary; others spend it every way they can, on armed vehicles to protect shopping malls, gas masks for police officers whose towns are smaller than Mayberry RFD, and bio-hazard suits for Podunk emergency personnel who will never have to pick up anything more toxic than a week-old burrito. The money is pouring into the provinces so fast that overwhelmed local officials can't spend it swiftly enough: North Carolina spent only 30 percent ($64.7 million of $217.4 million) of the federal homeland security monies it had received through 2004.[4]

The Bush administration has defined this protean term this way: "Homeland security encompasses those activities that are focused on combating terrorism and occur within the United States and its territories. Such activities include efforts to detect, deter, protect against and, if needed, respond to terrorist attacks."[5]

To this end, President Bush and the vast majority of Congress supported the creation of the Department of Homeland Security, the first new cabinet department since Veterans Affairs rose to that exalted status in 1989. The DHS was born full-grown, one might say: it was melded from twenty-two federal agencies employing more than 170,000 persons—and that was only its base. New agencies, new tasks, new offices have arrived every fiscal year. As Professor Donald F. Kettl wrote in a review of the Department of Homeland Security's first year, "unlike what happened in previous reorganizations, all of the agencies took on new and expanded homeland security responsibilities."[6]

The seemingly ageless West Virginia Democratic Senator Robert Byrd asked, "How is it that the Bush administration's No. 1 priority has evolved into a plan to create a giant, huge bureaucracy? How is it that Congress bought into the belief that to take a plethora of federal agencies and shuffle them around would make us safer from future terrorist attacks?"[7]

Good questions. But when Pork Barrel Bobby Byrd becomes the voice of fiscal sanity, we're in big trouble.

In his groundbreaking book, *Terrorism and Tyranny*, the investigative journalist James Bovard has written that "the war on terrorism is the first political growth industry of the new millennium."[8] It shows no signs of abating—whichever party is in power.

Under President George W. Bush, the Republicans have become the party of Big Government. Or at least they are trying to, though they find their path to that dubious mantle blocked at every step by the Democrats, whose chief complaint against the homeland security apparatus is that it is inadequately funded.

And hanging over our heads every single day of our modern American lives is the prophesy, as paraphrased by the *Pittsburgh Post-Gazette*, of the first Homeland Security Secretary Tom Ridge: "Even under the best of circumstances, a new attack by al Qaeda or another terrorist group is inevitable."[9]

Ridge assumed his job with no experience in the field, but then once upon a time "homeland security," though it is a new and unfamiliar locution, might have been considered synonymous with "national security." At what point "national security" came to exclude the protection of the United States is a question oddly unasked in the current debate.

Since September 11, we have sunk hundreds of billions of additional dollars into what President Dwight D. Eisenhower so presciently warned us against: the military-industrial complex.

Eisenhower's Farewell Address of January 17, 1961, remains one of the most extraordinary (if neglected) documents of our times. It is second only to Washington's Farewell Address as the greatest presidential valediction. Eisenhower, who had seen firsthand the growth of a government-subsidized defense industry, warned his countrymen that a vast "military-industrial complex" was inconsistent with liberty and republican government. He said:

> During the years of my Presidency, and especially the latter years, I began to feel more and more uneasiness about the effect on the nation of tremendous peacetime military expenditures.
>
> . . . Under the spur of profit potential, powerful lobbies spring up to argue for even larger munitions expenditures. And the web of special interests grows. . . . In the long run, the combinations of pressures for growth can create an almost overpowering influence. Unjustified military spending is nothing more than a distorted use of the nation's resources. . . .
>
> We annually spend on military security more than the net income of all U.S. corporations.
>
> This conjunction of an immense military establishment and a large arms industry is new in the American experience. The total influence—economic, political, even spiritual—is felt in every city, every state house, every office of the federal government. We recognize the imperative need for this development. Yet we must not fail to comprehend its grave implications. Our toil, resources, and livelihood are all involved; so is the very structure of our society.
>
> In the councils of government we must guard against the acquisition of unwarranted influence, whether sought or unsought, by the military-industrial complex. The potential for the disastrous rise of misplaced power exists and will persist.
>
> We must never let the weight of this combination endanger our liberties or democratic processes. We should take nothing for granted. . . .[10]

Today, almost forty-five years later, after sexual, technological, and political revolutions that have supposedly carried us far beyond the stodgy Eisenhower decade, any politician using such language would be confined to the fringes of American debate. Eisenhower's penultimate paragraph in this excerpt, with its very conscious echo of George Washington, would be enough to put him on a surveillance list at the Department of Homeland Security. In an age of big-government Republicans like Bush and Cheney and Ridge, Ike's is a voice of American radicalism.

"Military-industrial complex?" replies the homeland security crowd. "What military-industrial complex?" Or, more candidly, "Sure, there's a military-industrial complex. It keeps us free. Come and get your contracts, boys. . . ."

Do I exaggerate? Tom Ridge, secretary of Homeland Security, endorses the complex. As he says, "We look to American creativity to help solve our problems and to help make a profit in the process."[11] This "creativity," you understand, is not the result of the free play of market forces, of the happy intersection of hard work, inspiration, and the free exchange of goods and services, but rather it results from the subsidization of "creativity" by the federal government, and the application of this "creativity" to ever-more intrusive government programs.

If Americans have not entirely let their proud heritage crumble into the dust, they will reject such tyrannical assumptions. And they will begin looking at "homeland security," heretofore an unassailable sacred cow, with an eye that is at once skeptical and patriotic. They will act in the knowledge and the confidence that liberty is our birthright.

At the outset, to avoid confusion or misunderstanding, it is critical to emphasize that the primary function of every government is the protection of its citizens from aggression. Every nation has the fundamental right, indeed, the necessity and obligation, to defend itself and its citizens from terror and malicious assault. To even suggest otherwise is tantamount to throwing out the proverbial baby along with the bathwater. Mocking or degrading a nation's efforts to defend its citizens from hostile actions makes a mockery of self-defense. Homeland security is not only a worthy undertaking, but it is also essential in the increasingly uncertain contemporary world.

Having said that, however, it is also self-evident that no government can protect its citizens from every threat. Such an undertaking is both a technical and financial impossibility; so risks are inevitable. Irving Louis Horowitz, in his insightful essay, "The Texture of Terrorism: Socialization, Routinization, and Integration," has stated the matter perceptively and succinctly:

> Risk is part of the nature of the democratic system—to permit modes of behavior that are uncontrolled and experimental. What needs disaggregation, especially in terms of personal liberties, is society's willingness to respond to an immediate and dangerous threat with its capacity to build a social order that can absorb a certain level of risk while expanding its democratic potential. In short, to maintain an equilibrium between the passion for order and the compassion needed to instill change.... The ability to absorb some quanta of terrorism, like some protest violence, is a sign of a society's acceptance of the costs of liberty. It is also a measure of the citizenry's internalization of democratic norms, i.e., of its political socialization for democracy. And tough trade-offs are what characterize thriving open societies.[12]

Given that total protection from all threats is not possible, the tough trade-offs to which Horowitz refers must be made. This book is about those trade-offs and the way that governments at different levels have addressed homeland security issues. There is no question of the need for homeland security to combat terrorism.

First, there is evidence that some of the trade-offs between civil liberties and security have not been wisely made. For example, in a rush to "do something" about terrorism, Congress gave federal agents the authority to secretly question librarians about readership of books. But does anyone seriously believe that a terrorist contemplating mayhem would be so naïve as to check out a book that can be easily tucked under a jacket and taken without leaving a paper trail? This authority, which reduces civil liberties, is unlikely to do anything to reduce terrorism, but may well have unintended consequences that can exacerbate terrorism in the long run. Law-abiding citizens, such as researchers and students of terrorism, may be reluctant to check out and read certain books because doing so could potentially subject them to unwanted attention by government agents. Who needs that hassle? So, research and studies on terrorism could be adversely affected by such a law.

Second, homeland security, based on the "War on Terror," is being used to justify a huge expansion of government powers and spending, and these funds are often for programs far removed from anything that might be termed "defense" or "security" even under the most charitable definitions of those terms. Billions of taxpayers' dollars are flowing to state, county, and city governments that face no imaginable threat from anyone who might reasonably be called a "terrorist." Much of the homeland security initiative is doing little to make us safer, but a great deal to make us poorer, less free, and more dependent on the federal government.

Third, the primary beneficiaries of the homeland security are politicians, lobbyists, and a flourishing homeland security industry. Regardless of the color of the "security alert" issued by the Homeland Security czar, the spending light is always bright green, as pork barrel dollars are showered on programs of dubious worth. The vicious circle gets ever more vicious: lobbyists lobby for homeland secur-ity grants and contracts; corporations and state and local governments become more dependent on federal subsidies; the vested interest in prolonging and intensifying the home-land security "crisis" increases; and the lobbyists press for ever more money. Between January 2002 and June 2003, the number of registered lobbyists in the antiterrorism field increased by more than 500 percent, and the number of companies using the words "homeland," "security," or "terror" on their lobbyists' registration forms went from 157 to 569—the spendathon is on!

Fourth, with government money comes government controls. The nation's law enforcement and emergency response agencies at all levels of government are being effectively "nationalized." Police power is being concentrated, and the Department of Homeland Security (DHS) envisions a virtual "surveillance" state. Massive dossiers on the spending, travel, and health records of Americans and their communications with others are to be monitored, analyzed, punched, folded, stapled, and mutilated as never before in name of fighting terrorism.

Finally, despite all the spending and surveillance, the "War on Terror" cannot be won, because the foe cannot be beaten (we're having trouble even finding the enemy), cannot surrender, and can be characterized as having awesome powers to lay waste to American cities and citizens. The one constant is *fear*, which keeps the government spending pork barrel wide open and fully stocked. However, according to the U.S. State Department, in the two decades between 1980 and 2000, more people died of carbon monoxide poisoning each year than from terrorist activities throughout the world. Terrorism is just one of many other—and far more serious— threats to individuals and to nations. The "War on Terror" is also a "War on Privacy" and a "War on Liberty."

As Horowitz observes, we must accept risks and put them into perspective, weighing with extraordinary care the trade-offs between security and civil liberties. We must not dismantle the Homeland Security initiatives or repudiate its goals, but attempt to maintain economic equilibrium and political balance. Although corruption, waste, and pork barrel spending have, to some extent, always been associated with government spending, the excesses associated with Homeland Security are especially egregious and are the primary focus of this book. The analysis herein is primarily economic and from a public-choice perspective. At root, however, terrorism is a political issue, and attempts to solve a political issue with technology are unlikely to achieve dramatic success.

And now, let us crack open this barrel of pork.

Notes

1.   Hearing of the House Government Reform Committee, June 20, 2002, Federal News Service, p. 18.
2.   "Homeland Hypocrisy," [Madison, WI] *Capital Times*, editorial page, November 21, 2002.
3.   Douglas Valentine, "When the Phoenix Comes Home to Roost," www.douglasvalentine.com, March 25, 2004.
4.   "Security Funds Largely Unspent," Wire Reports, *Charlotte News-Observer*, www.newsobserver.com, October 20, 2004.
5.   President George W. Bush, "Securing the Homeland: Strengthening the Nation," (Washington, DC: White House, 2002), p. 27.
6.   Donald F. Kettl, *The Department of Homeland Security's First Year: A Report Ca*rd (New York: Century Foundation, 2004), pp. 7–8.
7.   Quoted in Traci Hukill, "Insecurity Complex," *Coast Weekly*, December 3, 2002, www.alternet.org.
8.   James Bovard, *Terrorism and Tyranny: Trampling Freedom, Justice, and Peace to Rid the World of Evil* (New York: Palgrave Macmillan, 2003), p. 1.
9.   James O'Toole, "'Not If, But When': Ridge Warns That Another Terror Attack Is Inevitable," *Pittsburgh-Post Gazette*, May 20, 2002, www.pittsburghpost-gazette.com.
10.   Quoted in Blanche Wiesen Cook, *The Declassified Eisenhower: A Startling Reappraisal of the Eisenhower Presidency* (New York: Penguin, 1984), pp. 345–6.
11.   Reg Whitaker, "After 9/11: A Surveillance State?" in *Lost Liberties: Ashcroft and the Assault on Personal Freedom*, edited by Cynthia Brown (New York: New Press, 2003), p. 70.
12.   Irving Louis Horowitz, "The Texture of Terrorism: Socialization, Routinization, and Integration," in *Political Learning in Adulthood: A Sourcebook of Theory and Research*, edited by Roberta S. Sigel (Chicago: University of Chicago Press, 1989), pp. 408–409.

2

Born to Spend Wild: The Messy Birth of the Department of Homeland Security

The creation of the Department of Homeland Security, the fifteenth Cabinet-level department and what one wag called "the Bush administration's secret plan to stamp out terrorism [by] getting 170,000 federal workers new letterhead,"[1] happened almost overnight, although its conceptual genesis may be said to have been a decade in the making. The tragic attacks of September 11, 2001, were the catalyst in the birth of a department that has become ground zero of the U.S. pork barrel.

Like the USA-PATRIOT Act, the Department of Homeland Security had long been in gestation. It was not a slapdash response to a sudden crisis. This is not to say that its swift passage was not in part a result of widespread panic by Congress, of a desire to Do Something and take credit for it at home. But such a department had been urged upon the Bush administration in early 2001 by the U.S. Commission on National Security/21st Century, chaired by the chin-rubbing wise men and ex-senators Warren Rudman (R-NH) and Gary Hart (D-CO). That Gary Hart—running mate of Warren Beatty, a roué whose career ended in spectacular squalor when photos surfaced of him frolicking with future anti-porno crusader Donna Rice aboard a boat infelicitously named "The Monkey Business"—is now regarded as a wise man illustrates starkly just how scarce a commodity sages are in these parlous times.

In any event, the $10 million, twelve-member Rudman-Hart Commission, which originated in the second term of President Bill Clinton, issued its final report on January 31, 2001. A central recommendation was "the creation of a new independent National Homeland Security Agency (NHSA) with responsibility for planning, coordinating, and integrating various U.S. government activities involved in homeland security. NHSA would be built upon the Federal Emergency Management Agency, with the three organizations currently on the front line of border security—the Coast Guard, the Customs Service, and the Border Patrol—transferred to it. NHSA would not only protect American lives, but also assume responsibility for overseeing the protection of the nation's critical infrastructure, including information technology."[2]

In expanded form, and with Cabinet status and a budget beyond the wildest dreams of the Hart-Rudman Commission (though soon enough Senator Rudman, erstwhile budget hawk, would complain that the DHS was underfunded), this became the Department of Homeland Security. Even the name Homeland Security, with its uncomfortable echoes of midcentury totalitarian states, was bequeathed Bush by these eminent bipartisans.

The Hart-Rudman Commission was responding to the scattered terrorist attacks of the 1990s, particularly the 1993 parking-garage bombing at the World Trade Center and the 1995 bombing of the federal building in Oklahoma City, Oklahoma.

Whether these operations represented failures on the part of U.S. intelligence or were carnage-littered demonstrations of the near-impossibility of stopping determined terrorists—especially men willing to sacrifice their lives in a religious cause—is an open question. What is not open to question, however, is that the FBI was devoting a disproportionate share of its money and manpower to investigating—and harassing—the bogeymen of the 1990s: militias and other right-wing populist groups. Reasonable people can disagree about the extent to which the militia movement, which at its peak in the first year of the Clinton administration may have included 100,000 adherents, posed a threat to the political order. The leftist columnist Alexander Cockburn of the *Nation* memorably characterized militias as inspiring groups of rural and working-class men and women who had taken up arms in defense of the Bill of Rights; the alarmists at Morris Dees's extravagant fund-raising machine, the Southern Poverty Law Center, viewed them as harbingers of working-class revolt.

In retrospect, however, the militia movement, which disintegrated after militia reject Timothy McVeigh blew up the Murrah Federal Building in Oklahoma City on April 19, 1995, killing 168 persons, including nineteen children, was a largely nonviolent protest movement of vaguely libertarian sympathies. Besides McVeigh, who had been turned away from the Michigan Militia as a nutcase, instances of violence by "right-wing extremists" were rare and uncoordinated. The militias made a useful hate object for upper-middle-class liberals who wished to feel threatened, but they were solidly in the American tradition of vigorous, vascular dissent.

Yet as intelligence analyst Marcus J. Ranum has written, "One reason we had our heads in the sand about the international threat in the early 1990s was that the U.S. government was paying too much attention to 'radical right wing militias.'. . . Mostly these groups could have been ignored, except that they had a bad habit of not paying taxes."[3]

Refusal to pay taxes was more than a "bad habit." It constituted a *casus belli* to the U.S. government, which devoted an absurdly disproportionate share of law enforcement resources to these essentially harmless tax protesters and Second Amendment devotees.

All the while, conspirators who meant to do the United States genuine, enormous, and lasting harm were plotting, quite without the militia lodestar of the Bill of Rights.

To its credit, the administration of President George W. Bush at first resisted the push to create a new department, arguing that its Office of Homeland Security, created at the executive's stroke of the pen on October 8, 2001, was sufficient to meet the terrorist threat. The office was charged with "coordinat[ing] the executive branch's efforts to detect, prepare for, prevent, protect against, respond to, and recover from terrorist attacks within the United States."[4]

The Bush administration presented its first "homeland security" budget—which did not include a new department—in "Securing the Homeland: Strengthening the Nation" (2002), which laid out the fiscal year 2003 budget request. The document appeared with presidential seal and imprimatur, and in tone, if not particulars, it set the stage for all subsequent debates of "homeland security" budgets. (I use the quotation marks around "homeland security" because it is so foreign a term; pre-9/11 Americans simply never used the word "homeland," and those of us whose memories stretch back beyond the age of George W. Bush may have a hard time getting our mouths around it.)

"Securing the Homeland: Strengthening the Nation" made it clear that the treasury had been thrown open; the spendathon was on. "A new wave of terrorism, involving new weapons, looms in America's future," warned the president, in best Harry Truman Arthur

Vandenberg "scare hell out of the American people" fashion. He continued, "We can never be sure that we have defeated all of our terrorist enemies, and therefore we can never again allow ourselves to become overconfident about the security of our homeland." This is a prescription for war without end—for spending without end—for a pork barrel as big as the Washington Monument.

Bush prepared the citizenry—or his subjects, as the case may be, for little in this seminal paper smacked of republican principle or representative democracy—for a long, expensive, harrowing trip. The "characteristics of American society we cherish—our freedom, our openness, our great cities and towering skyscrapers, our modern transportation systems—make us vulnerable to terrorism of catastrophic proportions." Now, bundling our freedoms with "skyscrapers" and "modern transportation systems" as the things that Americans cherish may seem odd: are Trump Towers and the New York City subway really that essential to Americanness? But nevertheless, the most basic features of our country are said to ensure that terrorism, which the document never bothers to define, is "a permanent condition to which America and the entire world must adjust."

Lest any naïvely hopeful reader think that al Qaeda can be broken and America can be America again, Bush emphasizes that "The need for homeland security. . . is not tied to any specific terrorist threat."[5] It cannot be defeated; it cannot be contained; it will not dissolve on its own.

"The Government of the United States has no more important mission than fighting terrorism overseas and securing the homeland from future terrorist attacks,"[6] states Bush. This would come as news to the authors of the Constitution, who envisioned the government's role as to "establish justice, insure domestic tranquility, provide for the common defense, promote the general welfare, and secure the blessings of liberty to ourselves and our posterity."[7] These tasks have been superseded—obviated, really—because of the events of one day in two American cities.

Bush proposed to meet the terrorist challenge though "major new programs and significant reforms by the Federal government."[8] It is no accident that the word "programs" precedes "reforms": elsewhere he boasts of the "massive infusion of Federal resources"—an increase from $19.5 billion in FY 2002 to $37.7 billion in FY 2003—into the heretofore unheard-of budget sector called "homeland security."

Pledging "a truly national plan"[9]—goodbye to local autonomy—
"Securing the Homeland: Strengthening the Nation" goes to absurd
lengths to demonstrate the national scope of the threat. "Virtually
every American has been involved in one way or another" in the
response to September 11, according to President Bush in this document. "Some rushed into burning buildings, putting themselves in
harm's way to save the lives of others. Others demonstrated their
solidarity by wearing an American flag in their lapel." Er, yes. They
also serve who wear flag lapels.

With the same degree of ridiculousness, Bush praises Congress
for "courage"[10] because it passed a $40 billion Emergency Re-
sponse Fund in the aftermath of 9/11. It seems that spending other
peoples' money has been elevated to a courageous act in the new
Washington.

Even at this early stage of the homeland security spending orgy,
the writing was on the Treasury building wall. The Bush report is
full of the buzzwords that always betoken government appropriations: infrastructure, twenty-first century, early warning system, seam-
less, investment. The document actually crows that Bush is asking
for (and would get) an "enormous Federal investment in technology."[11] As recently as the 1980s, Republicans mocked the Democrats for using the word "investment" as a euphemism for federal
spending. Now they've stolen the word and are themselves spending, as the gag goes, like drunken Democrats.

"Additional personnel"[12] is promised in "Securing the Homeland"
for the Immigration and Naturalization Service, which would also
soon get a new name. The FBI and DEA are to be bulked up, fortified with new agents and more intrusive powers of investigation. A
variety of impressive-sounding initiatives are to be funded at ever-
greater levels under the guise of "cyberspace-security": a Cyberspace
Warning Intelligence Network, a National Infrastructure Protection
Center, and a National Infrastructure Simulation and Analysis Center, to name but three. The administration proposed (and got)
Cybercorps Scholarships for Service, yet another tuition subsidy,
this one intended to encourage "college students to become high-
tech computer security professionals within government."[13]

I have seen the best minds of my generation destroyed by madness, as the late poet Allen Ginsberg declared at the outset of his
epic Beat poem "Howl." Had the grey potbellied pot-smoking poet
lived just a few more years, he'd have seen efforts to induce the best

minds of the new generation to go into government service, to take state jobs, to subordinate their inventiveness, creativity, and enterprise to bureaucracy.

Perhaps most chillingly, President Bush proposed a series of citizen-snoop programs that we will revisit in chapter 6. The notorious Operation TIPS (Terrorist Information and Prevention System) would have made mailmen, UPS drivers, telephone repairmen, and the meter-reading lady spies for the federal government, empowered to report on "suspicious activities." Pumped-up Neighborhood Watch programs were another component of the nationwide "Citizens Corps" designed by the Bush team, which was apparently heedless (or ignorant) of the Woodrow Wilson administration's disastrous experiments in citizen spying during the First World War.

All this and more was promised in the first post-9/11 report of the Bush administration. And for once, a politician kept his promise.

The first director of the Office of Homeland Security was Tom Ridge, a Vietnam veteran, former six-term member of the U.S. House of Representatives, and seven years the governor of Pennsylvania. Ridge had been on the short list of potential Bush running mates in 2000, but he was reportedly dropped in part because of concerns that he was not hawkish enough on foreign policy. Bizarrely, the decorated combat vet lost out to eventual vice president, Dick Cheney, who had received multiple deferments allowing him to avoid service in Vietnam.

Senator Joseph Lieberman (D-CT), the hawkish running mate of Albert Gore in 2000 and the early front-runner for the 2004 Democratic presidential nomination, introduced legislation to create a Department of Homeland Security in October 2001. No measly "office" was enough for Lieberman; only an additional chair in the Cabinet room would do. Although Lieberman's candidacy would flop in 2004, this seemed at the time a master political stroke: he had gotten out front on the first big issue of the new millennium, and his hobby-horse—let's create a new department!—was tried and true. Jimmy Carter had satisfied key constituencies with his departments of Energy and Education, the latter a payoff to the powerful National Education Association. In fact, the greatest single obstacle to passage of the DOE bill had been the rival American Federation of Teachers, which feared—with reason—NEA control of the department.

As puckish skeptics pointed out, the Department of Energy, born in 1977 during President Jimmy Carter's "energy crisis," which he termed the "moral equivalent of war," had extracted not a single barrel of oil from the earth in its quarter-century of existence. Indeed, the National Council of Research called it "one of the most inefficient organizations in the federal government,"[14] an ungainly Frankenstein monster whose limbs and appendages had missions ranging from nuclear energy to solar power to cleaning up nuclear wastes. It is incoherent, badly managed, and generally conceded to be a failure. Also midwifed by the Carter administration, the Department of Education, has spent almost $600 billion since its creation in 1980, yet average student scores on the SAT are lower than they were in 1970. And the Veterans Department, born in 1989, "is so bad that 90 percent of eligible veterans choose private health care instead,"[15] as a Cato Institute study announced.

Yet Ronald Reagan had thrown the nation's veterans a bone with the costly but politically cost-free elevation of Veterans' Affairs to Cabinet status. So what could be a more anodyne method of vanquishing terrorism than the birthing of a brand spanking new Cabinet department?

Lieberman, who plays the game of naked power politics cloaked in the garb of whiny sanctimony as well as anyone, tossed the usual bones to Democratic special interests in his Homeland Security bill. For instance, he proposed to expand the application of the Davis-Bacon Act, a Depression-era law which requires contractors on federal projects to pay "local prevailing wages," which are determined by the Department of Labor and are almost always significantly higher than the truly prevalent local wage.

Not wishing to follow the Lieberman lead, the White House insisted that its hastily cobbled together Office of Homeland Security was sufficient to the task. Critics pointed out that since budgetary authority would remain lodged in the agencies which Ridge had at least ostensible authority to oversee, he would be impotent, a mere figurehead pretending to orchestrate the nation's response to terrorism while the real conductors remained offstage.

Bush caved quickly on this. For there was no political downside to the creation of a Department of Homeland Security. The limited-government Republicans, to the extent any such grouping exists anymore, had largely lost their voice after 9/11. So President Bush proposed his own Department of Homeland Security—which promptly came under attack by Democrats for being too small and niggardly!

As a result of his Rove-ian political calculus, President Bush reversed field and welcomed a new department, saying, "The current structure of our government is a patchwork, to put it best, of overlapping responsibilities, and it really does hinder our ability to protect the homeland."[16]

In his June 6, 2002 address to the nation, Bush conjured the image of "a titanic struggle against terror." Bush said in his gravest, most smirk-less manner, "Tonight, I ask the Congress to join me in creating a single permanent department with an overriding and urgent mission—securing the American homeland and protecting the American people."

The stakes were nothing less than the survival of the citizenry. "Thousands of trained killers are plotting to attack us," Bush read from the teleprompter. "Employees of this new agency will come to work every morning knowing that their most important job is to protect their fellow citizens." If that didn't put a bounce into the step of your average GS-9, nothing would.

Remembering for a second that he was a Republican with a putative commitment to fiscal responsibility, the president added, "By ending duplication and overlap, we will spend less on overhead, and more on protecting America." As if to cast this assertion of parsimony into immediate doubt, Senator Ted Kennedy (D-MA) was among the first to welcome this "positive step long awaited by many of us in Congress." Kennedy, not theretofore noted for his exertions on behalf of the American taxpayer, seconded Bush: "We need a well-organized, efficiently run office that works in coordination with existing law enforcement and intelligence agencies, not another bureaucracy."[17]

When Ted Kennedy starts denouncing bureaucracy, you know the fix is in.

Yet Americans are not quite the fools our politicos like to think we are: In a Gallup Poll taken shortly after the creation of the new department, only 13 percent of respondents said that the Department of Homeland Security would make them feel safer.[18]

The Department sailed through the U.S. House of Representatives on November 14, 2002, by a vote of 299-121, with only six members of the "fiscally conservative" GOP dissenting. Five days later, the Senate passed the bill creating this new department by a vote of 90-9. The dissenting votes came from eight Democrats (Akaka, Byrd, Feingold, Hollings, Inouye, Kennedy, Levin, and dent of the United States,"[20] according to Tom Ridge. The CIA and FBI were statutorily obligated to share information with the new agency, but this sharing has been more in the line of perfunctory memos than anything else.

(One wonders just why the CIA has been restored to sacred cow status. Its record of misguided interventions and howling miscalculations is long and sordid. Its unconstitutional subversions in Iran [1953], Cuba [1961], Southeast Asia [1961-73], Afghanistan [1979], Central America [the early 1980s], and elsewhere have only served to make bad situations worse and given the world such dubious gifts as forty-plus years of the communist thug Fidel Castro; the Shah, the repressive Savak torture machine, and the Ayatollah Khomeini in Iran; and of course al Qaeda, the rotten fruit of CIA sponsorship of Muslim terrorism in Afghanistan. Its intelligence has been unworthy of the name: as Senator Daniel Patrick Moynihan [D-NY], former chairman of the Senate Select Committee on Intelligence, noted with disgust, the agency vastly overstated Soviet military and economic capability for four decades. By his career's end, the Cold Warrior Moynihan was calling for the abolition of the CIA, a move that foreign-policy analyst Chalmers Johnson notes would save the U.S. taxpayer as much as $30 billion a year. But in our topsy-turvy age, saving tax dollars is not part of even the red meat rhetorical strategy of either party.)

In any event, the DHS was seen by the senior intelligence services as something of a redheaded stepchild, if an extremely wealthy redheaded stepchild. John Mintz of the *Washington Post* reported that "more than 15 people declined requests to apply for the top post in its intelligence unit—and many others turned down offers to run several other key offices."[21]

Conceived in panic, the DHS was a mess from the start. This should have come as no surprise. A look back at the government reorganization to which the DHS was most frequently compared—the 1947 bureaucratic tremor that brought forth the Department of Defense—may be instructive. Indeed, Tom Ridge has called the creation of his department "the most historic—most significant transformation in the United States government since 1947."[22] The fact that Secretary of Defense Donald Rumsfeld has compared the swiftness and efficiency he found within his fiefdom to the Soviet bureaucracy makes for an illuminating comparison. So does the boast of one department publication that "DHS headquarters will focus on national policy

Sarbanes) and independent James Jeffords of Vermont
senators voted en masse for this massive new bureaucr

Democratic congressional leaders Tom Daschle (SD)
ate and Richard Gephardt (MO) in the House had pledged
the way to passage of this landmark legislation. In this, at
kept their promises.

The bumpersticker-spouting polemicists of TV talk sl
weekly 700-word columns pounced: the Department was to
They demanded the virtual merger of the FBI and CIA, a
absorption into the Department of Homeland Security, appar
blithe ignorance of their very different functions and bailiwic
FBI, within the Department of Justice, is the lead federal age
the investigation of domestic terrorism; the Department of State,
erly, is the lead agency in the area of international terrorism
National Security Council and the president's National Security
visor are also charged with assessing and formulating anti-terro
policies. The Central Intelligence Agency is, by its very title,
central agency in the gathering of foreign intelligence.

Bush's new department would not include the Federal Bureau
Investigation, the Central Intelligence Agency, or the National Sec
rity Agency, explained Bush White House chief of staff Andrew Ca
on June 9, 2002, for sound domestic reasons. "The FBI does mor
than worry about terrorist attacks," said Card on the ABC-TV gabfes
This Week. "And besides, we did not want to create a homeland security department that would look like the old Soviet-style ministry of
the interior."[19]

This refreshing reference to the totalitarian temptation was pretty
much the first and last time that an official of the Bush White House
would acknowledge the dangers of intrusive government.

The Act did create a Homeland Security Council, whose four standing members are the president, vice president, secretary of defense,
and attorney general. One would think that such a council would be
unnecessary, given the existence of a National Security Council, but
of course "national security" in the age of empire has little to do
with our nation and everything to do with the rest of the world.

The CIA was not included in the DHS because President Bush, or
those who act in his name, believed "that the CIA, the primary source
of foreign intelligence information, should remain directly accountable to one person in the executive branch of government, and that
is" ....Vice President Cheney. Oh, wait, no, the answer was "the presi-

through centralized planning."[23] When conservative Republicans adopt the language of the Politburo, bolt the doors and grab the rifle from the wall!

Crucially, Congress held more than two years of hearings on proposals to create a Department of Defense—almost two years more of careful consideration than the Congress gave to the legislation creating the Department of Homeland Security. The establishment of the Department of Defense is an interesting affair, and for policy wonks, think tank types, and others interested in the history of DoD, an appendix to this chapter contains some of the highlights. However, it is sufficient to note here that James Forrestal, first secretary of defense and the department's aggressive promoter, did offer a few words of wisdom that Tom Ridge might have found most useful. In congressional hearings on unification, Forrestal introduced a note of realism:

> It is my belief that in any field of human activity, whether it is business or government, there is a definite limit to the size of an administrative unit which can be successfully directed by one man. . . . There is a point, in other words, beyond which human beings cannot successfully direct an organization with the hope of having even casual knowledge of the operation of its component parts.[24]

The secretary of homeland security might remember that the next time he fumbles in answering consecutive questions about Coast Guard rescue missions, nuclear-power-plant security, and an elderly Ukrainian woman's visa problem.

The Department of Homeland Security possesses a bureaucratic complexity that makes the Department of Defense seem simple and transparent by comparison. Moreover, the many agencies and offices that were thrown together to construct this new department were not trimmed or whittled or downsized before the consolidation. It was, in the assessment of David Williams, vice president of policy for Citizens Against Government Waste, "like shuffling around the deck chairs on the Titanic."[25]

The DHS takes the concept of sprawl to an entirely new level. It was the first new department since 1989, when the Reagan administration gave us as a parting gift the woeful Department of Veterans Affairs. Cobbled together from pieces of eight other Cabinet departments and merging some twenty-two separate agencies (meaning that just six departments did not lose a limb to the newcomer), the DHS was quartered into four directorates. Yes, directorates: bureaucrats in the age of terrorism have no qualms about borrowing the language of étatism. These four directorates are Border and Transportation Security, Emergency Preparedness and Response, Science and Technology, and Information Analysis and Infrastructure Protection. Two other entities, the Secret Service and the Coast Guard, were transferred to Homeland Security but, in an assertion of bureaucratic muscle, they bypass the directorates and report directly to the Secretary.

The bits and pieces and chunks that went into this jerrybuilt department would make Dr. Frankenstein proud. The directorates consist of:

Border and Transportation Security
- U.S. Customs Service (formerly Department of Treasury)
- Immigration and Naturalization Service (part; the INS changed its name and birthed several spinoffs) (Justice)
- Federal Protective Service (GSA)
- Transportation Security Administration (Transportation)
- Federal Law Enforcement Training Center (Treasury)
- Animal and Plant Health Inspection Service (part) (Agriculture)
- Office for Domestic Preparedness (Justice)

Emergency Preparedness and Response
- Federal Emergency Management Agency (FEMA)
- Strategic National Stockpile and the National Disaster Medical System (Health and Human Services)
- Nuclear Incident Response Team (Energy)
- Domestic Energy Support Teams (Justice)
- National Domestic Preparedness Office (FBI)

Science and Technology
- Chemical, Biological, Radiological and Nuclear Countermeasures Program (Energy)
- Environmental Measurements Laboratory (Energy)
- National BW Defense Analysis Center (Defense)
- Plum Island Animal Disease Center (Agriculture)

Information Analysis and Infrastructure Protection
- Critical Infrastructure Assurance Office (Commerce)
- Federal Computer Incident Response Center (GSA)
- National Communications System (Defense)
- National Infrastructure Protection Center (FBI)
- Energy Security and Assurance Program (Energy)

Infrastructure, it should be noted, refers to networks both cyber and real, including not only information but also physical plants.

Title VII of the Homeland Security Act of 2002 established an undersecretary of management, a nominal directorate in itself, though the paper-pushing ring of this fiefdom renders it a dubious kind of semi-directorate, rather like George Best being the Fifth Beatle. Given that department publicists boast that it "is committed to becoming a model for efficiency and effectiveness in the federal government,"[26] enshrining Management as a coequal directorate seemed like a bad publicity move.

The DHS also includes three "mission agencies," two of which enjoy long histories of independence:

- The Coast Guard, founded in 1790 as the Revenue Marine and one of five armed services of the United States, and now the largest single agency within the DHS;
- The U.S. Secret Service, established as part of the Department of the Treasury in 1865 and best-known for its president-guarding agents, with their sunglasses and sang-froid (it should be noted that the Secret Service was intended to stamp out counterfeiters; it didn't start guarding the president until after McKinley was shot dead in Buffalo at the Pan-American Exhibition of 1901); and
- U.S. Citizenship and Immigration Services.

Each of these "mission agencies" performs missions far removed from the ostensible purposes of the Department of Homeland Security. The Coast Guard, in particular, is a stretch. While it has been retooled in the post-9/11 environment to respond to terrorist assaults in domestic ports or waterways, the job from which it derives its benign public identity—search-and-rescue missions at sea— remains its heart and soul.

The Coast Guard still asserts that its non-homeland security activities, which also include marine safety, navigational aid, marine environmental protection, and ice-breaking, are central to its mission.

Indeed, recent budgets have included $500 million for the "Deepwater" program under which the Coast Guard is modernizing its fleet of cutters and aircraft, $134 million for a maritime 911 system through which it may respond even faster to calls for help from distressed ships and sailors; and $20 million to hire more search-

and-rescue personnel. Whether or not one believes that these are legitimate expenditures of the taxpayers' money, they are emphatically not part of the War on Terror. (Unless the definition of that war has been stretched to include sharks and *Poseidon Adventure*-class waves.)

The Coast Guard has moved before: in 1967, it slid over to the Department of Transportation from the Department of the Treasury. Alan Dean, a fellow of the National Academy of Public Administration and an architect of the 1967 move, has been critical of the Coast Guard's change of port to the DHS.

"There is no government organization that cannot be made worse by a bad reorganization,"[27] Dean says, wondering if an emphasis on trendy homeland security chores will distract the Coast Guard from its historic mission of performing such mundane but necessary tasks as installing buoys and rescuing distressed mariners.

Since assuming homeland security duties, the Coast Guard seems to have developed something of an attitude. Consider the case of Rear Admiral Harvey Johnson, commander of District Seven of the U.S. Coast Guard, which covers South Carolina down through South America's Caribbean Rim. Johnson wears a second hat as well: director of Homeland Security Task Force Southeast. He is based in Miami and seems to be redefining the term "Miami Vice" to include incurable hubris and arrogance.

Johnson started making unwelcome waves upon his arrival in June 2003. He rejected the "flag quarters" traditionally occupied by the commander of District Seven: it was old, unhip, and one was surrounded by, well, Coast Guard types. "To unwind each day and to assure victory in the war on terror," as David Villano wrote in *Miami New Times*, "the commander would need something a little larger. And more modern. And with a pool. And for his wife, he'd like something not too far from fashionable shopping districts. And if possible he'd like neighbors a bit more socially connected than your average enlisted man."

The Coast Guard ghetto known as Richmond Heights would not do. Not for a swaggering Homeland Security stud like Commander Johnson. So he and his wife were ensconced in the exclusive Coral Gables area known as Cocoplum, in a 6,200 square-foot palace for which taxpayers pay an annual leasing fee of $111,600. The formula by which reimbursements for off-base housing are figured would peg Johnson's annual housing allowance at $32,0004, or

$2,667 per month, a healthy sum, it would seem, but nowhere near enough to rent a $2 million home in Cocoplum.

How would you like to be the military flack assigned to defend that kind of extravagance? The unpleasant chore fell to Captain Richard Murphy, commanding officer of the civil engineering unit in Miami. "The events of 9/11"—you knew that was coming—"and the transition into the Department of Homeland Security have greatly increased the visibility of the Coast Guard," stumbled Murphy, who pointed out that Johnson needs a mansion "given the order of magnitude of the job and the fact that he must represent the interests of the United States."

Johnson avoided the $32,004 maximum housing allowance by claiming that he was not leasing a house; no, it was a facility. As such, the civil engineering unit picked up the entire tab. Coast Guard bureaucrats in Washington, D.C. approved the scam, and so Johnson moved into Cocoplum, which wags have long dubbed "Cocaineplum," since its gaudy and tasteless homes are favored by some of Miami's most notorious drug kingpins.

But at least Commander Johnson has his pool.[28]

Within the Emergency Preparedness and Response Directorate, FEMA, or the Federal Emergency Management Agency, has found a new home. FEMA, which had been an independent agency since 1979, enjoys a Coast Guard-ish reputation among the public; its responsibility is "preparing for, mitigating the effects of, responding, to, and recovering from all domestic disasters whether natural or manmade, including acts of terror."[29] Its benign image is the result of handing out thousands of checks in the wake of hurricanes and tornadoes.

FEMA, too, has profited handsomely from its lodgment inside DHS. Its recent bounty includes an FY 2004 appropriation of $200 million to replace the country's Flood Insurance Rate Maps. Unless Osama bin Laden is directing tropical storms from his mountain hideout, this seems a far sight removed from "homeland security."

Bush officials assured Congress with what passes for straight faces in the Age of Terror that the DHS would be budget-neutral: a kind of reshuffling of deck chairs on an unsinkable *Titanic*. Of course, only the most credulous believed this, though the most disingenuous made use of this specious talking point.

In the words of the DHS website, its mission is "securing the homeland," a locution so foreign to Americans as to bring a shudder to the spine. Like any up-to-date bureaucracy, it even has its own "vision," which is expressed with a sort of fascist poeticism: "Preserving our freedoms, protecting America....we secure our homeland."[30] This might well pass as Oceania's slogan in George Orwell's *1984*. It sounds as if it comes straight out of a dystopian novel. While it may have the ring of Madison Avenue, it is certainly not a slogan fit for the government designed by Madison & Co.

The department also came with its own mission statement, which is not to be confused with what the first George Bush contemptuously referred to as "the vision thing." The DHS mission statement reads: "The Department of Homeland Security will lead the unified national effort to secure America. We will prevent and deter terrorist attacks and protect against and respond to threats and hazards to the nation. We will ensure safe and secure borders, welcome lawful immigrants and visitors, and promote the free flow of commerce."[31]

The catch-as-catch-can aspect of the department attracted criticism from a source usually friendly to any and all expansions of federal power: The Brookings Institution, that is, the Democratic subcabinet in exile, which released a report urging a smaller DHS. Paul C. Light, director of government studies at the Brookings Institution, called the department "a slapped-together approach that is destined for great confusion, great difficulty, and possible failure."[32] Light added that the proposal "relied more on hope and hubris than actual reasons to believe it would work."[33]

The department has not yet (and probably never will) figured out how to integrate its security and nonsecurity functions. Not that it hasn't spent money trying: the Congressional Budget Office reported that the cost of administrative reorganization was $3 billion. But the jumbled nature of its constituent programs destines it for failure. Light of the Brookings Institution notes that the most basic rule of governmental reorganization is to make sure that merged entities share at least 50 percent of the same mission. He estimates that the Coast Guard's homeland security responsibilities make up less than a quarter of its overall mission, while for FEMA the figure is less than 10 percent. One might just as well combine the National Endowment for the Humanities with the Centers for Disease Control.

Or one might simply transfer the Animal and Plant Health Inspection Service, whose duties include enforcing the Animal Welfare Act, to the Department of Homeland Security. Wait! The Animal and Plant Health Inspection Service has been transferred. As have a variety of tasks which include "rescuing drunken boaters in heavy surf, airlifting blankets to flood victims in Iowa, confiscating stolen antiquities from Cambodia and inducing counterfeiters to sell their product to undercover cops."[34] That's what happens when the Coast Guard, FEMA, and the Secret Service are thrown into the slumgullion stew.

The Department was up and running, or in the martial spirit of the times should we say rolling, on March 1, 2003. With approximately 180,000 employees and a budget of $31.2 billion, the DHS emerged full-fledged from the nest as the third-largest Cabinet agency. The envious GSes at Commerce, Labor, Energy, and other backwaters could only look on enviously.

The preternaturally swift passage of the Homeland Security Act had left time for only the most perfunctory congressional hearings on this momentous piece of legislation. Just two days after Congress got its first look at the bill—and isn't legislation supposed to originate in the Congress?—the House Government Reform Committee held a hearing that was almost breathtaking in its cursoriness, its inelegance, and its glibness.

The White House proposal weighed in at a modest thirty-two pages; the version that came out of committee was a bulky 282 pages; the legislation finally enacted exceeded 500 pages. Many congresspeople complained that the bill was not made available for inspection before passage, which meant that a landmark piece of legislation was voted upon and passed without the majority of members even knowing its contents.

The chairman of the Government Reform Committee, Rep. Dan Burton (R-IN), started things off on a suitably head-scratching note when he said, echoing President Bush, that the proposed new department would be "a Defense Department for the United States, if you will."[35]

Now, you might have thought that the Department of Defense established in 1947 was a "Defense Department for the United States," but you would be wrong. Just what country or countries the plain old Department of Defense is supposed to be defending remains something of a mystery.

The mood of bipartisanship at this and other hearings was so stifling as to put one in mind of a meeting of the Bulgarian National Assembly, circa 1958. The foamingly hawkish California Democrat Tom Lantos kidded Tom Ridge, who was about to be promoted from director of the Office of Homeland Security to Secretary of the Department of Homeland Security, "You currently have 100 employees. And you will have, I understand, about 170,000, which I think deserves a record in the *Guinness Book* as the fastest-growing entity in the federal government. And let the record show it happened under a Republican administration."

The crowd erupted in laughter, but Lantos made haste to reassure Ridge that he would enjoy "bipartisan support." After all, "We are dealing with the nation's security and we are all on the same side of this issue."[36]

Given that Secretary Ridge has been described, politely, by the *Washington Post* as "not detail-oriented,"[37] one might wonder if a member of Congress might have pressed him on just how he intended to manage a workforce of 170,000, but hard questions were as rare as burkas in that committee room.

Dissent had effectively been outlawed. Oh, the leftist Democratic Dennis Kucinich of Ohio added a forlorn hope that "these proceedings will include a discussion of causality as well as casualties,"[38] but he may as well have wished that the temperature would hit 90 degrees in Cleveland in mid-February.

The ranking minority member of the committee, Rep. Henry Waxman (D-CA), muttered a few doubts about the effectiveness of a "new bureaucracy," but given his record of support for almost every kind of federal spending and activity ever dreamt of by the mind of man, these weak cavils rang hollow. He did note, accurately, that "the White House proposal we are considering today was put together by a handful of political appointees working in secret,"[39] but his silence when, almost a decade earlier, Hillary Rodham Clinton had led a similarly secret gaggle of unelected wonks to cobble together the ill-fated Clinton health-care package robbed his words of whatever force they might have had.

Apropos nothing, the veteran liberal Patsy Mink (D-HI) observed that 2002 was the thirtieth anniversary of the Watergate break-in, which she linked to the Freedom of Information Act. The FOIA was to be curtailed by the DHS bill, under which concrete freedoms were sacrificed to an abstract, virtually meaningless "freedom" that was said to be under attack by foreign terrorists.

But the sharpest comments on the pending legislation came from the brave maverick Republican John Duncan of Tennessee. Duncan, who would be one of six House Republicans to vote against authorizing the 2003 invasion of Iraq, warned that "there seems to be a public relations rush to create this department by September 11th

[2002].'' (He was right, though the p.r. team missed by two months.) Rep. Duncan scoffed at the administration's claims that this new agency would not add to the bureaucracy.

"My staff has looked over the creation of every new department for the last 30 years," said Duncan, and in each of those departments "spending has gone up at many times the rate of inflation." Yet "those departments were created with words saying that they were going to increase efficiency and do away with overlapping and duplication of services and so forth . . . the same things we're hearing now."[40]

Tom Ridge would call these duplications "synergies." For instance, the DHS's absorption of the Animal Plant Health Inspection Services of the Department of Agriculture was not a case of administrative imperialism or a Frankenstein-like hybrid; no, said Ridge, it meant adding "some synergies" to the APHIS-DHS marriage. He noted that "identifying pests and pathogens that would affect animals and plant life" might also lead to the detection of terrorist activities: in a twist worthy of Kafka, the insect is revealed as terrorist.

Ridge did concede that swallowing the other twelve federal agencies that have responsibility for food safety "was just too much," though like any good turf-poacher, he allowed that "[i]t may be subject to consideration from Congress down the road."[41]

(The wags at Citizens for Legitimate Government crack that "it's nice to know that the Secret Service is now in the communications loop with the Plum Island Animal Disease Center," adding that "if the President gets mad cow disease, the SS will be the first to know."[42])

The well-being of federal employees was a persistent theme in this first congressional hearing. Rep. Lantos insisted that "one item will be nonnegotiable on the Democratic side, and that is the job security of every single federal employee in all of these agencies."[43]

Rep. Connie Morella (R-MD), whose distasteful job it was to represent the largest concentration of federal employees in any congressional district in America, cut right to the chase. No misty-eyed paeans to "freedom" or gruff denunciations of bearded Muslim fanatics for her; no, Congresswoman Morella fastened upon "the administration's plan...to grant the new secretary so much unprecedented managerial flexibility, which would include the power to remove existing federal personnel rules and regulations, including the current pay structure, labor management rules and performance appraisal system."

In a ghastly invocation of the Twin Towers' tragedy, Morella declared, "One of the many lessons of September 11th was the demonstrated strength and resolve and patriotism of our civil service." To Morella—and many others connected in some way with the GS system—government employees were the new heroes, brave souls with rippling muscles and keen wits. Gone forever was the invidious caricature of the pencil-pushing, clock-watching goldbricker: the federal employee of the twenty-first century was a cocky, can-do Tom Cruise, a perky and feisty Sandra Bullock. "[W]hy insinuate that federal personnel cannot be trusted to willingly protect our homeland when they so willingly have?"[44] asked Morella.

Eleanor Holmes Norton, the Democratic delegate from the District of Columbia, spoke gloomily of "the extraordinary flight from the federal government we are seeing." This flight—which was not visible to anyone outside the District of Columbia, nor was it evident to those who counted the number of federal employees—was not in response to a perceived terrorist threat against government buildings or the workers therein. Rather, it was part of the "real devolution of the government downward" that Del. Norton saw in the 1990s. She, if no one else, apparently believed Bill Clinton's famous pronouncement that the era of big government is over.

Del. Norton pressed Ridge on this crisis of confidence that was said to infect federal employeedom. "[T]he first thing people think about" during a reorganization of government, she lectured him, is whether "this is the time to get out of the government."[45]

Well, almost all of our valorous public servants suck it up and stick it out. But Norton did foreshadow a serious problem that would afflict the DHS in its first years of operation: the defection of high-level Ridge aides to lucrative lobbying positions, from which they helped funnel "homeland security" money to their clients. But more on this in chapter 3.

Bizarrely—sadly for those who cherish traditional American liberties—the single most controversial element of the entire Homeland Security package would be the proposed tweaking of the rules governing DHS employees. Rep. Albert Wynn, Maryland Democrat, went so far as to say, "This is supposed to be a bill about fighting terrorism. Unfortunately, this bill puts the administration at war with federal employees."[46] This may be the first time in recorded history that a government paid those with whom it was at war.

The Bush proposal called for DHS management rules "grounded in the public employment principles of merit and fitness."[47] This sounds like pabulum, but to those members of Congress for whom protecting federal employees is Job One, they were fighting words. The inclusion of the word "merit" meant that DHS management would have greater flexibility than other departments to give promotions and pay raises based on merit (or perceived merit) rather than seniority. As Mark Schmidt and Demian Brady, analysts with the National Taxpayers Union, put it, the government unions wanted the DHS to be another Post Office, with employee duties strictly spelled out, "a cumbersome process for disciplining or firing workers," the usual race and gender-based promotion policies, and "a rigid pay system based on automatic rather than merit-based raises."[48]

(When Rep. Morella later proposed an amendment to gut the flexible management provisions from the Bush homeland security legislation, the top twenty recipients of campaign contributions from government-employee unions all voted with Morella.)

To be fair, the public employees' unions did make one cogent point: the flexibility sought and achieved by the Bush administration may have the effect of silencing whistleblowers. The Homeland Security Act permits the secretary to ignore the Whistleblower Protection Act in the alleged interest of efficient deployment of human resources.

No one, however, was blowing the whistle on excessive spending at the congressional hearings on the proposed DHS.

Protecting the pork feasted upon by the ravening folks back home in the district was a central theme of these hearings. Rep. John Tierney (D-MA) worried that the transfer of the Coast Guard to the DHS might somehow imperil "the fishing families in my district."[49] Not to worry, Honorable Tierney: Ridge boasted to the committee that "the president in the 2003 budget has given the Coast Guard the largest increase they've ever received so they can attract new personnel and...acquire more equipment."[50]

Rep. Steven LaTourette (R-OH), who was not even a member of the committee, dropped by to complain that the number of officers in the Federal Protective Service, which was transferred to the DHS, had dropped from 600 to 200, largely as a result of a $10,000 pay differential in favor of the Capitol Hill police.

Rep. LaTourette noted that the FPS needed at least 1,000 officers to "protect our federal buildings and the federal structures,"[51] and the way to do that, of course, was to close the differential. If you thought that this Republican would propose to do that by reducing the salaries of Capitol Hill police officers then you are evidently not acquainted with the latest thinking in the party of Rockefeller and Dewey.

LaTourette's conception of the DHS was remarkably elastic. He also pestered Ridge to commit to federal subsidy for the fire departments located near the country's sixty-eight nuclear power plants. This was almost—almost—too much even for the Homeland Security chief, who first suggested that the "private companies" who operate the plants ought to bear that burden. On second thought, though, Ridge added, "yes, I think there would be dollars available to address, over time, that need."[52]

LaTourette's Syndrome: the rapid, seemingly unstoppable spewing of obscene amounts of money through the federal mouth.

As if functioning as a "Defense Department for the United States" were not mandate enough, a few foolhardy solons actually proposed to expand the DHS bailiwick ever further afield. The most astonishing such proposal was made by Rep. Mark Souder (R-IN).

Rep. Souder informed his colleagues that "more than 4,000 Americans die each year from drug abuse—at least the equivalent of a major terrorist attack. Our ranking member, Mr. [Elijah] Cummings [D-MD], has consistently pointed out we are already under chemical attack from international drug cartels, which also fund and are the sources of funding for catastrophic terrorism which this new department is created to counter. And we must make sure that this department fully addresses this potential conflict as we look forward to this."[53]

Rep. Benjamin Gilman (R-NY) seconded Souder's non sequitur. "About one-half of the foreign terrorist organizations have some link to . . . illicit drug distribution and the financing of their organizations through drugs," he said, without bothering to back up his statement with anything so simple as a supporting fact. Gilman went on to urge the DHS to "try to bring the DEA [Drug Enforcement Agency]"[54] into its capacious structure. This would expand the fiefdom—with a vengeance.

In plain English, Republican Reps. Souder and Gilman were proposing to add drug enforcement to the already long list of DHS functions. That drug enforcement was wholly unrelated to the purported mission of the department seemed not to matter: Any kind of war, metaphorical or not, was being refitted as part of the war on terror. Had Jimmy Carter been president, perhaps his symbolic energy war might have been loaded into the DHS. Gerald Ford might have tucked his war on inflation into the burgeoning department. And why not include the war on cancer? AIDS? Irritable bowel syndrome?

As we shall see, Rep. Souder's expansive vision of the regulatory and police possibilities of the Department of Homeland Security was shared by others. And in time, the DHS would range far afield from any ostensible focus on the al Qaedas of this world.

Tom Ridge testified at that slapdash House hearing. He sounded the efficiency theme, noting that "[r]esponsibility for homeland security...is currently dispersed among more than 100 different government organizations." The Founders, it was not noted, would be astonished to learn that 100 different government organizations even exist, let alone feed into a single bureaucratic river.

Ridge was in no mood for any nonsense about sunset laws or the finite life of a cabinet department. The DHS was being created to address "an enduring vulnerability...a permanent condition,"[55] he asserted, and it, too, promised to be a permanent presence in the administrative landscape. His bureaucracy was "a 21st century agency to deal with . . . a 21st century threat."[56] And it promised to be around for the twenty-second century as well.

Ridge's exchanges with committee members were notable only in that they showed, with grim starkness, the distance the Republican Party had travelled from the rhetoric of Barry Goldwater and Ronald Reagan.

Democrat Henry Waxman, playing the unfamiliar part of taxpayers' paladin, pointed out to Ridge that "the bill you have proposed includes 21 deputy, under, and assistant secretaries. This is more than double the number of deputy and assistant secretaries at Health and Human Services, which administers a budget that is three times bigger than the budget we expect for this agency. If the objective is not to grow government, why does the new department need so many deputy and assistant secretaries?"

Ridge's response, even in the edited transcript that was eventually published, is almost incoherent. He tosses out a few buzzwords—"a mission-driven, performance-driven organization," "flexibility," "internal leadership"—before mumbling to a close. But Waxman, who even his critics concede is a tenacious fellow, persists. He asks Ridge if perhaps the proposed department "doesn't have a clear enough focus," given that its bailiwick includes agencies whose tasks have included the eradication of boll weevils, the issuance of flood insurance to those reckless enough to build along the Mississippi River, and the cleanup of oil spills.

Though the close student of bureaucratic self-aggrandizement might expect Ridge to simply start calling boll weevils "terrorist beetles," he does not. He may as well have. The soon-to-be-secretary instead argues that the DHS is a manifestation of the U.S. "pushing our borders out."[57] Though this would seem to pose constitutional problems—to wit, the designation of these frontiers as states or territories before coming under U.S. jurisdiction—Ridge is stating the situation candidly. Just as Chairman Burton, in his opening remarks, revealed that the Department of Defense is not really a department dedicated to the defense of the United States, so does Ridge's formulation drive home the fact—an unpleasant fact for those who cherish the old, constitutional America—that the U.S. borders now encompass the entire world. Not a sparrow can fall in the furthest corner of the earth without the authorization of the U.S. government.

To Rep. Souder, the expanding borders of the United States ought to stretch at least into the Caribbean, for as he lectured Director Ridge, "I am concerned that there hasn't been much reference to the narcotics question" in the administration's DHS proposal. Absent a DHS-led crackdown on narco-terrorists, as the term of the day had it, "the Caribbean Sea becomes open waters for narcotics traffickers."[58] After all, our military expends only a billion dollars-plus on drug interdiction: isn't it time for the DHS to step up to the plate?

Ridge, perhaps mindful of the perils of stepping on bureaucratic toes, offered Souder the usual platitudes—"we have been under a chemical warfare attack for quite some time and that is in the drug war"; "we know that one of the funding sources of terrorist activity happens to be the drug trade"—but he promised only a "closer partnership"[59] with the DEA, not a wholesale merger or takeover. Cabinet-level voracity has its limits.

Ridge also testified before the House Select Committee on Homeland Security on July 15, 2002. He was again, in effect, testifying for a promotion from director to secretary. (The Select Committee was up for a promotion as well, though it has yet to receive one: it remains a Select Committee rather than a permanent committee of either chamber.)

And once again, Ridge laid the rhetorical groundwork for a cease-lessly expanding government in the name of "security."

"The United States is a nation at risk of terrorist attacks and will remain so for the foreseeable future," he intoned. The phraseology was borrowed from an earlier Republican administration: The Reagan educationists had produced "A Nation at Risk" (1983), their alarm-ist document demanding heavier spending on schooling, which had, before the Cold War, been largely the responsibility of families, par-ishes, townships, cities, and occasionally state governments.

"A Nation at Risk" changed the terms of debate in Washington. Conservative Republicans were no longer quite so ready to demand the abolition of the U.S. Department of Education. In fact, President George W. Bush made the expansion of the Education Department a central campaign plank in 2004.

Ridge and the administration for which he spoke envisioned "our enduring vulnerability" to terrorism. The implication was that the DHS, too, must be "enduring." He spoke of nameless homicidal fanatics laboring "to obtain chemical, biological, radiological, and nuclear weapons for the stated purpose of killing vast numbers of Americans." These Americans, he suggested, were sitting ducks. There they were, a nation of heedless millions hanging out at "schools, sporting arenas, malls, concert halls, office buildings, high-rise resi-dences, and places of worship"— have we left anyone out? –while dusky, bewhiskered Mohammedans were plotting mayhem. What were we but a nation of targets? And the targets were legion.

Lest the country cousins get the idea that only city slickers were at risk, and lest rural representatives look askance at swelling bud-gets, Ridge spoke darkly of the "agroterrorism" which "made our heartland a potential target."

Ridge was nothing if not Bushian in his claim that "The U.S. gov-ernment has no higher purpose than to ensure the security of our people and preserve our democratic way of life."[60] The word liberty is the dog that didn't bark in that sentence. Indeed, that dog is sitting in limbo in the euthanasia clinic as you read this.

The director-bucking-for-secretary spoke of "homeland security" as "a new mission." The "primary mission" of this department, he explained, was "to protect our homeland."[61] The Department of De-fense, one assumes, is out protecting someone else's homeland.

Ridge spent a good deal of his time defending the flexible em-ployment rules embedded within the Bush homeland security bill.

He noted that the Federal Aviation Administration, the Internal Revenue Service, the Central Intelligence Agency, and most federal banking agencies have "nontraditional" personnel rules. Speaking in the cant of the bureaucrat, in which people are "human resources," Ridge promised a department in which work rules and promotions would be guided by the lodestars of "merit and fitness,"[62] admirable principles, to be sure, though if the department's job consists primarily of doling out pork and violating the liberties of Americans, who really gives a damn about the efficacy of its workforce?

Subsequent appearances of Secretary Ridge before the pertinent congressional committees illustrate the maturation of the department. No longer a tyro, heady with its own importance but insecure of its permanence, the Department, as embodied in Ridge, has grown up and shows every sign of bloat, self-importance, and eventual ossification.

In his February 9, 2004 appearance before the Senate Governmental Affairs Committee, in which he requested a 10 percent increase in his department's budget (to $40.2 billion), Secretary Ridge spoke in his trademark mélange of cliché, dolor, and euphemism. The taxpayers' money was called "resources"; federal subsidies to well-connected private firms were "unprecedented partnerships"; and reviled proposals to encourage Americans to spy on their neighbors were "robust efforts to engage citizens in preparedness efforts."[63]

Committee members were every bit as obsequious as they had been two years earlier, when the DHS was begotten. Senator Joseph Lieberman (D-CT), who considered himself the Democratic father of the department, showed his plumage as a neoconservative Democrat when he criticized the Bush administration for being too niggardly with poor Secretary Ridge.

"Mr. Secretary, I believe that you have been given insufficient resources to do the job the Homeland Security Act requires you to do," stated Lieberman, condoling with Ridge. The Bushies were "shortchanging the homeland side in the war against terrorism," added Lieberman, leaving the country "dangerously unprepared." The Senator demonstrated, not for the last time, that you cannot outspend a hawkish Democrat. (Senator Durbin, the liberal Democrat from Illinois, went Lieberman a few billion better when he argued for a "Manhattan Project"-style budget and urgency for the department.)

Lieberman added a chilling coda, offering that "we ought to aspire to achieve the same standard of nonpartisanship in matters of homeland security that at our best we have achieved in matters of international security."[64] This is an updated version of the poisonously anti-democratic notion that politics stops at the water's edge, the platitude that for half a century was used to stifle debate over foreign policy. Now, apparently, it is to be used to stifle debate over domestic policy. Just what Senator Lieberman thinks we ought to be permitted to debate, to disagree over, one can hardly imagine. Perhaps the appropriate date on which to observe National Travel Agents Day? In any event, the best response to the "water's edge" bromide is that politics will stop at the water's edge the day policies do.

Needless to say, no one made that point to Senator Lieberman.

When Secretary Ridge talked up the Urban Area Security Initiative, which funneled DHS dollars into heavily populated areas, and even dared to opine that "the bulk of the dollars . . . should be distributed according to threat and risk,"[65] small-state senators were quick to circle the wagons 'round the pork barrel. Senator Susan Collins (R-ME), chairwoman of the committee, reminded Ridge that "the concerns and vulnerabilities of our small cities, small towns and small states must not be overlooked."[66] Senator Carl Levin (D-MI) lectured Ridge that Port Huron was among those vulnerable sites, while Senator Daniel Akaka (D-HI) was exercised over the prospect of less money for Hawaii under proposed grant-funding reforms. (The state-by-state peculiarities of homeland-security grant distribution will be discussed in chapter 3.)

Senator Akaka scraped the bottom of the government-waste barrel when he asked Ridge if the "new human resources system" at DHS might include, as a way of retaining employees, a "student loan repayment"[67] mechanism. No, sadly, it does not, replied Ridge, though Akaka's gall fair boggles the mind: Are taxpayers really to be burdened with the repayment of student loans taken out by employees of the Department of Homeland Security? Under what principle of government does this fall?

Secretary Ridge assured the senators that his goal, and that of the DHS, was "to make America stronger, safer, and better prepared every single day."[68] Note that he did not say "freer."

Americans are advised not to look to Congress for capable oversight of the Department of Homeland Security. Thirteen committees and sixty subcommittees of the U.S. House of Representatives and Senate have jurisdiction over at least bits and pieces and chunks and obtrusions of the DHS. With oversight spread so ludicrously thinly, we may assume that many departmental problems will slide by, the result of...well, an oversight.

As is often the case in American history, especially recent American history, those sifting the river of verbiage for nuggets of wisdom are advised to pan in dissident streams. Senator Robert Byrd (D-WV), who with his stentorian voice, leonine mane of white hair, and penchant for steering every stray federal dollar home to West Virginia has often seemed almost a caricature of the old-time senator, a virtual Foghorn Leghorn of the body, has in his octogenarian years matured into a kind of liberal statesman and guardian of the republic. He delivered one of his finest speeches in opposition to passage of the bill creating the Department of Homeland Security. Like the last of the small-r republicans in a brave new world of empire, Byrd implored his colleagues to stop and think about what they were doing: "The people are being offered a bureaucratic behemoth, complete with fancy, top-heavy directorates, officious new titles, and noble sounding missions. . . . How utterly irresponsible. How callous. How cavalier. . . . This Department is a bureaucratic behemoth cooked up by political advisors to satisfy several inside Washington agendas," among them:

- "It is intended to protect the president from criticism" in the event of another attack;
- "It will be used to channel federal research moneys and grants to big corporate contributors";
- "It will foster easier spying and information-gathering on ordinary citizens which may be used in ways which could have nothing whatsoever to do with homeland security."

Senator Byrd was under no illusions that his fine oratory might change minds. The die was cast; like Rosemary's baby, the DHS was going to be born. But Byrd had one final prediction: "the nation will have this behemoth bureaucratic bag of tricks, this huge Department of Homeland Security, and it will hulk across the landscape of this city, touting its noble mission, shining up its new seal, and eagerly gobbling up tax dollars for all manner of things, some of which will have very little to do with protecting or saving"[69] the country, people, and institutions of which Byrd had, late in his career, become a florid, if oddly touching, defender.

Outside Congress, voices of opposition were few and scattered. Father Andrew Greeley, he of the mildly salacious books about the priesthood, wrote in the *Chicago Sun-Times* that "the pretense that the nation will be safer because this new, super bureaucracy is creeping down the Mall in Washington like the Glob from Outer Space is either dishonest or stupid."[70]

Think tanks of libertarian or classical liberal bent were cautiously critical of the DHS, pointing out, as did the Cato Institute in its handbook for the 108th Congress, that it makes limited sense to meet the challenge posed by "agile, nonbureaucratic adversaries" such as al Qaeda with a sluggish, torpid "new super bureaucracy."[71]

But few on the Right were as plainspoken as the conservative, quoted by Kate O'Beirne of *National Review*, who told his colleagues on the Right, "I reminded them that we were watching the creation of a department we'll likely spend the rest of our careers criticizing."[72]

For his part, President Bush gave the department his own first-anniversary thumbs-up, saying "You've passed every single test." He gave the department "a gold star for a job well done."[73]

He also gave it a more conventional form of gold. Departmental news releases boasted that the budget "continues the dramatic growth for agencies that are now a part of DHS."[74] Its budget expanded from $31.2 billion in its infancy in FY 2003 to $36.5 billion in FY 2004 and $40.1 billion in FY 2005.

The greatest increases in the $40.1 billion fiscal year 2005 budget came in the areas of port security, aviation security, and biodefense. The Coast Guard received an eight percent boost for its high-profile port-security measures, while Project BioShield, the vaccine and antidote-stockpiling program discussed in chapter 6, also received a significant boost in appropriations. The sexy "first responders" grants, under which the traditionally local responsibility of fire fighting is gradually being nationalized, consumed $3.6 billion of the FY 2005 budget, with complaints coming from all quarters that this sum—which, as we shall see, is far more than the nation's first responders need or can even use—is insufficient.

But then this is what follows when the president announces that "The United States government has no more important mission than protecting the homeland from future terrorist attacks."[75] The budgetary implications of such a statement are momentous: the sky really is the limit. No expense is too great when it comes to protecting the country.

Broken down by function, the Coast Guard is the largest single component of the DHS, consuming 20 percent of its FY 2005 budget authority. FEMA is second at 18 percent, followed by U.S. Customs & Border Protection (15 percent), Transportation Security Administration (13 percent), U.S. Immigration and Customs Enforcement (10 percent), the Office for Domestic Preparedness (9 percent), U.S. Citizenship and Immigration Services (4 percent), Science and Technology Directorate (3 percent), U.S. Secret Service (3 percent), and various smaller bits and pieces whose most ardent hope is to grow into larger shares of the pie.

The Department is now ensconced in its pricey new digs on Nebraska Avenue in the District of Columbia. The FY 2005 budget called for a whopping $45.1 million increase (to $65.1 million) to pay for the consolidation of DHS functions at its headquarters.

Parenthetically, the location of the department was, at first, something of an afterthought. A junior White House aide chose Chantilly, Virginia, for the site of the headquarters. Perhaps he reasoned that government buildings ought to be dispersed in an age of kamikaze hijackers. Maybe he had a cousin who was a real-estate broker in Chantilly. Whatever the reason, Secretary Ridge blew up at the thought of being an hour's limo drive from the center of Washington, D.C., which is to say the center of the universe in the political mind. Chantilly was Out; Nebraska Avenue was In. Construction contractors in the D.C. area had a nice Christmas that year.

But then Santa Claus wears a pinstriped suit on Capitol Hill. It doesn't matter much anymore whether a member of Congress is a D or an R; if a program has even the most tenuous connection with the War on Terror, it winds up in the bag of goodies. No one dares say no.

The Democrats simply abdicated their role as the opposition party in the debate over the Department of Homeland Security. When it comes to expanding the size of government, there is no opposition party.

Consider the broken record that goes by the name of Nancy Pelosi (D-CA), the Democratic House Leader. "In Fall of 2001, Bush Requested Inadequate FY 2002 Homeland Security Funding," she headlined one report. The next year was no better: "In February 2002, the FY 2003 Bush Budget Request for Homeland Security was Once Again Inadequate." Pelosi and the Democrats offer not a choice but merely a profligate echo. She speaks for her party when she says, "Democrats believe that the federal government must do much more to help prepare our first responders—our police officers, fire fighters, and emergency medical personnel—ensuring that they have the training and equipment they need."[76] In other words, Bush has done an inadequate job in nationalizing these heretofore local responsibilities: the Democrats promise to hasten the nationalization of fire departments, police departments, and town and city ambulance services.

Pelosi and the Democrats offer no opposition to the perpetual war that the Bush Republicans have promised us. And make no mistake: they have promised us a lifetime of homeland security spending.

Vice President Cheney says that more attacks are "almost certain."[77] Department of Homeland Security Secretary Tom Ridge says that more attacks are "not a question of if, but a question of when."[78]

"The threat of terrorism is a permanent condition," declared President Bush. "It's not going to go away."[79]

Neither, it seems, is the "Defense Department for the United States." Its mission has no apparent end. President Bush said, on September 20, 2001, "Our war on terror begins with al Qaeda, but it does not end there. It will not end until every terrorist group of global reach has been found, stopped, and defeated."[80]

Texas Republican Congressman Ron Paul, a libertarian who played the Robert Byrd role in the House debate over the Department of Homeland Security, blames the "flawed foreign policy of interventionism" for the attacks of 9/11, and he wonders why so munificently endowed a department as Defense was helpless before nineteen fanatics with box-cutters. Pointing to "our inability to defend our own cities, while spending hundreds of billions of dollars providing more defense for others than for ourselves," Paul urged "the DOD to provide protection, not a huge, new, militarized domestic department." But that is precisely what we got, over the objections of Paul and a handful of congressional dissenters of both parties.

Rather than a DHS, Congressman Paul called for the U.S. to "bring our troops home, including our Coast Guard; close down the base in Saudi Arabia; stop expanding our presence in the Muslim portion of the former Soviet Union; and stop taking sides in the long, ongoing war in the Middle East."[81] Such steps would almost surely lessen, if not completely eliminate, the threat of Muslim-based terrorism. But absent a return to George Washingtonian principles in foreign policy, and a disengagement of the U.S. military from the Middle East, it is hard to see how liberty can stop taking a beating in the land of the free.

The DHS, like death and taxes, is now a fact of life. In fact, the DHS is death and taxes.

Notes

1.   Jeff A. Taylor, "Homeland Fries," www.reason.com, June 11, 2002.
2.   Jennifer Van Bergen, "Homeland Security Act: The Rise of the American Police State," Truthout Report, December 2–4, 2002, www.ratical.org.
3.   Marcus J. Ranum, *The Myth of Homeland Security* (Indianapolis: Wiley, 2004), p. 221.
4.   "Executive Order Establishing Office of Homeland Security," White House, October 8, 2001.
5.   "Securing the Homeland: Strengthening the Nation," p. 2.
6.   Ibid., p. 3.
7.   Preamble, The Constitution of the United States of America.
8.   "Securing the Homeland: Strengthening the Nation," p. 3.
9.   Ibid., p. 6.
10.   Ibid., p. 4
11.   Ibid., p. 19.
12.   Ibid., p. 17.
13.   Ibid., p. 22.
14.   Quoted in Jim Tyrell, "The Department of Homeland Security: New Solutions Meet Old Problems," National Taxpayers Union Policy Paper 109 (Washington, DC: NTU, January 6, 2003), p. 1.
15.   "Americans Who Support Bush's 'Homeland Security' Plan Are Gullible, Libertarians Say," Libertarian Party press release, June 10, 2002.
16.   Quoted in Kyle Williams, "Bush Whacks Conservative Principles," July 20, 2002, worldnetdaily.com.
17.   "Bush Wants Broad 'Homeland Security' Overhaul," CNN.com, June 7, 2002.
18.   "Tool Against Terror or Taxpayer Shakedown? Study Asks Hard Questions of Homeland Security Dept.," National Taxpayers Union press release, January 6, 2003.
19.   "Bush Wants to Avoid Soviet-Style Domestic Intelligence Agency, Card Says," Fox News, June 10, 2002.
20.   Hearing of the House Government Reform Committee, June 20, 2002, p. 26.
21.   John Mintz, "Government's Hobbled Giant: Homeland Security is Struggling," *Washington Post*, September 7, 2003, p. A1.
22.   Hearing of the House Government Relations Committee, June 20, 2002, p. 23.
23.   "DHS Organization," U.S. Department of Homeland Security, www.dhs.gov, December 3, 2003, p. 4.
24.   *The Forrestal Diaries*, edited by Walter Millis (New York: Viking 1951/1966), p. 280.
25.   Kelley Beaucar Vlahos, "Value of Department of Homeland Security Debated," Fox News, October 22, 2003.
26.   "DHS Organization," U.S. Department of Homeland Security, www.dhs.gov, undated.
27.   Guy Gugliotta, "Unintended Tasks Face New Security Agency," *Washington Post*, June 10, 2002, p. A1.
28.   David Villano, "The High Cost of Homeland Defense," *Miami New Times*, October 9, 2003.
29.   "Budget in Brief Fiscal Year 2005," U.S. Department of Homeland Security, p. 37.
30.   Ibid., p. 1.
31.   Ibid.
32.   Quoted in Kate O'Beirne, "The DHS Debacle," *National Review*, August 12, 2002, www.nationalreview.com.

33. Al Hunt, "Politics, Pork and Homeland Security," *Wall Street Journal*, November 21, 2002.
34. Guy Gugliotta, "Unintended Tasks Face New Security Agency," *Washington Post*, June 10, 2002, p. A1.
35. Hearing of the House Government Reform Committee, June 20, 2002, p. 1.
36. Ibid., p. 2.
37. John Mintz, "Government's Hobbled Giant: Homeland Security is Struggling," *Washington Post*, September 7, 2003, p. A1.
38. Hearing of the House Government Reform Committee, June 20, 2002, p. 6.
39. Ibid., p. 5.
40. Ibid., p. 22.
41. Ibid., p. 44.
42. "The Department of Homeland Security for Dummies," Citizens for Legitimate Government, www.legitgov.com, March 19, 2004.
43. Hearing of the House Government Reform Committee, June 20, 2002, p. 3.
44. Ibid., p. 17.
45. Ibid., p. 41.
46. "Securing the Homeland," News Hour Online, November 15, 2002, www.pbs.org, p. 2.
47. Testimony by Governor Tom Ridge, House Select Committee on Homeland Security, July 15, 2002, Federal Document Clearing House, p. 13.
48. Mark Schmidt and Demian Brady, "Homeland Insecurity: Why Are Some Members of Congress Putting Government Unions Ahead of the American People?" National Taxpayers Union Issue Brief 139 (Washington, DC: NTU, August 7, 2002), p. 1.
49. Hearing of the House Government Reform Committee, June 20, 2002, p. 8.
50. Ibid., p. 35.
51. Ibid., p. 21.
52. Ibid., p. 47.
53. Ibid., p. 13.
54. Ibid., p. 33.
55. Ibid., pp. 23–24.
56. Ibid., p. 29.
57. Ibid., pp. 29–30.
58. Ibid., p. 39.
59. Ibid., p. 40.
60. Testimony of Governor Tom Ridge, House Select Committee on Homeland Security, July 15, 2002, p. 2.
61. Ibid., p. 3.
62. Ibid., p. 13.
63. Hearing of the Senate Governmental Affairs Committee, February 9, 2004, Federal News Service, p. 8.
64. Ibid., pp. 3–4.
65. Ibid., p. 10.
66. Ibid., p. 2.
67. Ibid., p. 17.
68. Ibid., p. 9.
69. Senator Robert Byrd, "An Irresponsible Exercise in Political Chicanery," www.salon.com, November 21, 2002.
70. Andrew Greeley, "New Monster Bureaucracy Holds No Promise," *Chicago Sun-Times*, November 29, 2002, p. 65.

71. Ivan Eland, "Homeland Security," Cato Handbook for Congress (Washington, D.C.: Cato Institute, 2003), p. 62.

72. Kate O'Beirne, "The DHS Debacle," *National Review*, August 12, 2002.

73. Siobhan Gorman, "Homeland Security Still Seeking to Define, Measure Performance," *National Journal*, www.govexec.com, March 5, 2004, p. 2.

74. "Department of Homeland Security Announces FY 2005 Budget in Brief," press release, February 2, 2004.

75. George W. Bush, "National Strategy for Homeland Security," July 2002.

76. Nancy Pelosi, "President Bush Fails Homeland Security," www.democraticleader.house.gov, undated.

77. Quoted in Charles V. Pena, "Homeland Security Alert System: Why Bother?" www.cato.org, October 31, 2002.

78. Quoted in ibid.

79. Hearing of the House Government Reform Committee, June 20, 2002, p. 2.

80. Quoted in Elaine Cassel, "The Other War: The Bush Administration and the End of Civil Liberties," www.counterpunch.com, April 26, 2003.

81. Ron Paul, "Department of Homeland Security—Who Needs It?" www.antiwar.com, July 25, 2002.

Appendix: The Establishment of the Department of Defense

The National Security Act of 1947 brought the Army, Air Force, and the Navy (including its aviation division and the Marines) "under the general direction, authority, and control of the Secretary of Defense."[1] This secretary would have power "perhaps second only to that of the president,"[2] as Douglas Kinnard wrote in his history of this relative newcomer to the Cabinet.

In lifting air power to an equivalent rank, the 1947 Act recognized the altered military landscape. But although General Dwight D. Eisenhower viewed modern war as "essentially a matter of perfected teamwork,"[3] the war-making bureaucracy forged in 1947 was born in the usual administrative fractiousness.

The U.S. War Department had been created at our nation's founding; a Department of the Navy soon followed, in 1798, in the wake of naval operations against the Barbary Pirates. Over the years, occasional calls were heard for their merger under one department and a single secretary. These proposals grew in frequency between the First and Second World Wars. In 1932, one such plan even reached the floor of the House. Though it promised a savings of $100 million—a lot of money in those days, as the saying goes—it was defeated.

In June 1941, the Navy General Board called for a unification of the services under the Joint Chiefs of Staff, but war came and reorganization took a back seat. It would not be considered "until after the war,"[4] announced General George C. Marshall, Army chief of staff.

Defense historian C.W. Borklund summarizes the thrust of the arguments for unification of the armed services under a civilian secretary of defense: "to avoid expensive and useless duplication, especially in the logistics field; to help avoid a repetition of the Pearl Harbor disaster; to assure against military domination; and to avoid the haphazard and uncoordinated manner in which the military departments competed before Congress for appropriations."

On the other hand, writes Borklund, opponents of unification argued that "the Germans had established, on paper, just such a single-staff organization and it had not worked very well for them; the plan would concentrate too much power in the hands of a single person other than the President; and such a vast military organization would be too complex for any one man to handle."[5]

The air forces of the United States, embedded within the Army, favored unification as "the best way to assure their gaining full-fledged military partnership with their sister services."[6] Besides, by war's end the air force had The Bomb: it was ready to become a co-equal partner. The Navy, on the other hand, though it had proposed unification in 1941, resisted merger after the war. The Navy worried about losing the Marines, losing bomber aircraft and other sexy weapons, and its chieftains assumed that the Army, with its air forces allied, would win the bureaucratic battle.

The midshipmen dug in. The Navy, recognizing a last ditch when it saw one, put up its own unification plan: the Eberstadt Plan, which would elevate the secretaries of war, navy, and air to cabinet rank and create a National Security Council and a Central Intelligence Agency, among other bureaucracies. The Eberstadt whose name the plan bore was New York banker Ferdinand Eberstadt. His report would form the basis of the 1947 Act that created the postwar national security establishment.

This establishment stood at antipodes from the defense envisaged by the Founding Fathers of these United States. Thomas Jefferson wanted to "abolish standing armies in time of peace,"[7] and the vast majority of Founders shared his antipathy. But in 1947, such proposals never even made it to the table.

After the Second World War, the problems of coordination and interservice rivalry that had been glaringly obvious during the war made the political momentum for consolidation unstoppable. "Economy," which had been a mainstay of consolidation arguments for years, was a prime selling point. President Truman, whose spending habits (with other people's money, at least) have never been described as parsimonious, claimed to be appalled by "the extent of the waste and inefficiency existing as a result of the operation of two separate and uncoordinated military departments,"[8] and he threw his influence behind reorganization.

The combination of weariness and optimism that marked the postwar years gave tone to the debate. The public was sick of war, sick of militarism, sick of regimentation at home, sick of high taxes and absent sons and husbands and overweening bureaucracy. The number of men in uniform plummeted from 12 million at war's end to less than one-tenth that number two years later. This gave rise to a good deal of teeth-gnashing and brow-furrowing among elites, who hadn't the slightest intention of returning the U.S. to that policy set down by George Washington in his magnificent and utterly forgotten Farewell Address.

Demobilization—the cold, sterile word which defense bureaucrats use for reuniting fathers and sons and husbands and brothers with mothers and daughters and wives and sisters—proceeded at a pace which, while far too slow for civilians who wanted to get back to their former lives, is usually reckoned a sprint by military analysts. By 1947, although nine-tenths of those 12 million soldiers were out of the armed forces, in a sign of the changing times about half of those still in uniform were overseas, mostly in Europe or Asia. George Washington's farewell advice to steer clear of European conflicts was being ignored, and with a vengeance.

President Truman proposed that the U.S. continue to keep millions of men in the service of Uncle Sam through Universal Military Training, under which all males, on reaching age eighteen, would be drafted into military service for one year, following which time they would be in the reserves. But in those days the Republican Party was skeptical of the draft and what its leading spokesmen termed "militarism," so UMT died aborning, though its cousin, conscription, was soon to rear its Prussian head in the land of the free. As it may yet in the early years of the twenty-first century.

Given the vastly expanded role that the military was to play in post-World War II America, the wise men of the day set to devising a reorganization of the defense bureaucracy. Coordination of resources, manpower, and strategy was the stated goal; "integration" and "unification" were the new shibboleths.

General George Kenney spoke for the consolidationists when he told a Senate Military Affairs Committee hearing: "Such an organization we can achieve only with unified control in Washington—a control capable of planning and developing new weapons, and new tactics unlimited by the restrictions of jurisdiction and outlook of a single service. . . . Only through an organization which centralizes responsibility for our entire military structure—land, sea, air, guided missiles, atomic power—can we develop the vision to use all those resources to their fullest."[9]

Centralization was the theme running throughout the 1940s, as it is today. The military, then as now, was not immune.

Although General George C. Marshall had nixed a proposed reorganization in 1941, by 1943 he had become its prime advocate within the administration. The Marshall Plan—or Marshall plan, that is, for unlike his proposal for the revitalization of postwar Europe this one never achieved the success designated by capitalization of the letter "p"—contained the same unconscious mimicry of Christianity as the scheme eventually adopted. That is, the single department of war comprised a triune body consisting of the naval, air, and ground forces. A civilian secretary and military chief of staff were at the top of the pyramid.

While the airmen seized the reformist moment to elevate the profile of their branch of the service, the Navy, traditionally the most turf-conscious and congressman-friendly branch of the service, resisted, tactfully. The fear was that the Navy was going to be "not merged, but submerged."[10] Sensing that the momentum for reorganization was unstoppable, Secretary of the Navy James Forrestal enlisted investment banker Ferdinand Eberstadt, a friend, to draw up his more Navy-centric proposal.

Forrestal fought this battle with all the cunning of a seasoned politician, even though prior to joining the Roosevelt administration in 1940 he had been an investment banker. Secretary of the Navy Forrestal made tactical retreats, agreeing in mid-1946 to the inevitable single secretary of what was then to be called "National Defense," but his thrusts, parries, and cavils led to that strange setup in the National Security Act, later revised, that provided for cabinet-level rank for the secretaries of army, navy, and air, even though the chief assistant to the president in military matters was to be the secretary of defense, whose portfolio included the entire National Military Establishment.

The National Security Act achieved final congressional passage on July 25, 1947, and was signed into law by President Truman the next day aboard his plane, which was prophetically named the "Sacred Cow." For in the future, the most sacred cows in the entire U.S. budget would be those programs nearest and dearest to Truman's heart: the military and Social Security.

The 1947 Act also created a National Security Council, a Central Intelligence Agency, and a National Security Resources Board (NSRB). The Act, in a rare triumph of plain speaking, set up the secretary of defense as the head of what it frankly called "The National Military Establishment." The first Secretary would be none other than James Forrestal. Navy had skunked Army.

The 1947 Act, sold as a monumental and landmark step in U.S. military history, had a decidedly mixed legacy. It did not end interservice rivalry, though when vast sums of money are available to three competing entities, nothing will ever end such rivalries. They are the price of big government.

As historian Walter Millis notes, "Many Congressmen who supported the 1947 'unification' act did so under the impression that it was going to save money. But this was neither its primary purpose nor, markedly, its effect. Its aim was to provide the United States with a coherent and self-consistent system of military-political direction."[11]

Just how "coherent and self-consistent" the system was remained an open question. The 1947 Act was amended in 1949, 1953, 1958, and thereafter with a frequency that belied any claims to "coherence."

In 1949, during the first amendments to the Act, the name "National Military Establishment," with its awesomely Prussian implications, was changed to the "Department of Defense." The heads of the three branches were made clearly subordinate to the secretary of defense. Yet "the 1949 amendments did little to end these service conflicts,"[12] as even a historian sympathetic to the department has written. The 1947 Act would be amended periodically thereafter, in piecemeal fashion and also with more substantive changes, but even the reorganizations supported by President Eisenhower in 1953 and 1958 could not streamline this hydra-headed and enormous bureaucracy. We were told, with great fanfare, that the Goldwater-Nickles Act of 1986 finally set things right, but as even Bush Defense Secretary Donald Rumsfeld has conceded, the department is a bureaucratic nightmare. And this after almost six decades of fine-tuning!

James Forrestal was sworn in as secretary of defense on September 17, 1947. Less than two years later—on May 22, 1949—he leaped to his death from the sixteenth floor of the psychiatric wing of the Bethesda Naval Hospital. (He had resigned in March 1949.)

As the first chief of the National Military Establishment, Forrestal took as his duty the acquisition of additional money and power for his fiefdom. He was "a persistent lobbyist" for appropriations above and beyond the "budgetary ceilings imposed by President Truman."[13] His chief complaint with the reorganization was that the secretary of the NME lacked sufficient authority—a rather different position than he had taken as a turf-guarding secretary of the navy. But then men are wont to "grow" in office, as their flattering press often reminds us.

The James Forrestal saga has a tragic coda, of course. He began exhibiting symptoms of paranoia. Shadowy figures were following him, or so he thought. He was diagnosed with "a total psychotic breakdown . . . characterized by suicidal features,"[14] which is perhaps not the ideal personality type to occupy his office. The day of his death he had been copying a translation of Sophocles's "Chorus from Ajax," which includes the lines:

> Thy son is in a foreign clime
>> Where Ida feeds her countless flocks,
>> Far from thy dear, remembered rocks,
> Worn by the waste of time —
> Comfortless, nameless, hopeless save
> In the dark prospect of the yawning grave. . . .[15]

Conspiracy buffs have since had a field day with the Forrestal case, the circumstances surrounding his departure from the Truman administration, and his apparent suicide soon thereafter, but for our purposes James Forrestal is useful as an illustration of the iron law of bureaucracy: once created, it has a survival instinct with a fierceness dwarfing that of the most feral wolf. And unlike the wolf, it grows.

Walter Millis, the military affairs writer who edited Forrestal's diaries, which were published posthumously, wrote that although "a memorial bronze now stands at the Mall entrance of the Pentagon," the "real memorial [to Forrestal] is within, in the teeming offices of the vast establishment for defense, which owed so much to his patient architecture."[16] This is meant as a compliment, though those who have paid the onerous taxes necessary to support this "vast establishment" over the last six decades may register a muted dissent.

Notes

1. C. W. Borklund, *The Department of Defense* (New York: Praeger, 1968), p. v.
2. Douglas Kinnard, *The Secretary of Defense* (Lexington: University Press of Kentucky, 1980), p. 1.
3. Borklund, *The Department of Defense*, p. 17.
4. Ibid., p. 20.
5. Ibid., p. 28.
6. Ibid., p. 34.
7. *Thomas Jefferson to James Madison, The Political Writings of Thomas Jefferson*, edited by Edward Dumbauld (Indianapolis, IN: Bobbs-Merrill, 1955), p. 141.
8. Borklund, *The Department of Defense*, p. 15.
9. Ibid., p. 18.
10. Robert G. Albion and Robert H. Connery, *Forrestal and the Navy* (New York: Columbia University Press, 1962), p. 250.
11. Walter Millis, *Arms and Men: A Study in American Military History* (New Brunswick: Rutgers University Press, 1956/1981), p. 313.
12. Borklund, *The Department of Defense*, p. 57.
13. William A. Lucas, *The Organizational Politics of Defense* (Pittsburgh: International Studies Association, 1974), p. 30.
14. Ibid., p. 38.
15. *The Forrestal Diaries*, edited by Walter Millis, p. 555.
16. Ibid.

3

Wastin' Away Again in Homeland Securityville

Only in post-9/11 America can disaster relief be touted as a "springboard for economic development,"[1] but that's exactly how a fiscal analyst from the Louisiana state legislature described the vast opportunities opened up in the homeland security field. The grifters and grafters have sniffed out these opportunities: According to an Associated Press dispatch from Baton Rouge, upwards of a dozen lobbyists are present in Louisiana House and Senate committee rooms every time those magic words "homeland security" are uttered. Not to be outsubsidized, plenty of representatives from colleges and universities may be found at these meetings as well.

Security consultant Marcus J. Ranum, specialist in computer security and author of the provocative book, *The Myth of Homeland Security*, writes with some incredulity: "Somehow I have gotten on a 'homeland security' conference's mailing list. About once a month I get invitations to attend this important conference: 'The Grants Workshop will provide the attendee with important information about federal agency plans for over $3 billion in grants to first responders for training, communications, and outfitting. Attendees will learn where funding is located, how to apply for and win grants, and how to survive the audit process.' In other words, it's an entire conference devoted to teaching Beltway bandits and bandwagon-jumpers how to get their slice of the homeland security pork."[2]

This needn't surprise us, nor should we be shocked by conferences with such titles as "How to Sell Security to the Government." We do marvel, though, at the sheer tastelessness of the mad scramble for federal subsidies before all the bodies had even been excavated from Ground Zero. The rubble-dust had yet to settle, the tears had yet to dry, the endless reiterations of the event had yet to play out on television, before the lobbyists and subsidy-seeking businesses descended on Washington, D.C., in search of 9/11 loot.

In what must surely rank as one of the most callous remarks in modern lobbying, Andrew Sherman, an attorney with the firm of McDermott, Will & Emery who "helps Fortune 500 companies maneuver federal contracts," said in the aftermath of the Trade Center collapse, "How do we translate these unfortunate events into opportunities for our companies?"[3]

Well, give Mr. Sherman points for candor, if not sensitivity. He was far from alone in seeing that there was money to be made from disaster and fear. Homeland security became a growth industry during the first Bush administration. Of course, a certain etiquette attached itself to the homeland security lobbyists. Representatives of companies battling for government contracts were sure to pin American flags to their Brooks Brothers lapels, and the trade shows at which companies showed off their latest surveillance wares featured oversized American flags, patriotic music, and other overt symbols of national pride. Mustn't seem too brash, after all.

Still, time was a-wastin'. Though to many it seemed that Congress rushed through the legislation creating the Department of Homeland Security, to lobbyists the delay was galling. "There's no time to wait for the Department of Homeland Security," said an impatient Phil Whitebloom, chief of government sales for Sony Electronics, in the early summer of 2002: "Companies need to secure positions in the homeland security area now. You need to get in with the FBI, CIA, and National Security Agency."[4]

"Get in with": a nice choice of words, that. Those businesses for whom government contracts are the lifeblood—the charter members of the military-industrial complex against which President Eisenhower so vainly warned an unheeding posterity—were already "in with" the spooks and spies. As Gloria Lee of Taxpayers for Common Sense noted in July 2002, "small companies have yet to figure out how to position themselves next to more established government contractors like Lockheed Martin, Boeing, Northrop Grumman, and Raytheon."[5]

These quasi-governmental businesses were aboard the homeland security gravy train before sales reps from the smaller companies had even pinned on their plastic flags. Lockheed Martin nabbed a $79 million contract in March 2002 to supply three radar systems to the Tethered Aerostat Radar System, which monitors the Gulf Coastal border. Two months later, it was awarded a $490 million Transportation Security Administration contract to oversee the famously snafu-ridden conversion of private airport security forces into a federalized workforce. (This job—nationalizing a formerly private industry—was fitting for a state dependent like Lockheed Martin.) In July 2004, Lockheed Martin won a $15 million DARPA (Defense Advanced Research Projects Agency) contract to develop a laser-based communications system.

Boeing, meanwhile, which had been in a downward spiral before September 11, 2001, saw the homeland security boom as "an answer to its prayers."[6] In the first months of the homeland security bull market, it won a five-year, $1.37 billion contract to equip 429 U.S. airports with the bomb-screening devices that security experts have found to be almost laughably ineffective.

Nevertheless, the little guys wanted in on the action, too, so on July 10, 2002, the U.S. Senate sponsored a Small Business Homeland Security Expo for budding clients of the corporate welfare state. The Expo permitted fifty-four high-tech companies to show their wares under the auspices of the world's greatest deliberative body. The underlying message to the bureaucracy was clear: Consider these companies for contracts if you know what's good for your budget. The fifty-four companies were proudly sponsored by various members of the U.S. Senate: Democrat, Republican, liberal, conservative, peacenik, or warmonger—it didn't matter, so long as the pork barrel had its lid removed for easy dipping.

Liberal senators like Rhode Island Democrat Jack Reed and California Democrat Barbara Boxer proudly sponsored exhibitors from their home states: LiveWave, Inc. of Newport, Rhode Island, and Solid Terrain Modeling of Fillmore, California, respectively. The latter "brought in three-dimensional replicas of geographic areas created by satellite digital elevation and photometric data"[7] a useful tool in warfare, it would seem, though the fact that this was to be used for "homeland security" suggests that its use would be in domestic surveillance. Senator Boxer had been among the critics of the USA-PATRIOT Act, though it seems that principle bends its knee before the pork barrel.

That the Small Business Homeland Security Expo was a bazaar at which buyer and seller both profited, and the taxpayer—the only party absent from the premises—paid through the nose seemed not to unduly worry its sponsors. For after all, as National Security Advisor Condoleeza Rice said, "You can put no price on security."[8]

Actually, you can, if your calculator has room for enough zeroes. When homeland security pork is the prize, there are no dissenters in Washington, only supplicants. The big bad she-devil of right-wing Republican direct-mail campaigns, Senator Hillary Rodham Clinton (D-NY), is every bit as sedulous about steering homeland security bucks to her—well, adopted—state as is the most PAC-fattened old hawk.

The script from which our senators and representatives speak is of the one-size-fits-all variety. The "partisanship" which editorialists are always lamenting—as if having no debate is somehow healthy for a democratic republic—is conspicuously absent when talk turns to homeland security grants. So when Senator Clinton convened a June 2004 conference in Syracuse, New York, she told the more than 300 "business leaders, university researchers, and investors" that it was time to start bringing home the bacon.

Senator Clinton warned New York's businesses and universities that they were lagging in the race to lap up the most homeland security loot. Other states had done superior jobs in organizing their ostensibly private enterprises into government grant-seeking consortia, according to Senator Clinton. She noted the presence of numerous respected private secondary schools in upstate New York—Cornell University, the University of Rochester, Syracuse University, Rochester Institute of Technology, Rensselaer Polytechnic Institute—and encouraged these schools to be more aggressive in hunting down federal grants.

"There could not be a more urgent task," declared Senator Clinton, and for a moment there was confusion in the minds of the audience. Just what was this urgent task? The filling out of DHS applications? Marshalling the local congressional delegation in support of one's application? Tracking down and verifying all those Social Security numbers that must be plugged into the application before it is deemed complete? Well...yes and no. "The homeland security needs of our country are rather daunting," she continued. "I don't want to wake up one morning and think there are things we should have done."

Again, it's not clear if this prospective regret was for applications uncompleted or disasters that may yet befall us. In any event, lest anyone judge her a parochial hack, or a mere pork barrel politico in the fashion of the senior New York Senator, the tireless Democrat Charles Schumer, Senator Clinton intoned that it was "in the national interest to bring [our businesses and educational institutions] together to provide the innovations we need to enhance the security of our communities and country."[9]

Senator Clinton made much of the "partnership" that was developing in the burgeoning field of homeland security. Business, the federal government, and heavily subsidized research universities were joining—partnering, as the jargon goes—in unprecedented ways. The Senator accepted this partnership as perfectly natural, though sixty years ago we knew it by the f-word: fascism. Shorn of its German racialist additions, the fascist took as his central economic tenet that big business, big labor unions, the universities, and the central government ought to work together like the fingers on a hand. That these fingers might be encased in brass knuckles was simply a given. Partnership was the essence, and if a few heads had to be cracked in the process of cementing that partnership, well, that's the way it goes.

The fascist, as the brilliant *New Republic* columnist John T. Flynn wrote in his analysis of fascism, *As We Go Marching* (1944), wishes to

> commit this country to the rule of the bureaucratic state; interfering in the affairs of the states and cities; taking part in the management of industry and finance and agriculture; assuming the role of great national banker and investor, borrowing billions every year and spending them on all sorts of projects through which such a government can paralyze opposition and command public support; marshaling great armies and navies at crushing costs to support the industry of war and preparation for war which will become our greatest industry; and adding to all this the most romantic adventures in global planning, regeneration, and domination all to be done under the authority of a powerfully centralized government in which the executive will hold in effect all the powers with Congress reduced to the role of a debating society. There is your fascist.[10]

Allowing for Congress to add to its role of debating society the re-election-guaranteeing role of bacon provider, does Flynn's description seem rather timely?

Certainly the DHS is based on assumptions that fit Flynn's patterns of fascism. In its budget summaries, it calls for the U.S. government to "maintai[n] the nation's technological superiority in science and technology" and to "engage the private sector in innovative research and development, rapid prototyping of technologies, and systems acquisition."[11] Thus are big business and big government made mutual handmaidens.

In the early-to-mid-1980s, "privatization" was all the rage. Municipalities and state governments, especially, experimented with ways in which they might save money by contracting out services usually provided by government (e.g., trash collection, transportation) to private firms. Privatization worked—too well, it seems, for public employee unions mobilized as never before to halt privatization before it became anything resembling a permanent policy.

In the age of homeland security, we are experiencing just the opposite phenomenon: not so much nationalization as "governmentalization." Companies in what once was known as the "private security" realm have been co-opted into—or have sold out to—governments at all levels. Where just a few years ago they supplied private businesses and citizens with the equipment and the personnel necessary for an effective private defense against crime or trespass, today they largely have joined the rush to the homeland security bazaar. They are, for all intents and purposes, clients of the security state.

The transformation began almost overnight. Typically, the story ran like this one from December 11, 2001: "KPMG Consulting Hires Veteran Lobbyist," blared the headline. It seems that KPMG, a "global systems integrator with about 10,000 employees," didn't need a weatherman to tell which way the wind was blowing. Though its clients included various nonprofit and educational institutions, the share of KPMG's revenues "derived from the public sector" had climbed to 40 percent, and if not the sky then at least a percentage good enough for a B grade in most schools—say, 80?—seemed the limit. So KPMG hired a veteran lobbyist, one Charles Cantus, "to oversee the firm's lobbying efforts at all levels of government." Cantus's first job, according to the company line, would be to "emphasize KPMG Consulting's 'proven expertise' in homeland security."[12]

And so the vicious circle got more vicious. The lobbyist lobbies for homeland security grants, the company's dependence upon government subsidies deepens, its vested interest in prolonging the homeland security era grows greater, its lobbying team presses for ever more grants, and before long KPMG may as well cut its payroll checks from the U.S. Treasury.

Where, the naïf might ask, do these lobbyists come from? From the same bureaucratic swamp whither their ancestors hailed. Nineteen months after the events of September 11, 2001, Philip Shenon of the *New York Times* wrote a piece that fairly bristles with outrage beneath the gray prose of the gray lady of journalism:

> When Tom Ridge arrived here after the September 11 attacks and opened the White House Office of Homeland Security, the former Pennsylvania governor quickly surrounded himself with a group of trusted deputies, many of them drawn from the staff he assembled as governor.
>
> But when Mr. Ridge was sworn in this year as the first secretary of homeland security, some of his inner circle did not follow. Instead, they emerged as lobbyists whose corporate clients want contracts from Mr. Ridge's multibillion-dollar agency.
>
> They are a small part of a booming new lobbying business in Washington that is focused on helping large corporations get a share of the billions of dollars that will be spent by the vast domestic security bureaucracy that Mr. Ridge oversees.[13]

Of course, none of these men would dare exit the house without his American flag pinned to this lapel. Some may even tear up when the band plays Francis Scott Key's anthem. But they are, if one may use frank language in a cowardly time, scoundrels.

Homeland security can only be described as a boom market for lobbyists. Between January 2002 and June 2003, the number of registered lobbyists in the anti-terrorism field swelled by 500 percent, to 799. Over roughly that same period, the number of companies that used the words "homeland," "security," or "terror" on their lobbyist registration forms went from 157 to 569.[14] Their speech is as vulgar as their profession; as certain of these favor-seekers told Philip Shenon of the *New York Times*, they are all about "securing your piece of the homeland security pie" and helping clients "avoid the land mines and find the gold mines in homeland security."[15]

Whether Secretary Ridge places his countrymen on yellow alert or orange alert, the lobbying light is always green for go. Every month of the Ridge reign a few more high-level aides left the DHS for what was known, in those quaint days of yore, as Gucci Gulch. Blank Rome Government Relations, a powerhouse lobbying firm, includes Ridge's former chief of staff and two other influential Ridge aides. Secretary Ridge issued laughable statements denying that his associates had any inside track on DHS contracts, a claim that could convert even the terminally naïve to gruff skepticism.

Among the sleaze merchants is former Senator Tim Hutchinson (R-AK), who lost his seat after a messy sex scandal. Hutchinson, once a favorite of the Christian Right, divorced his wife of nearly thirty years to marry a much younger and comelier aide. Like most disgraced or simply retired politicians, Hutchinson did not return to live among the people who had sent him forth; instead, he traded on his Senate experience to become a high-priced lobbyist. In a stroke of good luck, Hutchinson's brother Asa was appointed undersecretary of Homeland Security. In summer 2003, an e-mail from lobbyist Tim boasted of the appointment he had set up for a manufacturer of germ-warfare antidotes to meet with brother Asa. The glare of publicity made the Hutchinsons uncomfortable, but only for a second, as is the case with their kind. In fact, the public scrutiny afforded that meeting probably helped Tim Hutchinson win new clients. The guy has ACCESS, and war or no war, isn't that what really counts?

Of course, both sides play this corrupt game. Democrats are no better, nor worse, than Republicans. Microsoft thought it had hit the jackpot in early 2004 when it hired Thomas Richey as its chieftain of homeland security technology. Richey, an ex-Coast Guard commander, had been an advisor to Massachusetts Senator John Kerry. If Kerry took the White House, Microsoft would be in the catbird's seat.

L-3 Communications, which manufactures explosive detectors for airports, hired Linda Daschle, wife of Senate Democratic Minority Leader Tom Daschle of South Dakota, as a lobbyist. (Covering all bases, L-3 has the good fortune to be located in the home district of House Appropriations Committee Chairman Bill Young [R-FL].) Another homeland-security firm, URS Corporation, was awarded a $600 million contract by the U.S. Army. What a coincidence: a partial owner of URS is the husband of California Democratic senator and security hawk Dianne Feinstein. Other Beltway fixtures who lobby for homeland security companies include General Barry McCaffrey, the "jail 'em all" drug czar of the Clinton administration; Louis Sullivan, secretary of health and human services under President Bush; Daniel Lungren, former California attorney general; and ex-INS general counsel William P. Cook.

Northrup Grumman created the position of vice president for homeland security in early 2003; he was worth it, for the company landed a $350 million contract to construct a DHS data network. "The Department of Homeland Security is the new cottage industry for government contractors, whether they are consultants who churn out paper or people who provide real services or hardware,"[16] says Charles Pena, director of defense studies at the Cato Institute.

Fred Wertheimer, long-time activist with the government reform group Common Cause, says, "When you see lobbying firms starting to create whole new departments for the sole purpose of lobbying for homeland security contracts, I think the signal for the American people is to watch out, to be vigilant that their taxpayer dollars for homeland security get the best possible results, as opposed to going to the best Washington lobbyists."[17]

Wertheimer means well but he is hopelessly naïve. "Citizen oversight" of these contracts and these lobbyists is non-existent—despite the best and well-funded efforts of Common Cause and the various organizations associated with Ralph Nader over the years. The only way to safeguard these taxpayer dollars is to return them to the taxpayers; to abolish the vast web of homeland security programs that do nothing to keep us secure.

War has always attracted scam artists and unscrupulous profiteers. President Lincoln was besieged with place and subsidy-seekers; after the First World War, Senator Gerald Nye (R-ND) made a name for himself with his investigation of the "merchants of death," those arms manufacturers who had lobbied for U.S. entry into the war as a means of enriching their own companies. On the brink of the Second World War, Kenneth A. Read, executive director of the Izaak Walton League, wrote in *Outdoor America*:

> Just as ghouls take advantage of a fire or disaster to prey upon the property of the unfortunate victims, so many of the exploiters are taking advantage of the present temper of the public mind and are attempting to slide their pet projects through as national defense measures.

> It's time to call a halt and comb off the national defense bandwagon those opportunists who have attached themselves to it like leeches in an attempt to further their own selfish interests.[18]

Mr. Reid, meet the Department of Homeland Security.

The leeches no longer even make much of an effort to disguise their leech-like intentions. They are bolder than the rashest thief. A website (www.HomelandDefenseStocks.com) is even devoted to this burgeoning field. For as Dennis Treece, director of corporate security for the Massachusetts Port Authority, marvels, "the feeding frenzy for Homeland Defense dollars in intense."[19]

In May 2004, Tel Aviv, Israel hosted the first in what is slated to be an annual international Homeland Security Conference. *Defense Daily International* described the mood as one of cautious optimism, as the gathered lobbyists, contractors, and government officials assessed "the emerging U.S. homeland security market."

This government-dominated "market" is a "minefield," remarked Dan Inbar of Homeland Security Research Corporation, a San Jose-based research firm. These "markets are legislation-driven," said Inbar in a vast understatement. Yet Israeli companies view the markets as containing many "entrepreneurial opportunities," according to *Defense Daily International*.[20]

It may seem borderline obscene to use the language of freedom—markets, entrepreneurship, opportunity—in discussing government programs designed to kill people and stifle liberties, but welcome to the twenty-first century. After his study of the homeland security megalith, computer security maven Marcus Ranum, no pacifist or libertarian purist, came to the conclusion (gasp!) that "there are gigantic bureaucracies that exist primarily for the sole purpose of prolonging their existence."[21] True. But their purposes may also be malign.

Few such phrases pack as much punch as "first responders." Think of the indelible images of September 11, 2001: New York City police officers trying valorously to create order out of the carnage; New York City fire fighters risking their lives—and in hundreds of cases losing those lives—to save those in distress, to quench seemingly unquenchable fires, to succeed or die trying in the rescue of innocent persons trapped in unthinkably dire circumstances. Not for nothing did the public image of New York City turn around almost overnight. Gone was the pushy, rude, arrogant obnoxious Manhattanite; the vile mugger slinking furtively through his subterranean world; the beady-eyed pervert trolling the sex shops of Times Square. Taking the place of these stereotypes was the stout-hearted, brave, and devoted fire fighters and police, the "first responder" who worked tirelessly despite the threat of death that was never far from his or her experience. This stereotype contained the same mixture of truth, exaggeration, and downright buncombe as the previous stereotypes, but who wanted to be so impolite as to point out this inconvenient fact? So around the country, men and women in Boise, in Buffalo, and in Birmingham—places condescended to, if not despised, by the New York City elites—wore their NYPD and NYFD ballcaps, proudly identifying themselves with the first responders whose grace under pressure and baptism under fire we had witnessed on our television screens.

The phrase "first responder" was compelling, powerful; its apotheosis occurred during the days following 9/11, but the groundwork for the public adulation of first responders had been laid by such earlier pop culture phenomena as the TV shows *Emergency* and *Rescue 911* with William Shatner. Politicians, with their unerring eye for the safe harbor in a time of storm, flocked to first responders. Liberals, conservatives, democratic socialists, big-business Republicans—no matter what their politics, they tried to be photographed next to as many police and fire fighters as possible. Senator John Kerry (D-MA) made the fire fighter a virtual emblem of his 2004 presidential campaign, surrounding himself with as many men and women in red coats and conical hats as possible. If Teresa Heinz Kerry had permitted it, no doubt he'd have adopted a Dalmatian during the campaign. Once he was in their presence the upper-class Kerry usually found he had nothing to say to these working-class stalwarts, but the media opportunities were too valuable to pass up. If ever there were a presidential candidate to whom those fearful of fire ought to attach themselves, it was John Kerry. A Bic couldn't be flicked within a mile of the Kerry campaign before whole departments of fire fighters aimed their hoses at the little flame.

Not only are these images political gold, but there's golden votes in them thar first responder hills. More than one million men and women serve as fire fighters in the United States, about three-quarters of whom are volunteers. There are more than 550,000 full-time employees in police departments across the country, of whom about 80 percent are sworn personnel. (In contrast to fire fighters, almost no police officers are volunteers.) There are approximately 300,000 employees of sheriff's departments in the United States, of whom about two-thirds are sworn personnel. And there are more than 150,000 national registered emergency medical technicians (EMTs) in this country.

"First responders" have been consistently featured in DHS publications and budgetary apologias. Typically, the Department of Homeland Security FY 2004 "Budget in Brief" leads off with the good news that the president proposed—and Congress ratified—a 1,000 percent increase for "the nation's first responders," who are described as "the police officers, fire fighters, and medical personnel who risk their lives every day defending our homeland." (The president spent his first term separating first responders from their homes. Almost 400,000 reserve and National Guard troops were called up in Bush's first term, depleting fire and police departments back home. A Police Executive Research Forum poll "found that 44 percent of police forces across the nation have lost officers as a result of deployment"[22] in the Afghanistan and Iraq wars.)

Don't think the first responders haven't noticed the adulation of the politicos and the media. They bask in it, yes, but at the same time their spokesmen seek ever more gold. Typically, in late 2002 the International Association of Fire Fighters demanded a $3 billion appropriation not for all first responders but solely for fire fighters. There's gold in them thar media puff jobs, too.

The vein seems deep indeed. First-responder training facilities are springing up like toadstools after a rainstorm. The Nevada Test Site in Mercury, Nevada, which trains 3,000 fire fighters, paramedics, and policemen annually, is slated to quintuple that number as the DHS money comes rolling in, courtesy of Senator Harry Reid (D-NV). A forsaken naval air base in Glenview, Illinois, is being spruced into "the Midwest's premier training academy." A police shooting range in Sunrise, Florida, has been rechristened an "antiterrorism center." At Oakland Community College in suburban Detroit, a $13 million antiterror-training center looks like a movie set, with its Potemkin complex of streets, buildings, homes, and a bank. Tasteless Michiganders can buy bricks at a memorial being constructed around a hunk of metal from the World Trade Center.

Such centers are popping up in every state, in every corner of every state, and in every congressional district with a member vigorous or shameless enough to lobby for subsidy. "The money is better spent in equipping hospitals and fire departments,"[23] Amy Smithson of the Henry L. Stimson Center told the *Christian Science Monitor*. Perhaps the hospitals should change their names to Anti-Terrorism Triage Centers and watch the DHS money roll in.

The money is falling from Washington like manna from heaven, or at least heaven's bureaucratic simulacrum. The regnant ideology of Washington in the Age of Terror was expressed by Rep. Jim Turner of Texas, ranking Democrat on the House Select Committee on Homeland Security: "The real question we must ask when we talk about funding a stronger homeland defense is, what is the cost of failure? The threat to lives, the threat of a catastrophic attack would be unthinkable. Whatever the cost is [sic] certainly worth it in terms of the lives and safety of the American people."[24] So let the greenbacks flow!

The chattering classes ensconced in Washington's gleaming cordillera of 501(c)(3) think tanks act as a pinstriped and power-shoed cheerleading squad for homeland security spending. What historian Arthur Schlesinger, Jr., once called the "Vital Center" is a vital force for centralism. Michael O'Hanlon, senior fellow of the Brookings Institution, told Cable News Network anchor Rhonda Schaffler that "if anything we should not worry about pork...because the national imperative to get secure is so pressing." He continued, "If anything, this [FY 2005] budget's too small."[25] Break open the checkbook, solons!

O'Hanlon envisions, with pleasure, what can only be called a freespending police state capable of protecting every skyscraper in America. His "conservative" counterparts in think tank land are just as spendthrift.

Following DHS Secretary Tom Ridge's tautology that "for the homeland to be secure, the hometown must be secure,"[26] members of Congress have also decided that one's re-election is more secure when one's hometown gets lots of moola. Bringing home the bacon is a time-honored way of bolstering one's political prospects, and it doesn't make a whole lot of difference if the bacon was sliced from a pig in the Department of Health and Human Services, the Department of Veterans Affairs, or the Department of Homeland Security.

Stories of money frantically chasing down unsuspecting or reluctant fire fighters are legion. For instance, Appleton, Wisconsin writer Jennifer Gritt took a tour of her region in rural Wisconsin to find DHS grants to be as common as—and sometimes no more welcome than—mud puddles.

In the village of Little Chute, Wisconsin, the fire department used its $38,000 grant to purchase new air tanks, although, as Gritt writes, "I'm pretty sure they would have already been equipped with ones that worked seeing how they are fire fighters and all."

Next door to Little Chute, the village of Combined Locks—how's that for a secure name?—"decided that the best way to protect residents from a biological attack was to install bulletproof glass in its police headquarters." Added Gritt, "And all I can say is, it's about time! Because the total number of drive-by shootings at that building last year came to a disturbing zero." Better safe than sorry, Tom Ridge would add.

Gritt notes what the regurgitators of DHS press releases seldom understand; to wit, that "even if a terrorist bombing did occur here, first responders in this area already have the equipment and training they need. These units have fully functioning emergency vehicles and they know how to rescue people from a burning building and treat the wounded." The DHS funds are a high-profile squandering of taxpayers' money. Their use comes in buying "equipment local fire and police departments could never afford or could never convince their local governments (and us residents) . . . were necessary."

Not that all fire and police chiefs are greedy grant-grubbers. Police Chief David Peterson of Wisconsin's Fox Valley Metro Police Department gave reporters an earful when asked what he thought of Homeland Security grants.

"In a nutshell, I think it's a joke," said Chief Peterson. "We're supposedly trying to cut back on a deficit," yet "every state wants a piece of the pie."

"Could I upgrade some equipment here?" Peterson asked rhetorically. "Sure. But I'll do it the right way."

Now that's a local hero.[27]

They were harder to find in flinty New Hampshire, as journalist Jordan Carleo-Evangelist found. For instance, the New Hampshire town of Bennington, with all of 1,272 souls and not an al Qaeda sympathizer among them, spent part of its $6,500 2003 Homeland Security grant to buy chemical weapons suits.

"I don't see no specific threats," admitted Steve Campbell, Bennington's chief of police. "It was just something they offered, so we figured we'd get on the bandwagon. Even though we're a small department, we take advantage of it."[28]

The Granite State is finding creative uses for DHS money. For instance, local police departments in New Hampshire will "get access to satellite television channels that transmit continuous news."[29] This is a new function for the federal government: add to the protection of life and liberty the provision of subsidized CNN.

Yet as the fire chief of Hampstead, New Hampshire, told Carleo-Evangelist, although Manhattan may have suffered "a tragic loss," nevertheless "when the sun shines we warm up. If they're giving, my palms are up because it helps the town and it helps the taxpayers."[30]

The Bethesda-Chevy Chase [Maryland] Fire Squad, described with evocative delicacy by the *Washington Post* as "politically active," actually lobbied the veteran U.S. Senator Barbara Mikulski (D-MD) for "protective clothing and equipment above that given to other Montgomery County stations—and got it."

This seems extraordinary: while distributive imbalances between states or regions are common, in part due to fierce lobbying and jockeying for position, one would assume that fire departments within a county would exhibit a greater decorum. But not in suburban Washington. Far from expressing shame or regret over his aggressiveness, the savvy chief of the Bethesda-Chevy Chase Fire Department, Ned Sherburne, boasted, "Frankly, the county was surprised at some of the political maneuvering we were able to do."

James S. Gilmore III, the former governor of Virginia, chairman of the Congressional Advisory Panel to Assess Domestic Response Capabilities for Terrorism Involving Weapons of Mass Destruction, and, most profitably, a homeland security consultant who heads something called USA Secure, told the *Washington Post*, "If you simply fund every local desire, the demand for money is going to be so great that you are going to break the back of the economy, which is exactly what the terrorists would like."[31] Although local departments must submit requests for DHS monies to the states and buy equipment from a list authorized by the federal government, many fire and emergency response chiefs have complained that this cumbersome process slows the passage of vitally needed funds to first responders. Though just how "vitally needed" these funds are makes for an interesting if seldom-asked question.

The range of outrageous DHS grants makes one wish that Senator Proxmire and his "Golden Fleece" award might be revivified. It also makes doubly amusing the straight-faced vow of Kyle Downey, a Republican staffer on the House Budget Committee, who told *USA Today* in April 2003 that "There's a renewed focus on rooting out waste, fraud and abuse. For the rest of the year, we will be watching this very, very closely."[32] Unfortunately for Mr. Downey and for the countless politicians who have pledged to cut government spending in mysterious ways, there is no line item in the budget reading "Waste, Fraud, and Abuse."

Colchester, Vermont, whose 18,000 citizens in perhaps the least strategically important and defense-dominated state in the union would seem to have precious little to fear from terrorists, received a $58,000 "search-and-rescue vehicle that can bore through concrete and search for victims in collapsed buildings." There is such a thing, as Colchester teaches us, as being too well-prepared for disaster.

Across America, towns and counties that might wait till the next millennium before showing up on a terror-target list are buying—or having forced upon them—emergency vehicles and equipment for which they are a ridiculously ill fit. For instance, Christian County,

Kentucky received $36,800 for apparatus to be used in the event of a chemical or biological catastrophe. The county's leaders, good and honest Christians, apparently, told *USA Today* that they neither needed nor wanted the equipment. And when the DHS gifted the Steamship Authority of Massachusetts with $900,000 in security money for the ferries that float mostly summer residents and vacationers to and fro Martha's Vineyard, the harbormaster told the newspaper, "Quite honestly, I don't know what we're going to do, but you don't turn down grant money."[33]

One of the oldest and most foolish of progressive delusions is that one can take politics out of government. Can't be done. The Progressives of the early twentieth century tried to do it with such anti-democratic reforms as the imposition of city manager systems and appointed instead of elected boards, but in these cases the politics simply found new, sometimes almost subterranean channels. (See, for instance, Arthur Ekirch Jr.'s *Progressivism in America* [1974].)

So it is futile to cry out against the grants that seep down to the Bennington, New Hampshires and Little Chute, Wisconsins. As long as Homeland Security grants exist, they will be parceled out by politicians in a manner that spreads the most credit to the most members of Congress.

That manner is very much in the tradition of the disbursal of federal funds from such tried-and-true government programs as highway construction, sewage treatment, and education. Sixty percent of the monies under the Homeland Security Grant Program, which was created under the USA-PATRIOT Act and which dispensed $8.3 billion from 2002–2004, are distributed to the fifty states, the District of Columbia, and U.S. territories and possessions (Puerto Rico, Virgin Islands, Guam, American Samoa, and the Northern Mariana Islands) on the basis of population. The other 40 percent is equally distributed to all recipients, regardless of population, and therein lies the rub, and the hubbub. For as David Williams of Citizens Against Government Waste remarks, "It's almost like an entitlement, like if you're below the poverty line you get food stamps."[34]

Or in one of the more decorous understatements of the year, Professor Donald F. Kettl of the University of Wisconsin, summing up the Department of Homeland Security's first year for the Century Foundation, wrote, "Money already distributed has been allocated more on the basis of pork than need."[35]

Wyoming, the Cowboy State, land of rugged frontier individual-ists, has become the poster child of homeland security grants run amok. Though she is the least populous state in the Union and no one's idea of a likely terrorist target, Wyoming receives more money per capita than any other state in homeland security grants: in 2004, that came to $45.22 for every citizen, as compared to $10.78 for each Californian, $11.25 for each New Yorker, $9.56 for each Texan, and $9.25 for each Floridian. Bringing up the rear is Michigan, which received a homeland security grant of $92.578 million in fiscal year 2004, or $9.18 per capita.

Other states with inflated per-capita grant totals in FY 2004 in-clude Rhode Island ($24.48), Delaware ($27.37), Montana ($27.66), South Dakota ($30.79), North Dakota ($33.05), Alaska ($38.34), and Vermont ($38.98). What outraged D.C.-based journalists usu-ally forget to mention when running their obligatory stories about grant-rich Wyoming is that a non-state—the District of Columbia—is far and away the biggest recipient of homeland security grants per capita, with a whopping $93.29 for every citizen.

Senators from populous states have led the cry against these for-mulae. Senator Dianne Feinstein (D-CA) argues that "It is ludicrous to pour homeland security money into small, rural states that are at little risk of terrorist attack and shortchange states that have densely populated centers and/or have critical infrastructure." Like, say, for instance, just to pick an example...California, which as Senator Feinstein notes, has "two of the biggest seaports in the country, Disneyland, the Golden Gate Bridge, two of the biggest airports in the country," and the list goes on.

Feinstein, with big-state senators Carl Levin (D-MI), Kay Bailey Hutchison (R-TX), and George Voinovich (R-OH), sought to amend the grant formula by directing the Department of Homeland Secu-rity to distribute grants "according to population, or, at a minimum, according to threat and vulnerability assessments, location of criti-cal infrastructure, and population density." In other words, she sought to amend the formula to steer the bulk of the grant money to the largest states, with none quite so large as her own. Even when speak-ing the language of reform and good government, politicians play the pork barrel game.

The current formula, which despite the best efforts of big-state legislators remains biased toward smaller states, "wastes taxpayers money by sending it to areas where it may not be needed,"[36] says Feinstein.

Smaller state representatives beg to differ. Senator Judd Gregg (R-NH), whose "Live Free or Die" state pocketed $28.422 million in homeland security grants in fiscal year 2004, or $22.07 per capita, protects the interests of his state from his perch on the Appropriations Committee's Subcommittee on Homeland Security. His goal, he says, is to "strike a delicate balance between protecting highly populated urban areas without neglecting still-vulnerable rural areas."

Those "still-vulnerable rural areas" include every single town or hamlet in New Hampshire, for the state simply divides its share of homeland security loot evenly among its towns. Hart's Location, New Hampshire, which at population thirty-nine is the smallest jurisdiction within the state, was made more secure by $182.82 in FY 2003; the second-smallest town, Ellsworth, which encompasses eighty-seven souls, received $407.82, which was used by the nearest fire volunteer department to purchase chemical decontamination equipment.

And yet even in New Hampshire, the Feinstein argument that populous areas should receive proportionately more money is problematic. Ronald O'Keefe, fire chief of Durham, points to the tiny neighboring town of Newington, whose petroleum storage facility would seem to make it a likelier (if still exceedingly unlikely) target for terrorism than most larger towns and cities in the state.

"Because their population is less than 1,000, they get considerably less money," O'Keefe told Jordan Carleo-Evangelist. "Now I think there needs to be a way of distributing it a little more fairly."

But again, one man's fairness is another man's imbalance. New York City Police Commissioner Raymond Kelly complained to a congressional committee of the "complete mismatch between the funding provided under this program and the need"[37]; New York City, in his view, was shortchanged, despite the massive infusion of federal money after September 11, 2001.

What Commissioner Kelly did not tell the committee was that not every dollar of this massive infusion was spent well or wisely. For instance, the police department paid $282,000 for emergency respirators for transit workers "only to find out later that the masks didn't even protect workers against tear gas." To be fair, Kelly was not commissioner at the time, and he has conceded, "They bought some things that in hindsight we might not have purchased."[38] But even NYPD and FDNY, those acronyms that grace ballcaps from sea to

shining sea, have succumbed to the temptation offered by available federal monies.

Rep. Peter King (R-NY) of Long Island, a political grandstander par excellence and member of the House Select Committee on Homeland Security, found in this debate his chance to impersonate a statesman.

"A lot of guys on both sides of the aisle only care about getting money for their districts," said King in a burst of self-righteousness that had the added benefit of being self-aggrandizing. "I come from Nassau County, I worked with Alfonse D'Amato, I understand pork-barrel spending. But this shouldn't be the case when it comes to homeland security."[39]

Perhaps not. But Rep. King's words might carry more weight if they didn't serve to justify the transfer of homeland security monies from elsewhere to his own district in the Long Island suburbs of New York City.

And even within the five boroughs of the City of New York, the ugly specter of rivalrousness has been known to rear its head. Rep. Vito Fosella (R-NY) of the Republican redoubt of Staten Island, one of those *rara avis* creatures known as a New York City Republican, succeeded in redirecting $450 million in federal aid ostensibly targeted for construction at Ground Zero into the reconstruction of the South Ferry subway station. New York's Democrats squawked, though one suspects it was less out of indignation than envy.

Newspapers across the country editorialized against the homeland-security distribution formula—or at least those newspapers located in large cities did so. The *Atlanta Journal-Constitution*, for instance, pointed to Georgia's "terrorist targets"[40]—the Centers for Disease Control, the nuclear submarine base at St. Mary's, the Savannah seaport, Fort MacPherson—and wondered why the state received so much less than—yes—Wyoming. (Georgia's FY 2004 per capita take was $9.52.) Would it be churlish to point out that those installations are all federally subsidized in the first place? That we the taxpayers have paid for the CDC, the nuclear subs, and the naval bases, which amounts to a federally mandated transfer of wealth to Georgia from states without such bases—for instance, Vermont?

Rep. Chris Cox (R-CA), chairman of the House Select Committee on Homeland Security, speaks in the classic language of ostensibly apolitical good-government reformers when he says, "We want to make sure first responders get the funding they need, when they need it, and we want to establish a grant-making system that meets homeland security objectives rather than political objectives."[41] To that end, he has sponsored legislation that would distribute homeland security grants by threat assessment and end the automatic set-aside for small states.

Cox has been rewarded for his canny stance by glowing press coverage. "His goal is to get Washington to be smarter about the way it distributes homeland-security money," coos the *National Journal*. Cox's proposal, which bears the clunkily propagandistic title of the Faster Smarter Funding for First Responders Act, "sounds like common sense,"[42] according to the magazine. Cox is painted therein as the paladin of common sense, wisdom, and the equitable distribution of tax dollars. His Solomonic proposal might be more compelling, however, if he were from a small state rather than the state which would be the largest beneficiary of that proposal.

Yet the small-state politicos have a point: Is Disneyland really any more of a target than, say, the Old Faithful Geyser in Wyoming's Yellowstone National Park? Defending the current formula, Rep. Harold Rogers (R-KY), chairman of the Homeland Security Subcommittee of the House Appropriations Committee, claimed that "hundreds of agricultural documents have been found in the al Qaeda caves."[43] These were probably lentil recipes and not maps of the tobacco fields of the Bluegrass State, but nevertheless, it is both naïve and urbanocentric to think that rural and small-state representatives will cede what everyone knows to be boondoggle money to big states. For their part, big-state interests have tried to buy off the likes of Rep. Rogers; for instance, New York City Mayor Michael Bloomberg donated $5,000 to the Kentuckian's campaign fund. To no avail.

Rep. Cox says, "We are not threatened in an inchoate sense from the entire planet from all sides in all ways. There are specific threats against the United States from specific people with specific capabilities, and we need to make sure our first-response monies are directed to those threats."[44] A good point: But if Idaho is to forego its DHS grants, will Cox urge rural Northern and Central California to do the same? (He won't if he has statewide political ambitions.) Moreover, rural members of Congress have learned how to play the What If? game, spinning dark scenarios of remote-controlled crop dusters waging chemical warfare against the nation's food supply.

Rep. Cox is nothing if not assiduous in seeking the transfer of funds from small states to large states. (His California residency has nothing to do with this noble effort, we may be assured.) "If we were talking about equipment and training for our armed forces, we wouldn't make the argument that it had to be done on a pork-barrel basis," he says, incorrectly, for what is a map of domestic U.S. military forts, camps, and bases if not a checkered portrait of the relative distribution of seats on the Armed Services and Appropriations Committees?

"The danger," continues Cox, "is that you solve a political problem but fail to achieve the homeland security mission because you are sending money to the wrong places for the wrong things."[45] Could those "wrong things" include the thirteen security booths that the Orange County, California, School Board bought with $160,000 in homeland security money?

Withal, the political spokesmen for urban areas kvetched about the slowness and inadequacy of aid to cities. James A. Garner, mayor of Hempstead, New York, a Long Island suburb of New York City, whined, "The money comes to the states by Federal Express, but the cities get the money by pony express."[46]

The Department of Homeland Security responded to big-state complaints about the malapportionment of funds in classic fashion: by giving more money to the big states. Under the Urban Area Securities Initiative (UASI), the DHS doled out $800 million in FY 2003 to large cities on the basis of their population density and estimated attractiveness to terrorists. The original UASI grants were to be limited to New York, Washington, Los Angeles, Seattle, Chicago, San Francisco, and Houston, but soon enough politicians from other large cities started squawking, and the 2003 field was enlarged to include twenty-nine other cities, among them Baltimore, Boston, Denver, Detroit, Honolulu, Memphis (Memphis? Does bin Laden hate Elvis?), Miami, Philadelphia, Phoenix, Sacramento, San Diego, and St. Louis.

By FY 2005, the Bush request had risen to $1.45 billion for UASI out of the $3.6 billion allotment for first responders. More than fifty cities splashed happily in the pool. The big-state lobby was pulling things its way. New Hampshire and Wyoming were shut out of this program, of course.

Rachael Sunbarg, a DHS spokeswoman, essentially conceded that the UASI was a sop to big cities: "If everything was just based on the Urban Area Security Initiative formula, then potentially states like New Hampshire and others would get very little from us," said Sunbarg. "It's...a good way to make sure that everybody gets a piece of the pie."[47]

And that's what it's all about, isn't it? Leave no supplicant behind. Fill every coffer. As one government consultant told Pam Zubeck of the *Colorado Springs Gazette*, "It doesn't take more than a year for [UASI] to become an entitlement. It's in the state and local government's interest to never have the threat go away, because if it does, the money goes away. We know Washington doesn't cut programs; it just adds to them."[48]

The dirty little secret of the USAI program is that it has very little to do with risk assessment. A city's share of USAI is determined by population, vulnerability, and threat, but these factors are by no means equal in importance. The complicated and still partially secret formula counts a city's population as three times more influential a factor than its "threat score." Thus King Numbers rules. The bigger the city, the larger the check, risk and vulnerability be damned. Houston profits, Dover loses.

And check out some of the grants made under UASI to the nation's transit systems. Prudent risk analysts would no doubt recommend that New York City's MTA receive money, as it did to the tune of $9.941 million. But Indianapolis? New Haven? The Greater Cleveland Regional Transit Authority? By what stretch of the terror-filled imagination are these targets of radical Muslims? Will they firebomb the Rock and Roll Hall of Fame? Release sarin gas at Yale? Storm the Benjamin Harrison Home? Unlikely. Yet each of these transit systems received $795,280, with repeat grants to come.

Despite the increased share of first-responder money going to big cities, Rep. Cox presses on. One DHS official told the *National Journal* that under the Cox proposal, "The system would literally screech to a halt."[49] The department's information and analysis sector simply isn't equipped to review thousands of detailed applications. It is far easier to simply dole out the money on the basis of population, with perhaps a perfunctory nod to risk and vulnerability.

It's hard to let go of the statesman crown, however, especially when it sits so lightly upon the head. The communications director for Cox's select committee declares in a fit of righteousness, "Basing funding on threat and vulnerability is right. And how do you argue against it out of anything but parochial politics?"[50]

Perhaps you can't. But then perhaps the Department of Homeland Security is all about parochial politics.

"Whenever it comes time to start writing checks," said University of Wisconsin political scientist Don Kettl, director of the Century Foundation's Project on Homeland Security, "it's very hard for a member of Congress to say the money ought to go someplace else." Outside observers, journalists, experts, and even ex-politicians have no such trouble: Indeed, former New Hampshire Senator Warren Rudman, whose post-Senate career seems to consist of serving on worthy establishment panels and delivering sententious advice, has criticized the small-state-biased DHS formula as "not rational,"[51] a clear case of a man gaining courage after he leaves office.

Even recipients of the DHS funds understand that something is amiss, though as long as the money is out there, they're going to grab for it. Mayor John DeStefano of New Haven, Connecticut, president of the National League of Cities, admits, "The money shouldn't be paying for police overtime in some neighborhood."[52] Yet Mayor DeStefano also complains that money isn't flowing fast enough to the cities, despite the abundant evidence that city governments are either unequipped to handle the influx of funds or unwilling to exercise even a modicum of control to ensure that the money is not spent on pork or routine functions.

Bruce Cheney, director of the Bureau of Emergency Communications in New Hampshire's Department of Safety, joked, "My view is that New York doesn't need any money and New Hampshire needs all of theirs. But I'm sure they feel the same way. There have been many programs in the past from which New Hampshire got nothing. So I'm not real sad about the fact that there may be some advantage to us in this go-around."[53]

Well said, Mr. Cheney. The real question is not so much how the money should be distributed as why it should be distributed.

But that is the kind of question that never gets asked in Washington, D.C. Instead, potential critics are struck dumb by the various talismanic phrases that find their way into the language every time a "crisis" advances the cause of government. Would that we had more chiefs of police like Kenneth Holding of Trenton, Florida, who refused the gift of M-16s (which the feds sell to local departments for less than $5 a rifle) with the remark, "I don't think terrorists are likely to visit here."[54]

The states are required by federal law to pass along at least four-fifths of their U.S. Homeland Security grant money to localities. This has encouraged numerous instances of accounting legerdemain—in Utah, for instance, the state pays the homeland security bills of municipalities and is in turn reimbursed by the feds. But the more serious problem is that local officials can't spend fast enough to satisfy Washington.

"There is so much homeland security money thrown at us that staying with present methods of accounting isn't realistic," Doug Allen, director of civil defense for Honolulu County, Hawaii, told *USA Today*. Not that Mr. Allen was advising Honolulu County to reject the money. Rather, he said, "What is needed is funding for a grants administrator."[55]

Not even the legendary skinflint H.R. Gross, the Iowa Republican congressman who was so cheap (or protective of his trust) that he voted against paying for the eternal flame at JFK's Arlington National Cemetery grave, could have imagined this state of affairs: local officials are so overwhelmed by the shower of federal cash coming their way that they want the feds to send them a grant writer to request even more money!

The run on corporate welfare triggered by the 9/11 attacks has even outraged citizens of Manhattan and its outskirts, who are usually far too jaded to be outraged by anything short of, say, Mel Gibson making a movie about Jesus Christ. In fiscal year 2004, homeland security monies flowed to such mainstays of Big Oil as Citgo ($17 million), Conoco-Phillips ($10 million), and Shell ($9 million). The funds were targeted for port refinery security: for instance, Citgo and Conoco Phillips used taxpayer money to reinforce security at their refineries in lovely Linden, New Jersey. All told, the various oil giants received $66 million to "pay for fencing, cameras, and gates around big oil's refineries."

The revelation that these companies were hitting up Uncle Sam to pay for security measures that, in most industries, are the responsibility of the owners involved elicited howls of protest from New York City-area politicians. But these howls were less the plaintive cries of wronged taxpayers than they were the jealous caterwauling of piglets who have been crowded out at the trough.

Westchester County Executive Andrew Spano sputtered to WABC-TV, "Why the federal government would give us something like $200,000—which is what we have gotten—and they give millions and millions to companies that are making exceptional amounts of money this year is beyond me." He added, "I think if you're making a lot of money, you don't go after that money."[56]

What Spano did not say is that the 2004 budget of Westchester County was $1.4 billion, which is "a lot of money" to most of us. The entirety of this county budget had been mulcted from unwilling givers, while at least part of any oil company's revenue stream comes from willing buyers of its products. This does not excuse the sorry spectacle of Shell and its ilk pursuing taxpayer subsidy, but it does cast doubt upon the purity of Spano's position.

The failure of the press to investigate, disclose, and mock without mercy the egregious waste, fraud, and abuse that goes on under the cloak of "homeland security" has been something of a mystery. Despite the generally liberal ideological coloration of most reporters, the press has, fitfully at least, in the past, exposed the misuse of government funds with gusto. From CBS-TV's *Sixty Minutes* to the supermarket tabloid the *National Enquirer* (whose fact-checkers shame the lax standards of, for example, the *New York Times*), the media have gone after $600 toilet seats purchased by the Pentagon, National Science Foundation studies seeking to answer thumpingly obvious questions, and the incompetencies (if not the *raison d'etre*) of NASA. For decades, flamboyant Senator William Proxmire (D-WI) garnered headlines with his "Golden Fleece" awards, which he doled out to the truly outrageous wasters of taxpayers' money.

So why haven't new Proxmires arisen to puncture the inflated threats concocted by grantees of the Department of Homeland Security? Where are the breathless, camera-jerking cinema verité TV specials in which the heirs to Mike Wallace make beady-eyed bureaucrats squirm under the bright lights of the idiot box? Where, for heaven's sake, is the *National Enquirer*?

Oh, sure, there is the occasional truth-telling local newspaper. The *Bangor Daily News*, for instance, editorialized against the purchase by the Maine Marine Resources and Inland Fisheries and Wildlife Department of a boat to patrol the Sebago Lake. Though the Sebago Lake is the source of drinking water for Portland, Maine, it "can't be very high on any terrorist's list of potential targets,"[57] asserted the newspaper. That Maine was spending its $22 million DHS 2004 allocation on such nongermane "homeland security" items earned the state government a deserved slap from the *Bangor Daily News*. But where is the national press on the national scandal of the DHS scam?

The answer seems to be that homeland security has been given, and still enjoys, a free pass. The department and its cousins can misspend, overspend, and tell fibs with impunity, confident in the knowledge that they are shielded by one very powerful amulet: the memory of 9/11.

"The whole world is watching!" shouted the student protesters as they were beaten by Chicago policemen during the Democratic National Convention in the summer of 1968, but they were wrong: only a slice of the world watched, and even fewer cared. But on September 11, 2001, and in the weeks thereafter, the whole world really was watching. Certainly almost every American citizen, from the hollows of Appalachia to the hollowness of Beverly Hills, was watching. The images of that day—the planes hitting the towers, the towers collapsing, the death, the tears, the unspeakable horrible sadness of it all—who among us does not still carry that in her heart? Even those of us who resist media hysteria or heavy-handed efforts to create a national consensus during times of crisis, real or manufactured, are caught short by the memory of 9/11. And so effectively did the Bush administration tie the indelible images of 9/11 to its subsequent policies on the matter of "homeland security" that even the most blithe dissident hesitates, if only for a moment, before uttering a discouraging word.

Our fearless press is not immune from this general dread, or at least strong reluctance, to ask of homeland security the questions we would ask of any other government activity. Add to this the atmosphere of conformity so sedulously encouraged by Attorney General John Ashcroft and you get a national press that is less watchdog than lapdog. Within the culture of the DHS, the spend light is always a bright green.

There have been the occasional, meritorious exceptions to the media torpor. One of the first, and still among the most powerful, exposes of homeland security waste came in that house organ of the permanent bureaucracy, the *Washington Post*.

Three reporters—Jo Becker, Sarah Cohen, and Spencer S. Hsu—dove into the bowels of the D.C. metro area bureaucracy, conducting more than 100 interviews and poring over virtual libraries worth of government documents to produce a major investigative report: "Anti-Terrorism Funds Buy Wide Array of Pet Projects," *Washington Post*, November 23, 2003.

Tracing the fate of the $324 million that Congress pumped into the D.C. area to fortify it against terrorism after the events of 9/11, the trio of reporters found that much of the money was either unspent (not that it was returned to the U.S. Treasury!) or "is funding projects with questionable connections to homeland security." Officials in Washington, Maryland, and Virginia took the money and "plugged budget holes, spent millions on pet projects and steered contracts to political allies."

This was a landmark story, and it is worth a careful exegesis. The tale of petty corruption, incompetence, and opportunism it paints is at odds with the heroic depiction of public officials that has recently become the rage. Not all of the blame, however, attaches to squalid local officials. As the *Post* reporters note, members of Congress were "shaken" by the "region's chaotic response" to the al Qaeda attack on the Pentagon. Although the target of the fourth hijacked plane has never been positively identified, the Capitol remains among the likeliest prospects. Fearful that a second wave of attacks was imminent, Congress emptied the Treasury upon local officials who were simply unprepared for such large infusions of federal aid. (They were also slowed by purchasing rules and the usual bureaucratic speed bumps.)

Of the $324 million earmarked for the D.C. region in the two years following September 2001, almost 40 percent was unspent as of November 2003. The Virginia and Maryland suburbs had spent only half of the appropriated monies, although the government of Washington, D.C., "which received the bulk of the money, has spent the vast majority of it." (And the sun will rise in the east tomorrow.)

But not all the unspent monies can be ascribed to bureaucratic screwups. For it seems, despite the din of dunning that comes whenever two or more government officials are gathered, that massive grants are unnecessary. The governments of Maryland and Virginia did not spend millions of available dollars, in part, because they had nothing to spend them on.

Oh, sure, the governments of the three regions dedicated part of the booty to commendable causes: training of first responders; purchase of compatible radio systems "so rescuers from different jurisdictions can communicate with each other in an emergency"; and buying more ambulances, bomb-defusers, and earth-movers in the event of a disaster. But a county only needs so many ambulances, so many paramedics, so many bomb-sniffing dogs. Mayors and county executives may whine for more money when the TV cameras roll, but when lightning strikes and they actually receive that money they are dumbfounded, tongue-tied, and at wit's end as to how to spend the damned lucre.

As the *Post* found, after the obvious purchases had been made, "The District funded a politically popular jobs program, outfitted police with leather jackets and assessed environmental problems on property prime for redevelopment. In Maryland, the money is buying Prince George's County prosecutors an office security system. In Virginia, a small volunteer fire department spent $350,000 on a custom-made fire boat. The Metropolitan Washington Council of Governments used some of the money for janitorial services."

The infusion of cash into the D.C. metro region was not solely due to its status as an obvious target of any future terrorist attacks. The region is also well represented on the House and Senate Appropriations Committees, a happy circumstance that keeps the spigot of money in a permanent "On" position and aimed at the home districts of its members.

The *Post*'s findings are not without their small amusements and ironies. For instance, the District of Columbia Hospital Association, unconsciously mimicking the much-derided Homeland Security formula under which each state gets a piece of the action, distributed part of an $8 million grant to every hospital in the city. While from one vantage point this might seem an admirable attempt to keep the big hospitals from gobbling all the homeland security money, it led to the absurdity of federal monies purchasing security cameras for the wards of the small, private Psychiatric Institute of Washington. Risibly, perhaps, the Psychiatric Institute also used these homeland security funds to buy a new van and "a garage gate that officials say will help keep out illegal parkers from nearby American University."

So there you have it. The Newest Frontier in Homeland Security: parking lot control.

The legendarily corrupt city government of Washington, D.C. sunk to predictable lows during the scramble for homeland security loot. Contracts were let to well-connected operators in the city whose experience in the matter at hand was, shall we say, limited.

Max Brown, the former legal counsel and deputy chief of staff to D.C. Mayor Anthony Williams, pocketed a quick $130,000 for his work with Kroll Government Services, a consulting firm that ran emergency preparedness seminars in the District. (Watchdogs of what were once called the taxpayers' dollars will be appalled to learn that Mayor Williams is a member of the Homeland Security Funding Task Force, which the DHS put together in March 2004 with the stated purpose of speeding the delivery of funds to the front lines. Or, perhaps more accurately, the front pockets of the well-connected.)

Even more egregious than Max Brown's $130,000, the incompetent former mayor, Sharon Pratt, who had the timely virtue of being a supporter of Mayor Williams, received a bioterrorism "consulting" contract—a no-bid bioterrorism consulting contract—worth $236,000. Her duties included not only advising the city on how it might best protect its citizenry in the event of a bioterror attack but also formulating strategies by which the District of Columbia might grab an ever greater share of federal dollars. That bears repeating: ex-Mayor Pratt received a federal subsidy to advise the city how it could receive more federal subsidies.

Pratt was awarded the contract after the intra-office lobbying of Kelvin J. Robinson, chief of staff to Mayor Williams. "Please tell me we've done this contract with Sharon's folks," Robinson e-mailed the city's Deputy Mayor, Carolyn N. Graham, who in turn contacted the D.C. health agency, ostensible overseer of the contract, with an imperative command: "We must move on it."

Pratt was an insistent supplicant. Robinson, Graham, and the city's bureaucracy, which can best be described as lumbering (except when big, no-bid contracts are at stake), were poked, prodded, and stabbed by Pratt along the way.

"This is a shabby way to treat any legitimate, quality contractor," Pratt raged in an e-mail on January 29, 2003. "It is an outrageous way to treat a former public official who has always faithfully served the City."

The City served her right back, it seems, with that $236,000 contract. Pratt, the *Post* reported, had lobbied for homeland security contracts amounting to $1.9 million. She denied that she was a mere grubby spelunker for government funds, just another seeker of political favor. "It requires someone who appreciates how to pull all the players together," she said. Indeed.

A spokesman for the D.C. department of health asserted that Pratt was awarded the contract because she "has the perspective of a former elected official."[58] The *Washington Post* editorial page begged to differ. The *Post* editors disparaged this "D.C. Boondoggle" which paid Pratt to "produce a homeland security-related program that any college intern with a C average could complete on spring break."[59]

The homeland security expenditures in the D.C. area boggle the mind; it's as if Senator Proxmire and his Golden Fleece have come back to life and are rehearsing a "Best Of" show. One can't help but laugh at the chutzpah, the sheer jaw-dropping audacity of it all. As the singer Elvis Costello once confessed, "I used to be disgusted—but now I'm just amused."

Among the disgusting/amusing purchases made by the District of Columbia government were $5,003 for five Smith & Wesson bicycles and bicycling gear for the mayor and his retinue. Only D.C., with its repressive gun control laws, would make Smith & Wesson a homeland security government contractor for items that haven't a thing to do with security.

On a related note, the District paid $37,502 for Honda scooters for officials of the health department to use in the event of an emergency. Apparently the health bureaucrats are not in half the shape that the mayor's team is: while hizzoner and his flunkies bike, strengthening those calf muscles, the health mandarins let the scooters do the driving. (You've got to hand it to Washington's city workers: come Armageddon, they'll be the best-dressed clean-up crew in America. The District spent $35,000 "outfitting health workers with lettered parkas, caps and polo and denim shirts.")

"If we can tie it to 9/11 and build capacity in our core functions, let's do it!" is how D.C. Department of Public Works director Leslie Hotaling explains her department's appalling misuse of homeland security funds. She sees nothing wrong, for instance, with spending $55,000 to teach her employees to read maps and handle "problem employees." (Perhaps one could simply use a bad map to misdirect the problem employee to the Psychiatric Institute of Washington's fortified parking garage.)

Hotaling's forces in the sanitation department were sent to Dale Carnegie management courses with homeland security monies. When the D.C. City Council, not usually a vigilant watchdog of the taxpayers' money, raised a few questions about this, the name "Dale Carnegie" was removed from the relevant documents. This is how history is rewritten on the first edit.

Hotaling, in best District fashion, seems to have a parking obsession. Under her keen eye, $300,000 in money purportedly used to Protect Us From Terrorism was put toward a computerized car towing system that had long been a pet project of Mayor Williams. She was nothing if not ingenious in defending this purchase, claiming that after the dirty bomb goes off, or the next plane crashes, or the bioterror rages through the leafy streets of Georgetown, the city will be most efficient at clearing the streets of automobiles and later re-uniting them with surviving owners. Whew. That ought to be load off the mind of those who suffer from terror nightmares.

And speaking of which, the District gave WUSA-TV $180,000 to advertise "a help line for people traumatized by the first anniversary of Sept. 11, 2001." Not people traumatized by Sept. 11, 2001. People traumatized by its first anniversary. That these are the same people who are traumatized by a dead woodchuck on the highway, the threat of Pat Sajak's retirement, or leaving the apartment to buy a loaf of bread should go unremarked. Their discomfort on the anniversary of days on which strangers experienced horrible tragedies is a matter best left to them and their analysts. But thanks to the compassionate conservative-bashers of the District of Columbia government, they—or at least those tuned to the witless offerings of WUSA-TV—knew where to turn for a sympathetic ear.

Continuing the traumatic theme, the D.C. Department of Mental Health spent $20,000 on a study to find whether or not 9/11 increased the city's jail population. This would seem to be a fairly simply matter of counting, but apparently the district's social scientists have more arcane methods of divining this information. In any event, Department of Mental Health director Martha B. Knisley told the *Post*, "At this point, we've made the results known, and discussions are continuing." Which clears that up.

Ms. Knisley's department also made a dubious funding choice when it paid $111,000 for an assessment of "environmental problems" at St. Elizabeth's Hospital. Knisley explained this profligacy by telling the *Post* that St. Elizabeth's would play an important role as a "mass casualty center" should the unthinkable happen—again. A reasonable explanation. Alas, Director Knisley failed to get her story straight with the relevant bureaucracy, in this case the D.C. Emergency Management Agency.

The acting director of that agency, one Barbara Childs-Pair, denied that St. Elizabeth's plays any such role in the District's emergency response plan. The likelier reason for the infusion of homeland security cash into St. Elizabeth's is that Mayor Williams and the city's archons hope to rejuvenate the hospital, "which has commanding views of the Anacostia and Potomac" rivers, as part of a larger development scheme. Casual Fridays at St. Elizabeth's? Yes. Casualties? No way.

Another $100,000 in homeland security funds supported a grand total of forty young people in the District through a summer employment program that seems to be, if this is possible, an even greater waste of money than are most summer jobs programs. These are, typically, slush funds for mayors, who are made to appear as virtual Lady Bountifuls, blessing the benighted teenagers of their purlieus with cushy, no-work jobs, and perhaps aiding a few children of prominent supporters, too. These "jobs" usually consist of picking up a little trash (but not enough to disturb the sanitation workers' union), playing ball with kids, or leaning on a broom between snack breaks: nothing onerous, nothing mind-stretching, nothing terribly destructive. Or productive.

The D.C. program, however, took the concept to a whole new, albeit rhythmical, level. After the D.C. Forty were instructed in rudimentary first-aid skills, they were "paid to rap and dance about emergency preparedness as part of outreach efforts."

Not to belittle the rappers: It's tough to find rhymes for "Cipro" and "al Qaeda." And quite possibly the emergency preparedness rap tunes that resulted were of a higher quality than much of the work subsidized by another Washington-based agency, the National Endowment for the Arts. But still: Is there any reasonable reading of the U.S. Constitution under which the sponsorship of this is a legitimate function of the federal government?

When confronted by *Post* reporters with these appalling misuses of federal monies, the D.C. political class not only failed to apologize; it positively crowed over its accomplishments.

"The District has done a remarkably good job," said Tony Bullock, a spokesman for Mayor Williams. Bullock, whose surname contains a wonderfully apt first syllable, went on to say, "We used these federal funds to achieve remarkable progress in preparing the District government's capacity to respond to potential terrorism incidents or similar emergencies."

Congressional overseers were not quite so sanguine. The District's flagrant misapplication of funds "make[s] me want to scream," said Rep. Christopher Shays (R-CT). "It's an outrage and a misuse of this money. The money should be used for things directly related to the terrorist threat." Though as we have seen and will see in pages to come, defining such words as "related," "terrorist," "threat," and even "things" is subject to so much confusion, obfuscation, and downright propaganda that one almost longs for the days when President Bill Clinton parsed the many meanings of the word "is."

The counties surrounding the nation's capital were hardly models of pure disinterested public service. (As if such a thing could exist anywhere.) Instead, they shared in what the *Washington Post* called the "culture of one-upmanship and giddy shopping" engendered by the post 9/11 windfall.

In a breathtaking example of either naïvcté or utter cynicism, representatives of suburban Maryland governmental jurisdictions (and other recipients of DHS aid) signed a pledge reading, "I hereby certify that Federal funds will not be used to replace or supplant state or local funds...that would, in the absence of federal aid, be made available for public safety purposes."

But of course they were. Police and fire departments used the federal funds to buy uniforms, guns, ammunition, vehicles: the sorts of things police and fire departments always buy. Oh, they might add a rhetorical gloss to these routine purchases: for instance, the Manassas Park, Virginia police department hired a deputy chief with federal monies, covering their bureaucratic posteriors by claiming that his duties included emergency preparedness.

In other cases, departments didn't even bother to pretend that homeland security monies were being spent on extraordinary, terrorism-related items. The Occoquan-Woodbridge-Lorton (Virginia) Volunteer Fire Department (and how do they ever fit that name across their windbreakers?) used its homeland security money to purchase a boat. A company owned by two members of this volunteer fire department equipped the vessel to the tune of almost $44,000. In Maryland, Prince George's County, whose officials had sounded the alarm of vulnerability in connection with Andrews Air Force Base, saw fit to spend $500,000 of its homeland security money on new digital cameras with which to take better mug shots of the drunks and petty felons who pass in and out of its criminal justice system. This frivolous purchase, according to the president of the local Fraternal Order of Police, forced the delay in obtaining the gas masks which had been identified as the department's principal anti-terrorism need.

Mayor Daley of Chicago used to say that government's prime function was to deliver "jobs for the boys." In this respect, at least, homeland security works. Take the Metropolitan Washington Council of Governments. This regional association of local government entities received $5 million from Congress to "enhance regional emergency preparedness, coordination and response." Right off the top, the MWCG "took a 35 percent management fee and applied it to salaries, fringe benefits and "indirect' costs, including $519,000 for expenses such as rent, insurance and janitorial services at its headquarters."[60]

Security comes in many forms. Job security, it seems, is Job One in our brave new world of homeland defense.

Few have jobs with quite so much job security these days as do "homeland security consultants." From Mayor Pratt to the most furtive Beltway bandit, these consultants profit handsomely every time the level of paranoia is ratcheted up. They have been especially effective in Washington, D.C., which is prone to collective panics in a way that cooler New Yorkers are not. For instance, a consultant convinced the authority that governs the metropolitan Washington subway to install chemical detectors. No doubt these sounded like a must-have for any twenty-first-century underground transportation network, but as Randall Larsen of the ANSER Institute for Homeland Security points out, "If someone releases a gas in the subway, people are going to start falling down and screaming and yelling." You don't need a detector in a chemical attack: "the bodies on the ground," as one reporter paraphrased Larsen, "would let authorities know a deadly gas had been released." (Larsen has also said that "uncontrolled spending"[61] is the greatest threat to homeland security. His words are not emblazoned over the front entrance of the Department of Homeland Security headquarters.)

I don't mean to pick on Washington, D.C. Well, actually, I do mean to pick on Washington, but no township or city government, however small or remote, is immune from homeland-security fever. Take the other Washington, the state located 3,000 miles west of Mayor Pratt's secure burg.

The state of Washington gives the lie, in a modest way, to the claim that urban areas are consistently shortchanged in homeland security dollars. Of the $462 million the state had received as of September 2004, $210 million, or almost half the total, had gone to Seattle-Tacoma International Airport.

Yet whether it is the languor-inducing effects of the drizzle, the mist, or the overrated coffee, Seattle residents have been slow in getting with the homeland security program. Eric Holdeman, director of Emergency Management Services in King County, complained, "People who live here don't think of themselves as being in the bull's-eye as Washington, D.C., and New York City might be... and that's not true."[62]

Well, Mr. Holdeman, actually, you see, it is true, but that hasn't stopped Washington state from spending every penny Washington, D.C. has sent along

For instance, the map-dot of Sammamish, an exurb of Seattle, received $102,784 in homeland security monies to install new cameras, locks, and alarms at its city hall. Now, one rather doubts that al Qaeda chieftains sitting in their Afghan caves have stuck prickpins in Sammamish, but assistant city manager Pete Butkus told the *Seattle Times*, "The threat to our City Hall could be from terrorists or it could be from run-of-the-mill street crazies. They're up there, too, you know."[63]

The last attack by "run-of-the-mill street crazies" on a U.S. City Hall was...well, it has never happened. Except perhaps in *Dawn of the Dead*. But that doesn't mean that the federal government can't spend $100,000-plus in every Podunk town to make sure it doesn't ever happen.

Somewhere south of Sammarish, in rural central California, the Kern County (Bakersfield) fire department spent $95,000 in homeland security grant money on a security system, complete with electronic key cards for employees. To date, Kern County has been conspicuously absent from lists of terrorist targets.

In even more rural Sutter County, California, the county seat of Yuba City spent its DHS money making its police station lobby bulletproof. It also fortified the police station with ten feet of steel-reinforced concrete. Don't even think about ramming a truck into the Yuba City police headquarters, bin Laden!

Across the county, city governments are spending homeland security monies on matters ranging from the trivial to the, well, trivial. The Bowling Green, Kentucky police department is getting new locks on its doors. The Washington Township-Avon Fire Department in Indiana is spending $900,000 in DHS grants received via Hendricks County Emergency Management to purchase 153 radios and a couple of sirens. Solano County, California is digitally photographing every single inch of itself from the air. It goes on and on and on.

And if radical Muslim sleeper agents are listening, steer clear of the fourth-largest shopping center in Minnesota or you'll be sorry.

That would be in Burnsville, which received $368,800 to buy a command vehicle described as "a 911 dispatch center on wheels."

The former police chief of Burnsville, Dan Johnson, now homeland security operations director for the state of Minnesota, was among those who chose the lucky recipients of homeland security grants, but he assured the *Minneapolis Star-Tribune* that he was not playing favorites.

The *Star-Tribune* revealed a number of questionable grants. The suburban city of Edina had approached Hennepin County for $189,000 with which to buy a Bearcat, "an armored car with rotating turrets and gun mounts," but the county's emergency services director said that "there was no way, don't even bother."

Then Edina discovered the pot of federal funds available from the state almost for the asking. Edina got its armored car.

Anoka County, Minnesota, got a demolition hammer, search cameras, and a reciprocating saw for a special team it had formed for the purpose of rescuing people from collapsed buildings and cave-ins. Evidently the visual images of the Twin Towers' collapse convinced the good officials of Anoka County that a similar fate might befall their somewhat smaller downtown buildings. The team has not had a single rescue in three years, but they're ready.

Rock County, Minnesota, got $164,800 in DHS funds to improve its 911 system. The county can now better locate cell phone callers when they phone in accidents. This was sold as an "anti-terrorism" measure, of course. Terri Ebert, chief dispatcher for the county, told the *Star-Tribune* that when she called the county administrator to tell him that the $164,800 check was in the mail, "he about drove in the ditch. He said, 'You've got to be kidding me.'"

If bin Laden isn't threatening the Gopher State, any terrorist will do. An Edina official noted, "They got the Posse Comitatus in the Dakotas,"[64] referring to an anti-tax group of the 1980s whose m.o. did not include assaults on suburban shopping centers.

Hardly was the ink dry on the Homeland Security Act of 2002 than the cry was raised: More Money!

Richard Clarke, the White House security advisor whose book, *Against All Enemies* (2004), jolted the Bush administration from the inside, took time out from writing his tell-all book to co-author, with former Senator Warren Rudman (R-NH), a July 2003 Council on Foreign Relations report which concluded, "The United States is drastically underfunding local emergency responders and remains dangerously unprepared to handle a catastrophic attack on American soil."

One wonders if any sum of money would be enough to "prepare" every state, county, city, town, village, and block for a "catastrophic" attack. Perhaps the wiser course would be to remove the incentives for terrorists to launch such assaults? But in any event, Rudman and Clarke, like drunken poker players playing with the bank's money, upped the ante. They demanded that the homeland security budget, already the fastest-growing part of the federal leviathan, be swelled by an additional $98.4 billion over the subsequent five years. So profligate was this demand that Gordon Johndroe, paid flack of the Department of Homeland Security, actually called it "grossly inflated,"[65] which was likely the first and last time that the "national greatness" conservatives of the Bush administration denounced a proposal for excessive spending.

John Mintz of the *Washington Post*, in an otherwise scathing article on DHS shortcomings, noted that despite its hypertrophied budget, "money is scarce and a constant preoccupation for department managers." Federal airport screeners, stepping out of their prescribed roles as front-line heroes in the war on terror, were busting the budget with overtime pay. Mintz, reverting to that established *Washington Post* role as house organ of the federal bureaucracy, decried "emergency cuts" and "cascading budget crises" that have resulted from the alleged parsimony of those notorious penny-pinchers in Congress and the White House.

The litany of departmental sacrifices is heartbreaking. It has too few employees. Some employees lack "secure telephone lines." Quarters are cramped. Buildings need repair. The third stall from the left in the fourth-floor men's room is out of toilet paper. And so on.

The solution, it seems, is ever higher budgets, lest the DHS remain perpetually "hobbled by money woes."[66] Only in Washington can an organization open shop with a $40 billion budget supplied by other people—the taxpayers—and within months whine that its belt is much too tight. That's homeland security for you.

Notes

1.   "Homeland Security Touted as Economic Development Tool for LA." Associated Press, August 24, 2004.
2.   Ranum, *The Myth of Homeland Security*, p. 31.
3.   Gloria Lee, "Homeland Security: A Boon for Businesses," Taxpayers for Common Sense Bailout Watch, July 19, 2002, www.bailoutwatch.org.

4.   Ibid.
5.   Ibid.
6.   Ibid.
7.   Ibid.
8.   Quoted in Christopher Preble, "Homeland Security: 'Welfare, Not Warfare,'" www.cato.org, September 17, 2003.
9.   "Clinton Urges Investments in Homeland Security Industry," Associated Press, *Rochester Democrat and Chronicle*, June 8, 2004, p. B7.
10.   John T. Flynn, *As We Go Marching* (New York: Free Life Editions, 1973/1944), p. 253.
11.   "DHS Organization," U.S. Department of Homeland Security, www.dhs.gov, undated, pp. 14–15.
12.   "KPMG Consulting Hires Veteran Lobbyist," Internet Week, www.internetwk.com, December 11, 2001.
13.   Philip Shenon, "Former Domestic Security Aides Switch to Lobbying," *New York Times*, April 28, 2003, p. A1.
14.   Llewellyn H. Rockwell, Jr., "Carving Up the Homeland Security Pie," www.mises.org, April 30, 2003.
15.   "Security Against Homeland Pork," *New York Times*, July 8, 2003, p. A22.
16.   Pam Zubeck, "The Big Business of Protection Against Terror," *Colorado Springs Gazette*, September 14, 2004, p. A1.
17.   Rockwell, "Carving Up the Homeland Security Pie," www.mises.org.
18.   Ranum, *The Myth of Homeland Security*, p. 183.
19.   Muphen Whitney, "Vendors Given a Reality Check at Homeland Security Summit," www.HomelandDefenseStocks.com, June 30, 2004.
20.   B.C. Kessner, "U.S. Homeland Security Market Described as a `Minefield,'" *Defense Daily International*, May 21, 2004.
21.   Ranum, *The Myth of Homeland Security*, p. xv.
22.   Erik Leaver, "Top 10 Reasons to Get Out of Iraq," *The Nation*, www.alternet.org, September 20, 2004.
23.   Abraham McLaughlin, "Homeland Security—Pork or Protection?" *Christian Science Monitor*, www.csmonitor.com, March 6, 2002.
24.   Katherine Pfleger, Associated Press, January 16, 2004.
25.   "Market Call," Cable News Network, Transcript 020410cb.105, February 4, 2004.
26.   Hearing of the Senate Governmental Affairs Committee, February 9, 2004, Federal News Service, p. 9.
27.   Jennifer Gritt, "Homeland Security Grants—A Not So Funny Joke," www.antiwar.com, March 3, 2004.
28.   Jordan Carleo-Evangelist, "No Town Left Behind in Terror Funding Flow," Boston University Washington Journalism Center, www.bu.edu/com/jo/washjocenter, Fall 2003.
29.   Jennifer Gritt, "Homeland Security Grants—A Not So Funny Joke."
30.   Jordan Carleo-Evangelist, "No Town Left Behind in Terror Funding Flow."
31.   Jo Becker, Sarah Cohen, and Spencer S. Hsu, "Anti-Terrorism Funds Buy Wide Array of Pet Projects," *Washington Post*, November 23, 2003, pp. A1, A16, A17.
32.   Mimi Hall, "Security Spending Raises Questions," *USA Today*, April 30, 2003, p. A4.
33.   Kate O'Beirne, "Introducing Pork-Barrel Homeland Security: A Little Here, a Little There..." *National Review*, August 11, 2003.
34.   Jordan Carleo-Evangelist, "No Town Left Behind in Terror Funding Flow."
35.   Donald F. Kettl, *The Department of Homeland Security's First Year: A Report Card*, p. 15.

36. "Citing Lack of Funding for California, Senator Feinstein Seeks Changes in Homeland Security Funding," press release, July 25, 2003.

37. Jordan Carleo-Evangelist, "No Town Left Behind in Terror Funding Flow."

38. Mimi Hall, "Security Spending Raises Questions," *USA Today*, April 30, 2003, p. A4.

39. Kate O'Beirne, "Introducing Pork-Barrel Homeland Security: A Little Here, a Lot There..." *National Review*, August 11, 2003.

40. "Homeland Security Grants Miss Needs," *Atlanta Journal-Constitution*, November 9, 2003, p. 10D.

41. Siobhan Gorman, "House Homeland Chair Seeks to Overhaul First Responder Funding," www.GovExec.com, October 9, 2003.

42. Siobhan Gorman, "Homeland Security Chair Calls for Restraint in Responder Spending," *National Journal*, www.govexec.com, November 14, 2003.

43. Richard Schwartz, "Congress Votes 'Me': Self-Indulgent House Keeps Sticking it to New York," *New York Daily News*, June 24, 2004, p. 45.

44. Kate O'Beirne, "Introducing Pork-Barrel Homeland Security: A Little Here, A Lot There..." *National Review*.

45. Jo Becker, Sarah Cohen, and Spencer S. Hsu, "Anti-Terrorism Funds Buy Wide Array of Pet Projects," *Washington Post*, November 23, 2003.

46. Douglas Turner, "Mayors Slam Bush Administration Over Lag in Homeland Security Grants," *Buffalo News*, January 23, 2004, p. C1.

47. Jordan Carleo-Evangelist, "No Town Left Behind in Terror Funding Flow."

48. Pam Zubeck, "The Big Business of Protection Against Terror," *Colorado Springs Gazette*.

49. Siobhan Gorman, "Homeland Security Chair Calls for Restrain in Responder Spending," *National Journal*.

50. Ibid.

51. Jordan Carleo-Evangelist, "No Town Left Behind in Terror Funding."

52. Mimi Hall, "Security Spending Raises Questions," *USA Today*.

53. Jordan Carleo-Evangelist, "No Town Left Behind in Terror Funding."

54. Gene Healy, "Deployed in the U.S.A.: The Creeping Militarization of the Home Front," Cato Policy Analysis No. 503 (Washington, DC: Cato Institute, December 17, 2003), p. 10.

55. Frank Oliveri, "Homeland Security Elusive Despite Available Cash," *USA Today*, www.usatoday, April 6, 2004.

56. Jim Hoffer, "Big Oil Companies Granted $66 Million by Homeland Security," WABC-TV, February 23, 2004.

57. "Boat Boondoggle," *Bangor Daily News*, April 6, 2004, p. A8.

58. Jo Becker, Sarah Cohen, and Spencer S. Hsu, "Anti-Terrorism Funds Buy Wide Array of Pet Projects," *Washington Post*, November 23, 2003, pp. A1, 16, 17.

59. Quoted in Mimi Hall, "Security Spending Raises Questions," *USA Today*.

60. Jo Becker, Sarah Cohen, and Spencer S. Hsu, "Anti-Terrorism Funds Buy Wide Array of Pet Projects," *Washington Post*.

61. Mimi Hall, "Security Spending Raises Questions," *USA Today*.

62. "State Has Received at Least $462 Million For Homeland Security," Associated Press, September 11, 2004.

63. Danny Westneat, "A New Call for Shared Sacrifice," *Seattle Times*, www.seattletimes.nwsource.com, August 27, 2004

64. Pat Doyle, Mike Kaszuba, and Ron Nixon, "9/11: A Special Report," *Minneapolis Star-Tribune*, September 12, 2004, p. 1A.

65. "Report: Homeland Security Grossly Underfunded," CNN.com, June 30, 2003.

66. John Mintz, "Government's Hobbled Giant," *Washington Post*.

4

(Expensive) Scenes from a
Twenty-First-Century Bureaucracy

"First responders" have replaced Chevys and joined motherhood and apple pie in the secular American trinity. The courage displayed by the fire fighters and police officers of the City of New York on September 11, 2001 was so inspiring as to shroud the brotherhood in a veil of holiness. No politician worth his PAC-money passed up the chance to be photographed standing next to a cop or a firetruck. In his pursuit of the presidency, Democratic nominee John Kerry was so often surrounded by fire hydrants that one could be forgiven for thinking him a dog. In fact, Kerry went so far as to make the alleged "preparedness gap" an issue in his 2004 presidential race. This "gap," which was every bit as contrived as the "missile gap" which a previous Massachusetts Democrat used to outhawk Richard Nixon in the 1960 presidential election, describes the supposed canyonesque chasm between our first-responder needs and our first-responder resources. As Kerry said in July 2003, "we still do not have a real plan and enough resources for preparedness against a terrorist attack."[1]

Going him a few billion extra, as *National Review's* Kate O'Beirne noted, a task force of the impeccably establishmentarian Council on Foreign Relations found us "Drastically Underfunded, Dangerously Unprepared," and noted "the United States could spend the entire gross national product and still be unprepared."[2]

Give Congress time, CFR, give them time.

Yet only on the fringes of politics did anyone raise a powerful and historically grounded objection to the profuse subsidies lavished on first responders: namely, that the Homeland Security and USA-PATRIOT Acts went a considerable ways toward the federalizing—that is, nationalizing—of local police and fire departments.

Recall the popular bumper stickers of the 1960s: "Support Your Local Police—and Keep Them Independent." On both right and left, Americans rightly feared the centralization of law enforcement.

That justified fear, like the defense of so many basic American liberties, has been pushed further and further to the margins of our political life. It took a writer for the John Birch Society, of all places, to note that the Homeland Security Act "mandates federal supervision, funding, and coordination of 'local first responders'—specifically police and emergency personnel." Picking up this concern from across the room, so to speak, was the leftish civil liberties lawyer Jennifer Van Bergen, who found in the HSA "reason for concern that central federal coordination could lead to loss of local control and to potential federal militarization, especially in view of the many other measures and events that support such a possibility,"[3] particularly the USA-PATRIOT Act and the military tribunals set up by the Bush administration.

Homeland Defense Secretary Tom Ridge unabashedly spoke for such centralized coordination. In a May 6, 2004 address to the National Volunteer Fire Council in Arlington, Virginia, Ridge disparaged the old days when volunteer fire departments acted as proudly independent avatars and protectors of their hometowns: "Before September 11th, counties, cities, and states for the most part worked independently to achieve their security goals and objectives," said Ridge. "The problem with that approach is that if security goals aren't integrated then there are going to be holes and weaknesses terrorists look to exploit. That's why after September 11th, it became abundantly clear that securing our homeland would require all those different entities to come together around a shared goal of protecting our nation and our citizens from those who would seek to do us harm."[4] Even volunteer fire departments in Alabama, New York, and Elba, Alabama, it seems, were to be enlisted in this national crusade.

In *Defending the Homeland: Domestic Intelligence, Law Enforcement, and Security* (2004), criminal justice scholar Jonathan R. White writes that "incorporating law enforcement in national defense will change the nature of American police work."[5] Approximately 600,000 Americans work as law-enforcement officers, and these are overwhelmingly local in scope and attachment. "Historically, the American police have never had a cohesive role in national policy,"[6] he notes, nor have they sought one. Yet they are, by inches and yards and leaps and bounds, undergoing a quasi-nationalization that is nothing less than revolutionary.

Given that Professor White wrote his book under a grant partially underwritten by the Federal Bureau of Investigation, he is hardly unsympathetic to the challenges faced by law enforcement. But in assaying the ways in which the War on Terror threatens to alter the traditionally localized nature of police in America, he raises troubling issues. The dispersed nature of the police function has certain policy implications. As White remarks, proponents of "decentralizing police power" believe that it "personalizes services and develops links to communities. They believe localized officers are more adept at recognizing and handling problems."[7] The Podunk Police Department understands the difference between a suspicious character and a local character; its officers are far less likely than national or state police to engage in racial profiling, for example, because they are familiar with the residents of a given village or city precinct.

Once upon a time, the local constabulary had its defenders even at the national level. Figures in both parties spoke for the wisdom of keeping the police power decentralized. Your city's cops were seen as more than mere adjuncts to the FBI, the DEA, and other agents of the federal government.

Yet in the early twenty-first century, the Republicans, the erstwhile professed party of limited government, were AWOL when it came time to voice even the tiniest complaint about the potential federal domination of state and local law enforcement. Instead, they entreated Uncle Sam for more money and swifter delivery. The weekend before Thanksgiving 2002 found the nation's Republican governors not so much in a thankful mood as in a beseeching frame of mind. As Robert Tanner of the Associated Press reported, "The three-day Republican Gov.'s Association conference...was largely devoted to celebrating the GOP's successes, but the governors also made pointed demands for faster and better federal support for law enforcement and public health needs."[8]

With federal support comes federal controls. When local police are effectively deputized by the national government, they often receive directions that in their maddening vagueness are virtual licenses to despotism. Take, for instance, these instructions to patrol officers assisting in national intelligence-gathering operations. They were directed to "look for":

- •   "Suspects who have money with no furnishings in apartments" (Bohemians beware!)
- •   "Radical literature" (First Amendment, we hardly knew ye...)
- •   "Hand-drawn maps" (Amateur cartographers, watch out!)
- •   "Loud and boisterous behavior in tight-knit groups" (Are teenagers to be locked up en masse?)
- •   "Alienated groups in school settings."[9] (Geeks have yet one more tormenter to fear.)

The National Strategy for Homeland Security calls upon "federal, state, and local law enforcement to share information." This may sound harmless, but the strategy goes on to announce as a basic principle of information sharing that relevant actors are to "View federal, state, and local governments as one entity."[10] If that phraseology doesn't set off alarm bells in whatever old-fashioned federalists are left in the U.S., nothing will.

Secretary Ridge boasts that his department has "redefined a new federalism."[11] In fact it is destroying true federalism. The pertinent question, however, is whether anyone in America cares anymore.

Professor White notes that "There are parallels with the federal call for homeland security and debates about state policing a century ago."[12]

Indeed, the parallels are both striking and chilling. Every state except Hawaii now has a state police department, but few know just how fierce were the battles over the creation of these centralized police forces.

"The idea of a state-controlled police force was an unprecedented and controversial development in nineteenth-century America,"[13] writes H. Kenneth Bechtel in his standard history of the state police movement. The first and most romantic such force was the Texas Rangers, who were formed in 1835, or one year before the Republic of Texas came into being. The Rangers were essentially a "frontier pacification force"[14] whose legend was built around tales of derring-do, Indian-fighting, and the pursuit of outlaws through storm and sagebrush.

The first modern state police force belonged to Pennsylvania, and its genesis was brutal and ugly, about as far as can be from Louis L'Amour novelizations of Texas Ranger heroism.

The Keystone State was the coal mining and steel manufacturing capital of the industrializing U.S. It was also the center of strikes, labor agitation, and union radicalism. Violence on both sides was not unknown. Enforcement of the law was the responsibility of local police and, in extreme cases, the National Guard, but as Jonathan R. White writes, "Since local police officers and guardsmen came from the working class, they frequently identified with striking workers."[15]

Elbert Gary, president of U.S. Steel, lobbied President Theodore Roosevelt to back the creation of paramilitary state police forces, unbound by local ties or loyalties, whose primary (if unstated) purpose would be to keep peace in the coal and steel industries. Roosevelt, who never met a proposal for a more muscular state authority that he didn't like, responded with great enthusiasm. The result was the Pennsylvania State Police, a "highly centralized, paramilitary, and impersonal" organization with "total powers of search, seizure, and arrest in any part of the state." Like the U.S. Army, the state police were "highly mobile, recruited nationwide, and without ties to any particular communities" so as to "eliminate any sympathy between police and public."[16] They were, in effect, an occupying army of police officers whose jurisdiction overlapped with the old decentralized police forces of the county and municipal level.

They were efficient, merciless, and not especially persuaded by appeals to personal liberty. They were, in short, a typical creation of the Progressive Movement. Critics of the state police, who tended to be rural, classical liberal, or localist, charged that they were (1) militaristic; (2) expensive; (3) open to political corruption and manipulation to a greater degree than sheriffs and elected law enforcement officials; and (4) a weapon used against strikers. Labor leaders called the Pennsylvania state police "American Cossacks" whose job it was to "terrorize and regulate workers."[17] But they were fast on their way to becoming a model for the nation.

Ex-President Roosevelt wrote the introduction to a classic propaganda text, Katherine Mayo's *Justice to All: The Story of the Pennsylvania State Police* (1917), which "play[ed] on the public's fear of foreigners"[18] in a wartime climate. Astonishingly, Mayo never mentions Elbert Gary or U.S. Steel in her book, preferring romanticized accounts of brave state policemen busting poachers, pickpockets, murderous lunatics, and other scofflaws that localized, dimwitted sheriffs were apparently unable to apprehend. Backed by Mayo and Roosevelt, the state police movement took off during wartime. Between 1917 and 1935, a majority of states created their own police forces. Some were paramilitary, along the lines of the Pennsylvania police, while others were highway patrolmen whose most sacred responsibility was ticketing speeders to fill the state's coffers. Many, as was the case in Nevada, where mine workers tended toward radicalism, were there to squash strikes.

The state police are by now so well entrenched an institution that almost no one questions their existence. They have not been an unmixed blessing for American law enforcement: Their jurisdictions frequently overlap with local police, leading to logistical headaches and fierce turf wars; like the Pennsylvania State Police of 1905, state police have been used to discipline protesters and petitioners when local police, who know a situation much more intimately, refuse to do so with much vigor. Decentralized police forces are part of the communities they serve; they are far better at placing incidents, suspicions, and unusual acts in context. They know the town eccentric; they understand patterns of life, of commerce, of culture, in a way that centralized outside forces never can. But in this age of homeland security, does such localized knowledge count for anything with the decision-makers of Washington?

Jonathan R. White points out that the Homeland Security Act mandates that "all levels of government—federal, state, and local—will work together." This seems inconsistent with the Tenth Amendment, which states, "The powers not delegated to the United States by the Constitution, nor prohibited by it to the States, are reserved to the States respectively, or to the people." (Those with a taste for bitter incongruities may recall Senator Bob Dole carrying around a copy of the Tenth Amendment in his pocket during his campaign for the 1996 Republican presidential nomination. Once he got the nomination he must have gotten his pants cleaned and lost the Amendment, for never since has a prominent Republican made mention of it.)

White makes note of the parallels between the state police movement and the homeland security initiatives, and he asks a series of questions that few others have bothered to ask, let alone answer: "Will police functions be centralized? Is efficiency the measure of police effectiveness? Will homeland defense result in a new type of police force or level of policing? Will state and local law enforcement remain autonomous?"[19]

The rise of state-level homeland security departments is particularly troublesome in light of the state police example. Yet another governmental function that has, traditionally, been best and most humanely performed at the local level is being centralized.

The quality of state homeland security czars seems to run from competent careerists to abject hacks. The most egregious and memorable example of the latter was the immortal Israeli fledgling poet, Golan Cipel, who is remembered for neither his sonnets nor his quatrains but rather his central role in the bizarre *opéra bouffe* in which New Jersey's Democratic Governor James E. McGreevey fell from grace and power in the late summer of 2004.

McGreevey, as gleeful scandalmongers had cause to learn, was the unprepossessing liberal governor of the Garden State. On August 12, 2004, he resigned his office (effective November 15) in a mawkish speech in which he revealed himself as a "gay American"— albeit a twice-married Catholic American with children. McGreevey sought to portray himself as a martyr for gay rights whose only crime had been to love perhaps too often, if not too well, but in fact the self-pitying gush of his resignation speech was meant to obscure an extraordinary scandal: He had appointed his alleged boytoy, the obscure foreign poet Golan Cipel, as the state's chief of homeland security. Cipel, McGreevey claimed, was now threatening a sexual harassment lawsuit against the governor unless the Gov forked over $50 million or $5 million or $2 million—the price flew downwards like a freefalling elevator, or like McGreevey's career. In any event, the McGreevey team refused to pay up, the governor resigned, and talk radio hosts had their topic for the week.

But the sexual aspect of the affair tended to eclipse a more revealing facet: that Governor McGreevey regarded the homeland security post as nothing more than a sinecure to which he might safely appoint his alleged boyfriend. While the mass media labor overtime to portray the mandarins of the homeland securiat as valorous if deskbound warriors fighting to keep us free, the politicos, à la McGreevey, know better: homeland security is just another name for pork.

Cipel was appointed to his position on January 15, 2002, when passions and fears still ran high in the aftermath of 9/11. For $110,000 annually, he was to "coordinate increased security with all branches of government," notes Justin Raimondo of antiwar.com. Local police departments and first responders were to look to the Israeli poet and McGreevey squeeze for direction. In a strange twist to the tale, McGreevey prevented the relevant authorities from conducting the usual background check on Cipel, whose visa was sponsored by New Jersey real estate developer Charles Kushner, the largest single contributor to Governor McGreevey's previous election campaign.

The flighty television personality and compassionate conservative turned limousine liberal Arianna Huffington said that Cipel's hiring "only makes sense as a taxpayer-funded cry for help."[20] The better explanation, perhaps, is that it shows in living color just how cavalierly politicians treat the hallowed position of state homeland security director. These would-be czars are a dime a dozen—well, in Golan Cipel's case, a bit more expensive than that—but the point is that Cipel's job, and that of most administrators in the War on Terror, is to dole out tax dollars to the most well-connected supplicants. Contrary to the cliché, September 11 did not "change everything." The pork barrel, it seems, is eternal and unchangeable.

The subordination of local police to state agencies and of state agencies to the federal government betokens a threatening concentration of police power. And this power is to be exercised in an unprecedented arena, for, as White writes, "[t]raditionally, the American police and the criminal justice system have had no role in national defense."[21]

At the same time, the armed forces have been forbidden from executing the laws of this country by the Posse Comitatus Act of 1878. In its entirety, the Act reads: "Whoever, except in cases and under circumstances expressly authorized by the Constitution or Act of Congress, willfully uses any part of the Army as a posse comitatus or otherwise to execute the laws shall be fined under this title or imprisoned not more than two years, or both."[22]

There was some debate in 1878 over whether the legislation was even necessary. As Gene Healy of the Cato Institute notes, Illinois Rep. Robert Townsend remarked that "it was the real design of those who framed our Constitution that the Federal Army should never be used for any purpose but to repel invasion and to suppress insurrection when it became too formidable for the State to suppress it."[23] But the Congress passed and President Hayes signed into law the act, which applies to the U.S. armed forces and the federalized National Guard.

Guard units under state control are not restricted by the Posse Comitatus Act. Thus over 7,000 National Guardsmen were stationed at the nation's airports by state governors after 9/11—a show of force that former Kansas City, Missouri chief of police Joseph McNamara criticized as "a pretense of doing something."[24] By contrast, the 2002 deployment of 1,600 federalized members of the National Guard along the U.S. borders with Mexico and Canada was, as analyst Gene

Healy points out, a violation of the Posse Comitatus Act. At last check, President Bush had been neither fined nor sentenced to two years in jail for this illegal act.

Soldiers and policemen perform fundamentally different roles: the former are trained killers, while the latter, who rarely if ever use deadly force, are expected to respect the constitutional rights of the citizens they serve—even of those they arrest. Argues Col. Patrick Finnegan, chair of the Department of Law at the U.S. Military Academy at West Point, "The military is designed and trained to defend our country by fighting and killing the enemy, usually faceless, with no individual rights. ...The training, mission, and role of the military and police are so dissimilar that it is not surprising that we do not, and should not, want the military to act as a police force."[25]

Well, some of us don't.

The Posse Comitatus Act was diluted in 1981 to allow the military—over the objections of much of its brass—to play a greater role in the domestic War on Drugs. Caspar Weinberger, secretary of defense in the Reagan Administration and nobody's sob-sister liberal, charges that deploying the armed forces in the drug war has been "detrimental to military readiness and an inappropriate use of the democratic system."[26]

The Posse Comitatus Act has also been amended to permit the armed forces to execute domestic laws in extraordinary cases of terrorism, for instance in a nuclear or chemical weapons attack.

As Gene Healy has pointed out, "deviation from our tradition of civilian law enforcement has had grave consequences,"[27] from the bloody clashes between troops and strikers in the late nineteenth century to the tragic murder of eighteen-year-old high-school student Esequiel Hernandez, Jr., who was shot by Marines in 1997 while tending goats on the Texas side of the Mexican border. The Marines who killed Esequiel were on an anti-drug patrol; they shot him because the young goatherd carried a .22 caliber rifle. The tragic 1993 assault on the Branch Davidian church at Waco, Texas, which left fifty-three adults and twenty-seven children incinerated, was done at the urging of U.S. Army Delta Force commanders, who were called in under one of the 1981 exceptions to the Posse Comitatus Act.

In the post-9/11 world, those who would forfeit our ancient liberties are calling for further amending, if not outright scrapping, the Posse Comitatus Act. We have all seen U.S. troops in airports: a deployment of dubious practical value but one of enormous symbolic importance. Their presence is less reassuring than it is a jarring reminder of those photos of circa 1960s Latin American police states.

General Ralph E. Eberhart, head of the "North Command," or those military forces stationed within the United States, has said, "We should always be reviewing things like the Posse Comitatus... if we think it ties our hands in protecting the American people."[28] That is troubling language: "ties our hands." The Bill of Rights certainly "ties the hands" of the police in the performance of their daily duties, but would we like to live in a country in which the police—or the military—act without restraint?

Since the events of September 11, 2001, government employees have been depicted in popular culture in an almost caricaturishly favorable light: every police officer and fire fighter is a saint; soldiers are selfless heroes "fighting for our freedom"; CIA agents are sexy, glamorous, and deeply ethical; even George W. Bush is a steely-eyed missile man, in the old Mercury Seven astronaut term of praise. One has to travel back to the years of the two world wars to find governmental officials treated with such reverence in the cinema. The Wilson administration's propaganda campaign paid off with such filmic classics as "To Hell with the Kaiser," "The Kaiser: Beast of Berlin," and of course "Mutt and Jeff at the Front." For modern versions thereof, please refer to the corpus of Tom Cruise.

But apparently even this kid-glove treatment is not enough for the James Bond-ian figures of our Department of Homeland Security. For in March 2004, word leaked that this department, whose charge it is to make us secure against terrorist threats, had advertised for an "entertainment liaison" with an annual salary of $136,466. This vital cog in our nation's defense was to "influence how Hollywood portrays the Department of Homeland Security," as reported by Lisa Friedman in the Los Angeles *Daily News*.

One might think that relevant experience for a job in the DHS would include bomb-detection, fluency in foreign languages, past police work, cloak-and-dagger stuff no one is allowed to talk about, or at least the ability to type sixty words a minute. But the Hollywood liaison is expected to have experience "developing or consulting on creative concepts and scripts"—preferably *Top Gun* rather than *M*A*S*H*—as well as "identifying external product placement opportunities in major motion pictures and television programs."

The mere existence of such a position raises First Amendment concerns. Is it really a legitimate function of the federal government to shape the political content of films? As Rep. Brad Sherman (D-CA) quite sensibly noted, "There's this growing tendency to spend government money to make government look good. It's hard for me to think this is the best possible use of taxpayer dollars."[29]

Alas, such propagandizing on the public dime has been going on for years. James Beck, former solicitor general of the United States, wrote in his 1933 muckraking book, *Our Wonderland of Bureaucracy*:

> Publicity has become a potent factor in the growth of bureaucracy . . . which loudly vaunts its usefulness from the housetops by newspaper articles, reports, radio broadcasting and bulletins. . . . To accomplish their ends they seize every opportunity, not only to promote the interests of their services but incidentally to suppress or explain away any news, which might reflect unfavorably on their bureau.
>
> The bureaucracy, at the expense of the taxpayers, is ever at work to increase the importance and prestige of their several bureaus and . . . to secure greater recognition. . . . If Congress at times weakly yields to these powerful propaganda organizations, it is because they are organized and are an appreciable force at the polls, while the taxpayers and consumers are unorganized and inarticulate.[30]

A congressman of Beck's era, Indiana Democrat Louis Ludlow, seconded his observation in words that could serve as a virtual motto of the Department of Homeland Security: "Bureaucracy thrives by tooting its own horn. No sooner is a bureau established than it goes in for publicity, the object being to glorify itself and make itself strong and secure by publicizing its glorious mission in the world and broadcasting its beneficent works."[31]

So the DHS Hollywood campaign is nothing new. Indeed, the Pentagon "has more than 20 people charged with projecting and protecting the agency's image in movies, music videos, television shows and other fictional portrayals."[32]

The press has been handmaiden to the propagandists in exaggerating the threats on which the homeland security bureaucracy thrives. But then this, too, is nothing new. As Marcus Ranum points out, the widespread scare of "computer hackers" in the early 1990s gave us "visions of aircraft falling out of the sky because their command systems had been wiped out with pulses of directed radiation and government agencies collapsing when a pimply-faced subculture hacked into their information resources."

No such horrors happened. Pustuled youths raised on video games never did find a way—if they even sought a way—of transferring the lessons of Mortal Kombat into the air traffic control system. Planes stayed the course, Social Security checks went out on time, or at least on the federal government's version of "on-time," and the sky did not fall. Yet "the spooks who were looking at budget cuts had found their foe. Best of all, because it was a nebulous foe—a threat that didn't really exist—it had advantages. It could not be beaten, could not surrender, and could be ascribed awesome, superhuman powers."[33]

Sound familiar? International terrorism has replaced—and is a much more effective bogeyman than—the acne-scarred hacker. After all, every week seems to bring another worm, another virus threatening to shut down our computers, yet somehow Americans and our economy muddle through.

Marcus Ranum, who has extensive experience advising public and private clients in the area of computer security, is withering in his view of government cybersecurity initiatives, which he calls "Chicken Little make-work program[s] for Beltway bandits and high-tech firms."[34] As far back as the Reagan administration, the Defense Advanced Research Project Agency (DARPA), of which we shall hear much more anon, sponsored costly research into the ways and means of preventing terrorist subversion of information systems.

This research was about as cutting-edge as the films of Mary-Kate and Ashley Olsen. For one thing, most of the top-flight IT people within the federal government had flocked to the private sector by the early nineties, lured not only by vastly higher remuneration but also the relatively unshackled environment of Silicon Valley.

Once liberated, many of them realized that the vaunted chess match between government supersleuths and brilliant hacker-terrorists was almost wholly a figment of Hollywood's imagination. As Ranum remarks, "the FBI constantly panders to the press by portraying the hackers they are up against as 'brilliant' or 'geniuses' or 'whiz kids.' In fact, a lot of the hackers are simply persistent and are going up against defenses that are incredibly weak and poorly maintained."[35]

On the other side of the illusion, although "Hollywood almost always represents government (CIA and NSA computers, particularly) as supersecure, with capabilities right out of science fiction novels," in fact "some of the worst computer security in the world is that used by the U.S. federal government."[36]

The GAO blasted the FBI's National Infrastructure Protection Center as, in the words of computer-industry journalist Declan McCullagh, "a federal backwater that is surprisingly ineffective in pursuing malicious hackers or devising a plan to shield the Internet from attacks."[37] The Center is now a centerpiece of the DHS infrastructure protection strategy.

In any event, computer companies are taking advantage of the hysteria over homeland security to seek subsidies that are right out of the old industrial America playbook. As a Cato Institute report notes, "the cybersecurity threat can also be an occasion for shifting to the government the costs of what are—or should be—private sector responsibilities, such as bolstering corporate networks or hiring and training individuals capable of doing the job."[38]

The DHS publicity machine has learned one valuable lesson in its first three years: all the fawning press in the world can't compete with a ten percent pay raise.

After the initial skirmishing between the Bush administration and union-backed members of Congress over the former's request for greater latitude in the assignment of civil servants, the two sides have come closer. While disagreements over flexibility and a performance-based pay system persist, the administration's pledge to "inves[t] in human capital"[39] within the DHS seems to have quieted the liberal opposition. The prospect of an expanding payroll and workforce has that effect on government-employee unions.

And the prospect of enlisting government employee unions in one's presidential quest has a remarkably sobering effect on ambitious politicians. In April 2002, Senator Joseph Lieberman (D-CT), father, in a way, of the Department of Homeland Security, said that the DHS would "need the power to knock heads to overcome bureaucratic resistance, to eliminate wasteful duplication of effort and target precious resources."[40] As the lure of the 2004 Democratic presidential nomination grew stronger, he dropped the posturing about "head-knocking" and took up the cause of the aggrieved bureaucrats. So sedulous was his advocacy that he was honored with the designation "Porker of the Month" by the watchdog group Citizens Against Government Waste.

As the Department of Homeland Security matured, disputes over work rules heated up once more. On February 20, 2004, the DHS and the Office of Personnel Management published a proposed regulation change that would significantly change pay, promotion, and disciplinary rules governing 110,000 of the DHS's 180,000 and climbing) employees. The DHS and OPM proposed to scrap the General Schedule pay system, with its fifteen grades, and compensate the affected DHS workers with a "pay banding" system under which their pay rates would be determined by "market demand" and job performance. Management—that is, government—would also find it easier to transfer workers and fire or demote workers without the usual lengthy appeal process. The new rules took effect for a pilot group of 8,000 DHS workers in late 2004; they were to be in place for the other 170,000 or so employees by late 2005.

Government employees' unions objected strenuously, as did their spokesmen in Congress. A joint statement of John Gage, president of the American Federation of Government Employees; Colleen M. Kelley, president of the National Treasury Employees Union; and Michael Randall, president of the National Association of Agriculture Employees, asserted that "the proposed system fails to advance the public's interest in protecting homeland security."

How thoughtful of the AFGE, NTEU, and NAAE to put the public first! But in urging the rejection of the new rules, the troika went even further. The new system "would be complex and costly to administer," they argued, adding, "A new bureaucracy would be created."[41]

Now, in every other instance ever recorded, the fact that a new bureaucracy would be created is reason enough for these unions to support a proposed rule. This was a novel argument indeed. Alas for the unions, the rule changes took effect in late 2004.

Hiring at the new department was done "quickly and haphazardly," according to White House leakers. But then beggars can't be choosers: The *Washington Post* reported that "many potential recruits decline because they consider Homeland Security a government backwater."[42] The money may be there, but the action isn't. For instance, 795 employees in the FBI's cybersecurity office were said by the White House to be moving to DHS; a grand total of twenty-two actually made the move.

If "first responders" is gold, "transportation security" is a strong silver medalist in the pork barrel Olympics. Even as the years that separate us from the events of September 11, 2001, lengthen, the image of the planes hitting the towers remains horrifyingly fresh in the mind's eye. And so it has become even easier for politicos to squeeze money for projects back home into homeland security or transportation bills.

In a sense, pork has been part and parcel of homeland security from the beginning. The June 2002 $28-billion emergency spending bill, which canny lawmakers denominated a homeland security Christmas tree, was "disgraceful," according to Senator John McCain (R-AZ), who added, "There are policy changes which have nothing to do with any national emergency."[43] The anti-terror "emergencies" funded included:

- $5 million for farmers' markets and roadside vegetable stands, disproportionately located in Wisconsin, home state of ranking Democrat David Obey on the House Appropriations Committee.
- $2.5 million to map coral reefs off Hawaii.
- $7.2 million to the National Oceanic and Atmospheric Administration for the purchase of a weather-forecasting computer.
- $1 billion in aid to veterans, perhaps in acknowledgement that federal policy was about to create a new generation of disabled vets.
- $10 million to help farmers along the Rio Grande.

The pork barrel has stayed full ever since. For instance, the FY 2004 Homeland Security Appropriations bill earmarked repair money for numerous bridges: $5 million for the Florida Avenue Railway/Highway bridge in New Orleans, Louisiana; $1.5 million for the EJ&E railroad bridge in Morris, Illinois; $2 million for the John F. Limehouse bridge in Charleston, South Carolina; $2.5 million for the Chelsea Street bridge in Boston, Massachusetts; $2.5 million for the Sidney Lanier Highway bridge in Brunswick, Georgia; and $7 million for the Fourteen Mile CSX Railroad bridge in Mobile, Alabama.

As Senator McCain noted, these bridges had not undergone any kind of risk or vulnerability assessment. The spend-happy Bush administration had not requested that homeland security monies be spent on these bridges. Rather, they were located in the districts of influential members of Congress who served on the appropriations committees.

But that's kid's stuff, the merest scraps from the table, when it comes to the single most reviled agency within the DHS: the Transportation Security Administration (TSA).

Few homeland security agencies have come in for such upbraiding as has the Transportation Security Administration, the Bush-created entity whose job it is to ensure the security of U.S. air, land, and sea borders as well as the network of transportation systems.

The TSA was born out of a dubious philosophy: When in doubt, reorganize. Once the manifold failures of the Federal Aviation Administration had been so widely aired as to render the concept of

"airline security" oxymoronic, responsibility for preventing a se-
quel to 9/11 was transferred to the new Transportation Security
Agency.[44]

The Agency has been characterized by an expansion so rapid that
one might be forgiven for believing that someday, each and every
American will be an employee of the TSA. As Rep. John Duncan
(R-TN) noted with exasperation, "[W]hen we created the Transportation Security Administration, they told us that they needed . . .
33,000 [screeners]. Then after we passed the bill, they told us 40,000.
And then last month [May 2002] they came to the appropriations
subcommittee and said they need 72,000 employees in that short a
time."[45] As of November 2004, the TSA was making do, grumblingly,
with 45,000 screeners.

Airline Security Report complained right off the bat that it took
seven months for the TSA to even figure out just what it was supposed to do, but that didn't stanch the flow of funds. Appropriations
for aviation security have risen up, up, and away in each year since
2001. The Bush administration boasted that its fiscal year 2005 budget contained a 20 percent increase (or $890 million) for aviation
security, which lifts this former budgetary backwater into the $5.3
billion range. A few hundred million here and a few hundred million
there, to paraphrase Senator Everett Dirksen, and pretty soon we're
talking real money.

Bureaucrats overseeing other modes of transportation can barely
contain their envy. Daniel Duff, vice president for government affairs of the American Public Transportation Association, told the
Subcommittee on Railroads of the House Transportation and Infrastructure Committee that "32 million times each day, Americans take
public transportation, compared to the 2 million daily passengers
who use the nation's commercial air travel system. The federal government needs to do more to support a secure environment for public transportation's tens of millions of riders."[46]

Duff's jealousy is palpable. If only those damned planes hadn't
crashed into the World Trade Center then all that DHS money would
be going to subways and city buses! Duff identified $6 billion worth
of "security" needs of our public transportation system. These included personnel, new radio systems, security cameras, personnel,
overtime, training, and—did we mention?—personnel costs.

Eat your heart out, Duff. The TSA is so spendthrift it makes George
W. Bush look like Ron Paul.

Barely was the paint dry on the personal parking space signs in the TSA lot than the first director of the agency, John Magaw, spent $420,000 (not of his own money) to redecorate his office. Wrong move, Magaw: He was dismissed.

In November 2003, the TSA hosted a lavish party at a downtown Washington, D.C. hotel that cost more than $200,000. The purpose of this party was to honor over 350 TSA employees for outstanding work. Presumably these were not the baggage screeners whose qualifying tests were chockfull of "simply inane" questions, according to a TSA internal audit. This same report found that $9 million of the $18 million in expenses incurred by one TSA contractor were the result of "wasteful and abusive spending practices."[47] And no, that contractor was not catering the TSA bash in Washington—though the finger food cost $33 per person.

All this spending on transportation security has had doubtful impact upon making transportation more secure.

Airplanes and other modes of transport can never be made truly terrorist-proof. The Libyans who blew up Pan Am Flight 103 over the skies of Lockerbie, Scotland, in 1988 did so with a bomb that had been hidden inside a portable radio stuffed into checked luggage. The nineteen homicidal suicides of 9/11 were armed with little more than box-cutters and the willingness to die for a cause, however perverted. The incompetent Brit Richard Reid had filled his shoes with the explosive triacetone triperoxide (TAE) in his unsuccessful December 22, 2001 attempt to blow up a American Airlines flight from Paris to Miami. (As Ranum has written, "We can all be grateful that Reid didn't place his explosives in his underpants or the experience of travel would have been changed dramatically for the worse for many of us."[48])

Airplanes make fine, if unwieldy, weapons, as murderers and madmen have discovered.

The delays, massive inconveniences, and petty harassments of air travel are well known to all who fly the no longer so friendly skies. James Bovard has documented them in *Terrorism and Tyranny*. Toenail clippers have become contraband, Rockport shoes set off alarms that rival London during the Blitz, and in one memorable instance, on November 16, 2001, a Mr. Michael Lasseter, thirty-two, of Gainesville, Georgia, sprinted past a security checkpoint because he was late for the plane that would take him to Memphis for the University of Georgia-Ole Miss football game. The ensuing chaos shut down the Atlanta Hartsfield airport for hours, delaying and canceling flights for 10,000 passengers.

The TSA was singled out for chastisement in "The Department of Homeland Security's First Year: A Report Card," a project overseen by University of Wisconsin-Madison Professor of Public Affairs and Political Science Donald F. Kettl for the Century Foundation. (The Century Foundation, it is amusing to note, was the new name hung upon the Twentieth Century Fund once the twenty-first century dawned. It faced the same nomenclatorial dilemma as Twentieth Century Fox, though the Fund both graduated into a Foundation and also solved the problem of anachronism once and for all by opting for the unadorned "Century." Presumably it is now refitted for foundational eternity.)

In any event, the Century Foundation's report card punished the DHS with the grade of "D" in its performance of several aviation security tasks:

- Conduct timely screener background checks
- Ensure security in general aviation (private planes)
- Ensure security in cargo.[49]

While giving the Transportation Security Administration credit for hiring 4,000 undercover air marshals (and later adding 7,000 more "reserve" marshals who fly during times of perceived security risks), Kettl scored it for lax to non-existent examination of air freight and also noted that "security remains loose for private planes and some small airports."[50]

Meanwhile, the billions of dollars being spent on air security and the millions of inconveniences experienced by travellers have given us...well, it's not clear. Marcus J. Ranum has written, "I tried desperately to find even one example where U.S. airport passenger screening had actually prevented a terrorist incident. We have this gigantic, expensive bureaucracy and infrastructure that has no actual history of serving a purpose other than keeping up appearances."[51]

The TSA's "No Fly List," which was secretly instituted in November 2001, has kept numerous Americans off planes for no reason beyond the usual bureaucratic foul-ups. Once on the list, the hapless grounded citizen has no way to get his or her name removed from the list. Nor does she have a right to find out why she is even on the list. This is Kafka at the airport.

Newspapers have been filled with stories of hapless travelers who are not permitted on flights because their names are uncomfortably similar to those of persons on the "No Fly List." Although the first reaction of many Americans is probably "thank God my first name isn't Mohammed," in fact many persons with typical, ordinary, regular-guy American names like Joe and Bob have been delayed, hassled, or even kept off flights for—literally—nominal reasons.

The No Fly list has a political bent that ought to be unacceptable in a land with an operative First Amendment. Stories of dissidents refused entry onto a plane are legion.[52]

The No Fly List is compiled by the Transportation Security Administration in consultation with the Department of Homeland Security. It is distributed to the commercial airlines and airport security, which are instructed to either keep listees from boarding airplanes or to search them as thoroughly as possible. There is no appeals process for those on the list, even though in certain instances people have landed on the list due to misspellings and other cacographic mix-ups. For instance, those who joined the American Civil Liberties Union in filing an April 6, 2004 class-action lawsuit against the TSA and DHS over the No Fly list include a retired Presbyterian minister, a Master Sergeant in the U.S. Air Force, and—more suspiciously—a staff attorney with the ACLU's National Prison Project and a coordinator for the pacifist American Friends Service Committee.[53]

Have these last two, and others like them, been harassed for their political beliefs? It seems, ahem, possible. After all, Cat Stevens, a.k.a. Yusuf Islam, was denied entry to the United States in September 2004—not for the crime of the mawkish "Peace Train" but rather for his Islamist sympathies.

If American citizens are to be denied access to U.S. airlines for their political views, what's next? Why not also deny them access to the voting booth?

All in good time, friend, all in good time.

Bolstering the No Fly List is the incipient Computer Assisted Passenger Prescreening System II (CAPPS II), which was announced in the August 1, 2003 *Federal Register*. CAPPS II "would for the first time put the government in the business of conducting regular background checks on everyday citizens," as the American Civil Liberties Union notes. Under CAPPS II, the TSA would monitor every single airline passenger in the country. Drawing upon a vast database contributed to by governmental and commercial sources, the TSA would subject all passengers to a "risk assessment function." The three or four percent with the riskiest profiles would be placed under the most severe scrutiny.

The ACLU emphasized the jaw-droppingly large potential for invasions of privacy implied by CAPPS II, which relies heavily on credit information. It pointed to an instance in which JetBlue, the commercial carrier, shared more than five million passenger records with Torch Concepts, a subcontractor of the U.S. Army. Torch Concepts used the information supplied by JetBlue to create "an extremely detailed and intrusive dossier on the lives of many Jet Blue passengers." Northwest Airlines also gave ostensibly private passenger information to firms associated with CAPPS II.

As the ACLU dryly noted, "surveillance programs, once initiated, always grow in scope." A critical General Accounting Office report of February 2004 made the same point: mission creep is already seeping into CAPPS II, and it is barely out of its infancy.

CAPPS II will not stop at detecting terrorists. Its bailiwick will soon extend to dope dealers, deadbeat dads, credit-card scammers, "and so on down the scale of wrongdoing until it becomes a comprehensive net for enforcing even the most obscure rules and regulations."[54] Passengers with outstanding parking tickets can expect to be handcuffed and led away from the airline terminal once CAPPS II is up and running.

As of this writing, the European Union is refusing to participate in CAPPS II. The EU, which has not been known as a haven of transatlantic Jeffersonianism, has cited privacy concerns. We are arrived at a strange state of affairs when the Old World outflanks the Land of Liberty in its regard for the rights of the individual.

The TSA's powers are those of a black-helicopter-paranoid's nightmares. The agency may even separate children from parents during the boarding of airplanes; parents who complain may be, and have been in some instances, charged with the obstruction of federal law enforcement. When family-values conservatives meet homeland security conservatives, the former fall faster than Sonny Liston at the hands of Cassius Clay.

Instead of relying on market forces, the Bush administration and the bipartisan consensus in Congress has rushed to subsidize the airline industry as if it were some dilapidated tractor factory on the outskirts of Brezhnev-era Siberia. Take, for instance, the FY 2003

DHS Supplemental Appropriation, which pumped an extra $6.71 billion into DHS programs. This supplemental spending bill was a response to the Iraq War and was part of Operation Liberty Shield, the Orwellian-named domestic counterpart of the war—that is, the very expensive extra security provisions in the event of a terrorist or Iraqi retaliation.

Fully one-third of this abnormally large supplemental appropriation ($2.4 billion) went to "the airline industry to help with costs associated with enhancing the capabilities of the airline industry to combat terrorism."[55] While a small portion of this ($100 million) was dedicated to reimbursement of the airlines for the strengthening of flight-deck doors, the vast majority of the money was distributed to the airlines for vaguely defined "security" measures that, one might argue, fall within the range of activities that a company ought to undertake on its own, and pay for out of its own corporate pocket.

As Texas Republican Congressman Ron Paul charged, "The airlines are bailed out and given guaranteed insurance against all threats. We have made the airline industry a public utility that gets to keep its profits and pass on its losses to the taxpayers, like Amtrak and the post office."[56]

Other mendicants watched the flow of tax dollars into the airline industry and took note. Los Angeles Mayor James Hahn said in December 2002, "We've had to pay for a lot of extra security in a tough budget year. The airlines got a $5 billion bailout almost immediately after 9-11. When is it going to be our turn?"[57]

The insurance industry got its turn in 2002, when Congress passed and President Bush signed legislation taking insurance companies off the hook for 90 percent of any terrorism-related claims over the next three years, for up to $100 billion. Now that's insurance. It also serves as a disincentive for insurance companies to press clients for more effective security measures because—what the hell?—Uncle Sam is picking up most of the tab.

The assumption underlying virtually every homeland security proposal to emanate from Democrats and Republicans is that more money equals more security. One would have thought that politicians had learned the speciousness of this belief as far back as the Great Society, but alas, when it comes to homeland security dollars, the philosophy of FDR hatchetman Harold Ickes prevails: Spend and elect, spend and elect.

Yet as former Rep. Bob Barr (R-GA) pointed out, "we can spend all the money we want, all the money the taxpayers allow us to spend, we can have all of these elaborate security measures, but if the people on the ground don't care about what they're doing and are not held accountable—i.e., fired if they allow something...to happen—I think we're going to have problems."

Barr was referring to a spring 2002 undercover investigation by the General Accounting Office (GAO) in which three former Secret Service agents easily secured "full access at any time of the day or night to every federal building in Atlanta that they attempted to gain access to."[58]

The GAO also produced a perhaps unintentionally devastating account of DHS mismanagement of funds in a September 10, 2003 report titled "Department of Homeland Security: Challenges and Steps in Establishing Sound Financial Management." The report, presented to Congress by McCoy Williams, GAO Director of Financial Management and Assurance, was requested by the House Subcommittee on Government Efficiency and Financial Management. This subcommittee, with its Gingrichian moniker, noted that the DHS has no presidentially appointed and Senate-approved Chief Financial Officer and is, according to GAO, "the largest entity in the federal government that is not subject to the Chief Financial Officers (CFO) Act of 1990." (No doubt submitting to sound financial practices would impede the war on terror!)

The accounting challenges facing DHS were daunting. The GAO deemed it a "high risk" operation and an "enormous undertaking."[59] Achieving efficiency, like defeating terrorism, is at best a very long-term goal.

To be fair, the DHS inherited "many known financial weaknesses and vulnerabilities," in the words of the GAO report. Four of the seven major agencies absorbed by the new department—the Immigration and Naturalization Service, the Transportation Security Administration, the Customs Service, and the Federal Emergency Management Agency—were cited for 18 "material weaknesses" by GAO auditors in 2002. Moreover, five of those seven agencies "were not in substantial compliance with the Federal Financial Management Improvement Act (FFMIA) of 1996."[60] (The FFMIA is supposed to assure that federal agencies are following applicable federal accounting standards.)

The GAO found an accounting mess throughout the various limbs of the jerrybuilt DHS. "For the most part," according to the report, "DHS's component entities are using legacy financial management systems that have a myriad of problems, such as disparate, nonintegrated, outdated, and inefficient systems and processes."[61] They "have a history of poor systems and inadequate financial management."[62]

For instance, auditors discovered in 2001 and again in 2002 that FEMA lacked even the rudiments of an accounting system: property, plant, and equipment were neither recorded nor depreciated in accordance with federal accounting practices. "As a result, FEMA's property management system cannot track items to supporting documentation or to a current location."[63] Not only does the left hand not know what the right hand is doing, but it's also not even certain that it has a right hand.

The debacle that is the Transportation Security Administration was a prime exhibit in GAO's catalogue of DHS accounting woes. Its utter inability to provide oversight of security screener contracts "enabled contractors to charge TSA up to 97 percent more than the contractors charged air carriers prior to the federalization of the screener workforce."[64] So much for the virtues of nationalizing the air security force!

The GAO was not sanguine about the prospects for a quick turnaround. In contrast to Tom Ridge's Pollyanna-ish claims of efficiency, efficacy, and budget neutrality, the GAO stated flatly, "It is well recognized that mergers of the magnitude of DHS carry significant risks, including lost productivity and inefficiencies. Successful transformation of large organizations generally can take from 5 to 7 years to achieve."[65]

How long the unsuccessful mergers take is best left to the imagination.

There is a hoary cliché, trotted out by imagination-deprived political speechwriters, that America is "a nation of immigrants." Like many clichés, it has a basis in fact. In 1600, when the Pilgrims were learning just how gnarled an oxymoron is "Dutch hospitality" and John Smith was just another English soldier, no more noteworthy than the next Smith, the aboriginal dwellers on this continent numbered five million, by the most reliable current estimates. Three centuries later, the American Indian population stood at about 250,000—a drop in the bucket of a circa 1900 United States that was 76 million strong and growing.

Until the late nineteenth century, the U.S. had virtually no immigration policy. No border guards, no nationality quotas, no INS. America was a beacon, a refuge, and those who made the long ocean voyage to the new land were of hardier stock than Emma Lazarus gave them credit for with that strange phrase "wretched refuse." With sweat and genius, hard work and inspiration, these immigrants helped build America, and in turn they became Americans, changing—with each successive wave of immigration—the composite face and accent, if not the essence, of their new country.

The first serious attempt at controlling immigration came in the 1850s, as the American Party, popularly known as the Know Nothings, proposed legislative remedies to what they saw as the un-American-ness of Catholic immigrants, especially those from Ireland. The central Know Nothing plank was the requirement that an immigrant must have resided in the United States for twenty-one years before becoming eligible for citizenship. Yet as historian Otis L. Graham has written, "They proposed little in the way of immigration restriction, never even mentioning immigration in the party's 1856 platform."[66]

The Catholics assimilated, eventually, though fear of their popish loyalties persisted well into the twentieth century. Anti-Catholicism was the prime motive behind the recrudescence of the Ku Klux Klan in the 1920s as well as the state of Oregon's remarkable 1922 law that effectively outlawed Catholic schools, which was overturned by a unanimous U.S. Supreme Court in *Pierce v. Society of Sisters* (1925).

The Chinese, at least on appearances, were less miscible than the Catholics. The Chinese had been a significant building block of nineteenth-century California, but by the last decades of the century labor union concerns that Chinese workers were driving down wages led to an exclusion movement culminating with the landmark 1882 legislation that established the first real controls on immigration in U.S. history.

The tidal wave of immigration during the years 1880–1920 filled the plains and the tenements from sea to shining sea; it altered American culture in fundamental ways, introducing Americans to everything from spaghetti to "Jewish humor," from the mafia to Scandinavian socialism. Worries that the melting pot was consuming the old, pre-Ellis Island America led to the passage of the Johnson-Reed Act of 1924, which set strict limits on immigration from non-Western hemisphere countries, virtually ended Chinese immigration, gave preference to immigrants with useful skills, and capped total immigration to the U.S. for the first time in our history. This act was administered by the Immigration and Naturalization Service, which had been created in 1891.

Immigration law was greatly liberalized—and the complexion of the United States altered in profound ways—by the Immigration Act of 1965. Limits on immigration due to national origin were out; kinship and family connections now took precedence over skills in applications for residence in the U.S. The sources of immigrants to the United States shifted radically: whereas in the 1950s, 70.2 percent of newcomers hailed from Europe or Canada, by the 1990s only 17.1 percent came from these regions. Latin America and the Caribbean became the largest supplier of new Americans, contributing 47.2 percent of immigrants in the fin de siècle, while 30.7 percent came from Asia, a continent that had supplied only 6.2 percent of U.S. immigrants in the 1950s.[67]

Immigration has only accelerated since the historic 1965 act. The INS, with its legendary inefficiencies, its hopeless backlog, and its stunning incompetence, was the lead agency in accepting (or rejecting) the tens of millions of aspiring U.S. citizens. This was a legendary backwater of the bureaucracy: Three months after 9/11, INS officials confessed that they were unable to find more than 300,000 "fugitive deportees" in the United States. These were people who were scheduled to be deported but never bothered to show up for the actual deportation.

Glen Fine, inspector-general of the U.S. Department of Justice, said that the INS had "a Byzantine management structure with overlapping functions and disconnected chains of command."[68] Duplication was its middle name; a 1997 General Accounting Office study found that the INS wasted $100 million annually through mismanagement in the deportation of criminals.

In one of those almost winsome displays of the Republican belief that renaming a bureaucracy is tantamount to an invigorating overhaul, the INS disappeared into that great administrative hole in the sky where CETA and the ICC and the CCC went to die. It emerged as U.S. Citizenship and Immigration Services, since the GOP, under the influence of former Speaker Newt Gingrich, has for a decade now inserted words like "services" and "opportunity" into the dun grey names of white elephants. USCIS processes applications for asylum, refugee status, work documents, and immigration; its separated-at-DHS birth twin, the Border and Transportation Security

Directorate, was fissioned into a Bureau of Customs and Border Protection and a Bureau of Immigration and Customs Enforcement. The former performs inspection and security-related measures along the border; the latter enforces immigration and customs laws. Both bureaus have seen double-digit annual budgetary increases since their creation.

The bailiwick of our immigration department, whatever name it might go under, is, admittedly, enormous. The U.S. shares a 7,500-mile border on land and in air with Mexico and Canada. Our navigable shoreline and rivers total 95,000 miles. The land border is crossed by 11.2 million trucks, 130 million motor vehicles, 2.5 million rail cars, and 5.7 million cargo containers every year; U.S. ports are visited by 7,500 foreign-flag ships making more than 50,000 calls each year. Upwards of 95 percent of U.S. trade goes through various of the country's 361 ports.

More than half a billion people are admitted into the U.S. each year; about two-thirds of them are noncitizens whose stays will be temporary. Unless we turn every other American into a border guard, patrolling our land borders is an impossible job: At present, the U.S. deploys an average of one guard for every thousand feet along the Mexican border but only one guard for every sixteen miles along the border with Canada.

In a task that fair begs the description "impossible," the DHS, through its Container Security Initiative (CSI), seeks to pre-screen those containers originating at ports with high volume or those that pose strategic concerns. Yet in port security, as elsewhere, the only truly effective strategy must be comprehensive: inspect every container. Protect every reservoir. Frisk every passenger. And so on. The alternative to this prohibitively costly and intrusive strategy is to remove the causes of terrorism—that is, U.S. intervention in the Middle East. But to even raise the question is an objectively pro-terrorist act, according to our attorney general, so we shall return to the bankrupting measures of the Department of Homeland Security.

The Port Authority of New York has estimated that it would take $100 million to bring security at New York's ports up to standards. Given that DHS aid to New York's ports has been about $10 million a year, the gap between what the Port Authority wants and what the Port Authority gets is canyonesque.

New York officials point out that New York's harbors handle 13 percent of the nation's cargo, or about $90 billion annually. Rick

Larrabee, commerce chief of the Port Authority, raises the specter of "a container being used to transport a weapon of mass destruction into the United States." The cost to the economy, or so estimates the consulting firm of Booz Allen Hamilton, would be $58 billion.

One suspects that even $58 billion in aid would not satisfy the avaricious New Yorkers. No amount of money can ensure the inspection of every container. (In summer 2003, a TV news crew easily smuggled fifteen pounds of uranium into New York Harbor.)

Nevertheless, the struggle for more money has given us the delicious image of New York Democratic Senator Chuck Schumer, probably the most shameless camera-hogging pork-barrel-dipping member of the entire Congress, posing as a good-government reformer. "Instead of spending the money as they should in the largest ports, the administration is scattering it around like political pork," wails Schumer. "It's a national disgrace and a threat to national security."[69]

Thus speaketh a statesman.

Among the other initiatives in the field of port and border security is the Aerial Surveillance and Sensor Technology program, which consumed $64.2 million tax dollars in FY 2005. This program, which purports to use unmanned aerial vehicles and sensor technology to shore up U.S. borders, illustrates the insidious way in which the war on terror bleeds into other real and metaphorical wars waged by the U.S. government. According to the Department of Homeland Security's Fiscal Year 2005 "Budget in Brief," Aerial Surveillance and Sensor Technology also "supports other missions such as drug interdiction."[70] Stopping bin Laden's minions is not task enough, it seems; the DHS is also using funds dedicated for the war on terror to stamp out the trade in marijuana, cocaine, and other banned substances. Whatever one thinks of the never-ending War on Drugs, this is a clear case of dissimulation. But then, one supposes, all is fair in love and war.

The drug war is routinely lumped in with DHS activities, even though the Drug Enforcement Administration remains outside the ever-expanding Department of Homeland Security.

Drug interdiction is in fact a primary mission of the Coast Guard, along with search and rescue, marine safety, port and coastal security, environmental protection, and even icebreaking. With its humanitarian image—when most Americans think of the Coast Guard the image that comes unbidden to mind is of fresh-faced competent young sailors rescuing some lost soul adrift at sea—the Coast Guard seems primed for growth well beyond its 40,086 active military employees in FY 2005.

Americans do not generally mistake the Coast Guard for the door-busting goons of the DEA, but in fact it is in the area of "drug interdiction" that the Coast Guard experienced its second-largest budgetary boost (from $906 million to $966 million) from FY 2004 to FY 2005. As long as the drug war is entwined with the war on terror, and the Coast Guard is buoyed by both, the Coast Guard has nothing but calm waters and budget hikes as far out on the horizon as the eye can see.

The Middle East, defined as Pakistan, Bangladesh, Afghanistan, Turkey, the Levant, the Arabian Peninsula, and Arab North Africa, had never been a source of significant U.S. immigration. Before 1970, barely 200,000 Americans traced their ancestry to this region. In the last thirty-five years, the Middle Eastern population within the United States—including those here illegally—has ballooned to over 1.5 million. And as Otis L. Graham, Jr., points out, while most of the Middle Easterners in the U.S. before 1970 were Christian, today the immigrant Middle Eastern population is 75 percent Muslim.[71]

While the vast majority of immigrants and visitors from Middle Eastern and Muslim nations are peaceable, the plain fact is that the terrorists of 9/11 and the 1993 parking-garage bombing of the World Trade Center were of Islamic faith and Middle Eastern nationality. They evaded the INS as easily as a sprinter might evade a purblind 400-pound security guard.

"They came as students, tourists, and business visitors,"[72] in the words of Steven Camarota, research director of the Center for Immigration Studies. Some overstayed visas, some entered in marriages of convenience with U.S. citizens, some became citizens themselves. Camarota found that of the forty-eight convicted or admitted terrorists who committed their acts on U.S. soil since 1993, twenty-one were here illegally. A failure of the system, perhaps, but that also means that the majority of terrorists were here legally. As the historian Otis L. Graham, Jr., an immigration restrictionist, sums up, "there are many ways for terrorists to get into America, legally or illegally, and many ways to stay there, some lawful and some not. It is an easy country to attack, from within."[73]

The petty harassment of visitors from nations that haven't a speck of connection with al Qaeda is perhaps typical of the bureaucratic mis-response to any crisis or perceived crisis. Carlos A. Ball, editor of a Florida-based Spanish-language news organization, notes that the number of nonimmigrant visas has plummeted by 36 percent, or 2.7 million annually, since 2001. A triumph of the INS and its clean and cogent, opportunity-society successors? Or the same old bureaucratic blunderbuss? As Mr. Ball asks, "Are those millions of people [no longer being issued nonimmigrant visas] enemies of the United States or are they, in part, the executives and scientists that used to hold their annual conferences in New York, Miami, Los Angeles, Las Vegas, or Hawaii and now prefer to meet elsewhere because of the difficulties imposed by U.S. officials?"

Recounting the—sadly—all too common horror stories of travel hassles experienced by Spanish-speaking visitors since September 2001, Ball notes archly that "None of the 19 al Qaeda assassins came from Latin America, and all of them entered the country with valid visas."[74] Three of them, in fact, had secured entry though the "visa express" program—from a travel agent in Saudi Arabia.

William Reinsch, president of the National Foreign Trade Council, has estimated that U.S. businesses have lost $30.7 billion in "lost contracts, delayed shipments and other areas"[75] due to visa delays since 9/11.

Though Tom Ridge pledged that "[a]ll aspects of border control, including the issuing of visas, would be perfected,"[76] his faith in the perfectibility of bureaucracy was not borne out in the messy real world. Responsibility remains divided: The DHS sets out the rules for visa eligibility, but the State Department gives applicants the green or red light.

A departmental pledge to reduce the processing time for immigration applications to six months by 2006 stands as one of those agency promises that everyone knows (but no one will admit) is impossible.

There was much ballyhoo over revised procedures in the INS and its successor agency: lots of talk of "streamlining" (which one would think would save money; alas, the federal government version of streamlining is always nothing if not expensive), of tamper-resistant passports and other travel documents, of shared information and new tracking systems and a crackdown on foreign students with unnatural interests in esoteric toxins and homemade explosives. Just how effective these policy changes are cannot be properly reckoned for several years.

Many of these changes are commonsensical. The State Department has discontinued its "Visa Express" program by which visas could be obtained without hassle through foreign travel agents. (And were obtained by those Saudi hijackers of 9/11.)

Under the "one face at the border" program, a trio of formerly separate inspections—immigrations, customs, and agriculture—will be performed by a single agent. This agent, denominated a CBP (U.S. Customs and Border Protection inspection officer), took the field in September 2003. It seems unlikely that the CBP program can be less efficient than Customs has been in the past.

(Amusingly, in 2004 the Department of Homeland Security awarded its largest single contract yet—$10 million—to Accenture, which is developing supposedly more efficient means of controlling exits and entries along the U.S. border. Accenture was incorporated in Bermuda to avoid the burden of paying U.S. taxes and had been a leading lobbyist against a provision in the Homeland Security Act that would have barred firms incorporated offshore from sharing in the homeland security pie. The provision was dropped during the House-Senate conference committee, much to Accenture's eventual profit. Among those lobbying against the tax-haven stricture were Republicans Bob Dole, ex-House Ways and Means Chairman Bill Archer, lobbyist Charles Black, ex-House Appropriations Committee Chairman Robert L. Livingston, and former Arizona Democratic Senator Dennis DeConcini of Keating Five infamy. Independent presidential candidate Ralph Nader called the Accenture contract "shameful,"[77] but Accenture officials took the shame, and the $10 million, in stride.)

This is a tough time for advocates of open borders and the enriching effects of immigration. The public, which has always been far more restrictionist on immigration than the elites, has become even more hostile to the free flow of persons across borders. And given the shock and aftershocks of the September 11 attacks, who can blame them?

Still, one indicator of our integrity is the way we treat marginalized persons in time of crisis. It is all very easy for us to be sunshine libertarians, to borrow Thomas Paine's clement imagery: It requires no fortitude whatsoever to defend the right to speech, to petition, to trial by jury, when all is well with the world and when those who wish to exercise those rights are friends and comrades. But when the specter of war dominates the sky, and those looming clouds of oppression threaten those with whom we have little in common, the sunshine libertarian, as with Paine's sunshine patriot, seeks shelter and clams up.

The treatment of immigrants, both legal and illegal, is one standard by which our fidelity to basic American principles is measured.

If Americans are to be watched, monitored, and never allowed to leave the federal government's radar screen, the reverse, alas, is not the case. The federal government is actually withdrawing itself from the scrutiny of the citizenry.

"If you like the idea of a government agency that is 100 percent secret and 0 percent accountable, you'll love the new Homeland Security Department,"[78] remarked Timothy Edgar, legislative counsel of the Americans for Civil Liberties.

Edgar was referring to the exemptions granted the DHS from the Freedom of Information Act (FOIA). "Nothing un-American can live in the sunlight," the jaunty New York governor and FDR nemesis Al Smith used to say, and if the FOIA has not exposed all of our government's secrets to the purifying rays of the sun, at least it has given us a glimpse of what really goes on in the bowels of the middle to upper level bureaucracy. The Act, which requires federal agencies to fulfill requests by citizens for nonclassified documents and information, has proven invaluable to me in previous books detailing the chicanery and grant-gathering of the big health nonprofits.

The Freedom of Information Act was gutted thusly: Any information that is voluntarily submitted to the DHS about computer systems, power plants, transportation infrastructure, banks, telecommunications, and other "critical" facilities is now exempted from the FOIA. It should be noted that trade secrets, commercial and financial information, and banking records are already protected from revelation under the FOIA. Protecting the privacy of corporations was not the intention of the Bush exemption.

Secretary Ridge justified this exemption by saying that the protected information must be "only used by the federal government in order to help prevent or be prepared for a terrorist attack."[79] He implied that the FOIA would somehow hinder the DHS in its mission and also aid in the leaking of company trade secrets to competitors—leaking which was already prohibited.

Though this was an unprecedentedly wide exemption, it was to be expected of the Bush administration, which had earlier "blocked the scheduled release of presidential and vice-presidential records from the Reagan administration,"[80] as Jeffrey Benner wrote in *Reason*.

Vitiating the Freedom of Information Act in the manner of the Homeland Security Act would "encourage government complicity with private firms to keep secret information about critical infrastructure vulnerabilities," charged Senator Patrick Leahy (D-VT). It would, consequently, "reduce the incentive to fix the problems and end up hurting rather than helping our national security."[81]

But this exemption was part and parcel of the Bush administration's war on the Freedom of Information Act and the various "open government" statutes enacted after Vietnam and Watergate had demonstrated, to even the most obsessive obscurantist in the federal labyrinth, the dangers of government secrecy.

The Supreme Court has declared that "Disclosure, not secrecy, is the dominant objective of the Act,"[82] but Attorney General Ashcroft turned FOIA protocol on its head. Whereas the Clinton administration ordered agencies to withhold FOIA documents only in the case of "foreseeable harm," Ashcroft advised them to do so if there was any "sound legal basis" for the withholding.

The Bush-Ashcroft assault on FOIA raised alarms on both left and right. Mark Tapscott, director of the Heritage Foundation Center for Media and Public Policy, told Jeffrey Benner of *Reason*, "This concerns me deeply as a conservative Republican. This is so broad it amounts to an exemption without end. Information about any company that could even tangentially identify itself with the war on terrorism could conceivably be put behind closed doors."

Added Steven Aftergood of the left-of-center Federation of American Scientists, "I understand the need for increased security in narrowly defined areas, like production of biological weapons, for example. But what is happening is that a blanket is being thrown over all kinds of things that have nothing to do with terrorism."[83]

In this respect, the evisceration of FOIA is of a nasty piece with so many other initiatives of the War on Terror. That gasping sound you hear is liberty suffocating under the blanket of anti-terrorism.

Notes

1.   Kate O'Beirne, "Introducing Pork-Barrel Homeland Security: A Little Here, a Lot There..." *National Review*.
2.   Ibid.
3.   Jennifer Van Bergen, "Homeland Security Act: The Rise of the American Police State," truthout Report, www.ratical.org, December 2–4, 2002.

4. "Ridge Speaks to Volunteer Fire fighters," press release, U.S. Department of Homeland Security, May 6, 2004.
5. Jonathan R. White, *Defending the Homeland: Domestic Intelligence, Law Enforcement, and Security* (Belmont, CA: Wadsworth/Thomson, 2004), p. ix.
6. Ibid., p. 5.
7. Ibid., p. 36.
8. Robert Tanner, "GOP Governors Worry About Funding Woes," Associated Press, November 23, 2002.
9. White, *Defending the Homeland: Domestic Intelligence, Law Enforcement, and Security*, p. 42.
10. Ibid., p. 80.
11. Siobhan Gorman, "Homeland Security Still Seeking to Define, Measure Performance."
12. White, *Defending the Homeland: Domestic Intelligence, Law Enforcement, and Security*, p. 38.
13. H. Kenneth Bechtel, *State Police in the United States: A Socio-Historical Analysis* (Westport, CT: Greenwood Press, 1995), p. 49.
14. Ibid., p. 34.
15. Jonathan R. White, *Defending the Homeland: Domestic Intelligence, Law Enforcement, and Security*, p. 37.
16. H. Kenneth Bechtel, *State Police in the United States: A Socio-Historical Analysis*, p. 37.
17. Jonathan R. White, *Defending the Homeland: Domestic Intelligence, Law Enforcement, and Security*, pp. 37–38.
18. H. Kenneth Bechtel, *State Police in the United States: A Socio-Historical Analysis*, p. 16.
19. Jonathan R. White, *Defending the Homeland: Domestic Intelligence, Law Enforcement, and Security*, p. 38.
20. Justin Raimondo, "Sex, Lies, and Terrorism," www.antiwar.com, August 16, 2004.
21. Jonathan R. White, *Defending the Homeland: Domestic Intelligence, Law Enforcement, and Security*, p. 55.
22. Quoted in Gene Healy, "Deployed in the U.S.A.: The Creeping Militarization of the Home Front," Cato Policy Analysis No. 503, pp. 4–5.
23. Ibid., p .5.
24. Ibid., p. 6.
25. Ibid., p. 2.
26. Ibid., p. 15.
27. Gene Healy, "Misguided Mission for Military," www.cato.org, July 31, 2002.
28. Gene Healy, "Deployed in the U.S.A.: The Creeping Militarization of the Home Front," p. 2.
29. Lisa Friedman, "Security With a Spin?" *Los Angeles Daily News*, www.dailynews.com, March 22, 2004.
30. James M. Beck, *Our Wonderland of Bureaucracy: A Study of the Growth of Bureaucracy in the Federal Government and Its Destructive Effect Upon the Constitution* (New York: Macmillan, 1933), p. 87.
31. Quoted in Tom G. Palmer, "Uncle Sam's Ever-Expanding P.R. Machine," *Wall Street Journal*, January 10, 1985, editorial page.
32. Lisa Friedman, "Security With a Spin?"
33. Marcus Ranum, *The Myth of Homeland Security*, p. 2.
34. Ibid., p. 4.
35. Ibid., p. 22.
36. Ibid., p. 25.

37.   Declan McCullagh, "Homeland Security—Big Brother is Here?" ZDNet.com, November 18, 2002.
38.   Quoted in "Take the Pork Out of Homeland Security," *Detroit News*, November 25, 2002, editorial page.
39.   "Budget in Brief," U.S. Department of Homeland Security, Fiscal Year 2005, p. 10.
40.   "Sen. Joe Lieberman is August Porker of the Month," Citizens Against Government Waste, press release, August 15, 2002.
41.   Stephen Barr, "Three Unions Come Out Against Proposed Homeland Security Personnel Rules," *Washington Post*, March 23, 2004, p. B2.
42.   John Mintz, "Government's Hobbled Giant: Homeland Security is Struggling," *Washington Post*, September 7, 2003, p. A1.
43.   William M. Welch and Jim Drinkard, "Security Bill Has Plenty of Pork," *USA Today*, www.usatoday.com, June 2, 2002.
44.   Secretary of Transportation Norman Mineta, eager to pin a winsome motto on the new agency (which would be installed in the DHS, not the DOT), suggested "no weapons, no waiting," though frustrated travelers and eye-rolling airline employees soon suggested more accurate alternative mottos: "DMV from Hell" and, cronymically, "Thousands Standing Around." James Bovard, *Terrorism and Tyranny*, p. 181.
45.   Hearing of the House Government Reform Committee, June 20, 2002, p. 22.
46.   "APTA Testimony Highlights Critical Needs in Security Funding for U.S. Public Transportation," American Public Transportation Association press release, May 5, 2004.
47.   "Reckless Spending at the TSA?" WJLA-TV, www.wjla.com, February 12, 2004.
48.   Marcus Ranum, *The Myth of Homeland Security*, p. 75.
49.   Donald F. Kettl, *The Department of Homeland Security's First Year: A Report Card*, p. 10.
50.   Ibid., p. 14.
51.   Marcus Ranum, *The Myth of Homeland Security*, p. 92.
52.   James Bovard cites the example of twenty members of a Milwaukee Catholic peace group—Peace Action Milwaukee—who were harassed by TSA screeners on April 19, 2002. These dangerous characters—priests, nuns, and high school students—were told by one law enforcement official, "You're probably being stpped because you are a peace group and you're protesting against your country." James Bovard, *Terrorism and Tyranny*, p. 199.
53.   American Civil Liberties Union class action complaint, *Michelle D. Green; John F. Shaw; David C. Fathi; Sarosh Syed; Mohamed Ibrahim; David Nelson; and Alexandra Hay v. Transportation Security Administration*, United States District Court for the Western District of Washington at Seattle, April 6, 2004.
54.   "ACLU Comments to Department of Homeland Security on the 'Passenger and Aviation Security Screening Records,'" American Civil Liberties Union, www.aclu.org, September 30, 2003.
55.   "Department of Homeland Security FY '03 Supplemental Funding Fact Sheet," U.S. Department of Homeland Security, press release, April 16, 2003, p. 1.
56.   Rep. Ron Paul, "Department of Homeland Security—Who Needs It?" www.antiwar.com, July 25, 2002.
57.   Bill Hillburg, "No Help for Security Since 9-11: Mayors Still Wait for Funds," *Los Angeles Daily News*, December 16, 2002, p. N3.
58.   Hearing of the House Government Reform Committee, June 20, 2002, p. 42.
59.   Testimony of McCoy Williams, "Department of Homeland Security: Challenges and Steps in Establishing Sound Financial Management," General Accounting Office, September 10, 2003, "Highlights" page.

60.   Ibid., p. 2.
61.   Ibid., p. 3.
62.   Ibid., p. 13.
63.   Ibid., p. 5.
64.   Ibid., p. 8.
65.   Ibid., p. 16.
66.   Otis L. Graham, Jr., *Unguarded Gates: A History of America's Immigration Crisis* (Lanham, MD: Rowman & Littlefield, 2004), p. 31.
67.   Ibid., p. 94.
68.   Jim Tyrell, "The Department of Homeland Security: New Solutions Meet Old Problems," National Taxpayers Union, NTU Policy Paper 109, January 6, 2003, p. 3.
69.   Brian Kates, "Harbor Fears High, Terror Funding Low," *New York Daily News*, December 21, 2003, p. 33.
70.   "Budget in Brief," U.S. Department of Homeland Security, Fiscal Year 2005, p. 7.
71.   Otis L. Graham, Jr., *Unguarded Gates: A History of America's Immigration Crisis*, p. 174.
72.   Ibid., p. 165.
73.   Ibid., p. 166.
74.   Carlos A. Ball, "Antagonizing Traditional Friends," www.cato.org, November 17, 2003.
75.   Evelyn Iritani, "Visa Denied," *Los Angeles Times*, www.abs-cbnnews.com, October 21, 2004.
76.   Hearing of the House Government Reform Committee, June 20, 2002, p. 24.
77.   "Nader Urges Bush to Cancel Homeland Security Contract With Accenture," Nader for President 2004 press release, June 7, 2004.
78.   "ACLU Says Homeland Security Department Long on Secrecy, Short on Needed Accountability," ACLU press release, June 25, 2002.
79.   Hearing of the House Government Reform Committee, June 20, 2002, p. 48.
80.   Jeffrey Benner, "Closing the Books," *Reason*, www.reason.com, October 2002.
81.   Jennifer Van Bergen, "Homeland Security Act: The Rise of the American Police State."
82.   Timothy Edgar, "Testimony on the President's Proposal for a Homeland Security Department," Before Congressional Committees, June 25–28, p. 2.
83.   Jeffrey Benner, "Closing the Books," *Reason*.

5

Life (and Lost Liberties) During Wartime

"The natural progress of things is for liberty to yield and government to gain ground,"[1] Thomas Jefferson famously wrote from Paris in 1788. At no time does this natural progression move with such alarming alacrity as during war.

With the USA-PATRIOT Act and the Department of Homeland Security, not only was the door to the U.S. Treasury thrown open, but fundamental American liberties were trampled in the rush. As Rep. Ron Paul charged while the bipartisans were congratulating themselves over enactment of the DHS legislation, "our most basic freedoms as Americans—privacy in our homes, persons, and possessions; confidentiality in our financial and medical affairs; openness in our conversations, telephone, and Internet use; unfettered travel; indeed the basic freedom not to be monitored as we go through our daily lives—have been dramatically changed."

Paul, like some Paul Revere whose words, borne on the night wind, might someday strike the ears of posterity as prescient and brave, continued, "The list of dangerous and unconstitutional powers granted to the new Homeland Security department is lengthy. Warrantless searches, forced vaccinations of whole communities, federal neighborhood snitch programs, federal information databases, and a sinister new 'Information Awareness Office' at the Pentagon that uses military intelligence to spy on domestic citizens are just a few of the troubling aspects of this new legislation."[2]

The existence of an Office of Civil Rights and Liberties within the DHS hardly assuages the fears of liberty-loving Americans. Unlike other such officers in other departments, the DHS officer for civil rights and liberties may not investigate violations of civil rights by department officials. He or she is as toothless as a centenarian, and about as vigorous, too. The Office is the barest window dressing for a department which, upon its creation, had the questionable distinction of having more armed federal agents with the power to arrest citizens than any other federal department.

Yet these curtailments of American liberties were to be expected. War and preparations for war always curb freedoms, centralize power, cast suspicion upon dissenters, and encourage the naturally tyrannical bent of government.

Wars also cost tremendous sums of money. Not for nothing have big-spending presidents placed war and military expenditures atop their agendas. Alas, Congress, with a few notable exceptions, rubberstamped the programs, restrictions, and expenditures embedded in the War on Terror. Had any of the honorable members bothered to investigate—or asked the Congressional Research Service to investigate for them—they would have found that our history is littered with tales of the wartime constriction of liberties.

As Arthur A. Ekirch, Jr., dean of American classical liberal historians, wrote, "depressions and wars...have occasioned both massive governmental spending and increased regimentation of American life and thought."[3]

In the same vein, Robert Higgs, an economist and historian, sought to explain "the rise of that awesome aggregation of forces, programs, and activities we know as Big Government."[4] Its growth, as he discovered and then wrote in *Crisis and Leviathan*, was not a steady, predictable expansion due to Washington's sedulous attention to "traditional governmental functions." Rather, it grew in fits and starts and great spurts, "taking on new functions, activities, and programs—some of them completely novel, others previously the responsibility of private citizens."

Although Higgs wrote his pathbreaking book in 1987, the post-9/11 hypertrophying of government settles perfectly into his thesis. His "central emphasis" was "on how governmental officials and citizens have reacted to national emergencies."[5] Thus his conclusion: crisis begets leviathan.

Higgs pinpoints World War I, Woodrow Wilson's mad crusade to "make the world safe for democracy," as a—perhaps *the*—prime culprit that "undercut American liberties and fed the growth of Big Government." In 1916, Higgs argues, the U.S. economy was recognizably a market system: not wholly, not pristinely, but primarily so. Within two years that system had undergone a metamorphosis into what can only be called "war socialism." As Higgs summarizes,

By the time of the armistice the government had taken over the ocean shipping, railroad, telephone, and telegraph industries; commandeered hundreds of manufacturing plants; entered into massive economic enterprises on its own account in such varied departments as shipbuilding, wheat trading, and building construction; undertaken to lend huge sums to businesses directly or indirectly and to regulate the private issuance of securities; established official priorities for the use of transportation facilities, food, fuel, and many raw materials; fixed the prices of dozens of important commodities; intervened in hundreds of labor disputes; and conscripted millions of men for service in the armed forces.

The market, like the hated Hun, like the perfidious Kaiser, became an enemy in wartime. Wise observers were absolutely stunned by the swiftness with which traditional liberties and American freedoms were locked away in the closet for the duration of Mr. Wilson's War.

More than even the phalanx of programs and interventions it spawned, the war effected a change in the American psyche. Historian Arthur A. Ekirch, Jr. notes that "never until World War I did the suppression of freedom enjoy the almost unanimous support of the various agencies of government—national, state, and local."[6] Petty and large infringements upon liberty alike were accorded a respect unthinkable even a decade earlier.

As Senator James Vardaman (D-MS) predicted, "preparedness," as a euphemism for national defense, is "a word that will stand as a colossal blood-stained monument marking the turning point in the life of this Government."[7]

The defenders of war socialism—and they are everywhere today, not least in the pages of conservative magazines whose ardor for the Iraq War and the "War on Terrorism" has driven out any vestigial commitment to limited government—will say that Big Government, while an essential feature of a wartime society, is easily cut back to size once the war is over. Put aside, for a moment, the problematic aspects of the war on terror, which President Bush, Vice President Cheney, and Secretary of Homeland Security Thomas Ridge have assured us will be fought by generations yet unborn. (Does this mean that Big Government is also to be bequeathed to our guiltless posterity?) Higgs, in *Crisis and Leviathan*, demonstrates, in copious and irrefutable detail, that crisis-driven government interventions are not temporary. They are not repealed immediately upon the cessation of hostilities. Oh, certain of the most egregious features of a wartime economy—say, gasoline rationing—may disappear with peace, but on the whole, an intervention once made is seldom unmade. Contrary to the famous phrase that helped Warren G. Harding win the presidency in 1920, there is never a "return to normalcy."

The First World War, as Higgs points out, had the same "ratcheting" effect as other crises have had throughout our history. Government had jumped to the next level in size and scope, and it was not about to surrender its new puissance. For instance, federal revenues skyrocketed from a high of $762 million before World War I to at least $2.8 billion every year of the placid 1920s. The war was funded in significant part by the new income tax, which was to be thereafter the prime source of federal revenue. Rent controls, national prohibition, an array of wartime regulatory agencies: these, too, had become so well established during the crisis of war that they became permanent features (except, thank God, for Prohibition) of the American landscape. As Navy Secretary Josephus Daniels exulted, "We will not be afraid in peace to do revolutionary things that help mankind, seeing we have become accustomed to doing them in war."[8] Once eroded, the habits of liberty are difficult to reacquire.

As Robert Higgs notes, "each genuine crisis has been the occasion for another ratchet toward Bigger Government.... Knowing how much a crisis facilitates Bigger Government, special interests always use such propitious occasions to seek whatever governmental assistance they think will promote their own ends. Once undertaken, governmental programs are hard to terminate."[9]

"Conservative" supporters of the Department of Homeland Security would do well to ponder Higgs' words. As they would the warning of Herbert Hoover, who understood that "Every collectivist revolution rides in on a Trojan horse of 'Emergency.' It was a tactic of Lenin, Hitler, and Mussolini. In the collectivist sweep over a dozen minor countries of Europe, it was the cry of the men striving to get on horseback. And 'Emergency' became the justification of the subsequent steps. This technique of creating emergency is the greatest achievement that demagoguery attains."[10]

President Nixon, who self-dramatizingly titled his first memoir *Six Crises*, took a perverse pleasure in such crises. Twice he declared national emergencies as president. Both occasions, in retrospect, were ridiculously short of a true emergency. Once (March 23, 1970) he did so over a postal workers' strike (how could the public tell they were striking, one wonders) and the second time, on August 15, 1971, he used the emergency declaration to impose an import surcharge.

Conservatives might also consider the effectiveness of these emergency-response programs and laws. In the pitifully brief de bate over the USA-PATRIOT Act, the Comprehensive Terrorism Prevention Act of 1995 escaped scrutiny. This act, passed in knee-jerk response to the Oklahoma City bombing of April 19, 1995, restricted the writ of *habeas corpus* for terrorism suspects, threatened countries that refused to cooperate in the War on Terror with embargoes, and pumped $1 billion into the nascent but growing anti-terrorism industry. This law failed to prevent the terrorist acts of six-and-a-half years later, but its failure was not taken as a sign of ineffectualness, as a spur to look critically at anti-terrorism laws. Instead, it was amplified, magnified, and multiplied by the USA-PATRIOT Act.

Note, too, the bipartisan nature of these laws. The 1995 Act was a meeting of the minds, as it were, of Republican Senators Bob Dole (KS) and Orrin Hatch (UT) and Democratic President Bill Clinton. It was also an echo of the draconian Terrorism Prevention and Protection Act of 1993, which grandstanding Democratic Rep. Charles Schumer (now a U.S. senator) introduced in headline-making response to the first bombing of the World Trade Center. Schumer, perhaps the most dedicated enemy the Bill of Rights has in Congress, would have "federalized all violent offenses, allowed the use of secret evidence in deportation proceedings, and increased the surveillance powers of the Federal Bureau of Investigation," according to Timothy Lynch of the Cato Institute.[11]

The first term of President George W. Bush, or Lyndon Baines Bush as he may be known to historians, is a clear—if depressing—lesson in the ways in which crisis feeds leviathan. Bush was elected in 2000 over Democratic Vice President Albert Gore as the purported candidate of both fiscal responsibility and a more "humble" foreign policy than that of the nation-building, Serbia-bombing, promiscuously interventionist Clinton administration. Yet once in office, Bush set a course for Leviathan, expanding the federal state as have few presidents this side of LBJ.

Whereas federal expenditures rose by an average of 3.4 percent annually during the Clinton years of 1993 to 2001, they spiked by 7.9 percent in 2002, 7.3 percent in 2003, and 6.3 percent in 2004. Federal spending as a percentage of the gross national product has risen from 18.6 percent when Clinton left office to 20.5 percent at the end of Bush's first term.

This cannot be blamed on the events of 9/11, though the Bush administration took advantage of the post-attack atmosphere of fear and a desire for security to boost spending even in fields far removed—ostensibly—from national defense, for example, education and space. The Republican budgets signed into law by Bush in his first two years in office increased defense spending by 34 percent, but as Stephen Moore of the pro-capitalist Club for Growth points outs, "under President Bush inflation-adjusted domestic discretionary spending has grown faster than under any other president in 40 years."[12] Domestic discretionary spending actually rose at a higher rate (39 percent) during Bush's first term than did defense spending.

There was, of a sudden, no major political party even nominally dedicated to parsimony—even moderation—in government spending. As Doug Bandow, a former special assistant to President Reagan, lamented in 2004, "Conservatives once fought passionately to preserve the United States as a limited, constitutional republic. No longer. Many 'conservative' Republicans now view themselves as the party of government. That means constant war and massive social engineering abroad and vast new social programs and regulatory regimes at home."[13]

The footprints of Ronald Reagan, which were imprinted with his fine rhetorical commitment to limited government and liberty, have been washed away by the tidal wave of Big Government Republicanism.

But we, the people, must take a measure of blame as well. Opinion polls in the wake of the World Trade Center attack showed Americans flocking to the security blanket of government.

And this, even though the later revelations of career bureaucrat Richard Clarke established that 9/11 was a classic case of the government doing badly the one thing that most people agree is its primary function: providing for the common defense!

Somehow, in the wake of 9/11, the idea took hold that the government is the great protector of life. Our Savior, in an earthly sense. Just how obscene such a notion is can be demonstrated, with abundant and disheartening evidence, by the landmark work of political scientist R.J. Rummel of the University of Hawaii.

Rummel is a pioneer in the field of what he calls, with a knack for coining a phrase, "democide." That is, death by government. His proposition is simple, and irrefutable: "Power kills, and absolute power kills absolutely."[14]

What Rummel has done is tabulate the astronomical numbers of people killed by governments—both their own and others. "Democide" includes the genocide practiced by the Nazis, Cambodians, Turks, and others, but it also takes in the state-sponsored killings of the Soviet Union and other totalitarian states, the vast carnage of warfare (which is, after all, an activity of the state), and the "political murders" that one finds in Latin American and other states.

In *Death by Government*, Rummel's summing up of his life's work, he organizes the twentieth-century's homicidal states by their grisly accomplishments. There are the dekamegamurderers, a kind of gold medal elite of evil: these are the states that killed more than ten million persons, citizens and foreigners alike. The Soviet Union sits atop the trash-heap with an astonishing 61.9 million murders to its discredit. The vast majority of these—54.8 million—were citizens of the Soviet Union. Under the Communists, homicide, like charity elsewhere, began at home.

Communist China takes second place in the dekamegamurderer tally, with a death toll of 35.24 million, followed by Nazi Germany (20.95 million) and Nationalist China (10.075). Other twentieth-century governments which killed more than one million persons include the militaristic Japan of 1936–45 (5.97 million), Cambodia under the Khmer Rouge (2.04 million), Turkey in its genocide against the Armenians (1.88 million), Vietnam during its wars (1.68 million), Soviet-controlled Poland from 1945–48, when it massacred German ethnics (1.59 million), Pakistan between 1958 and 1987 (1.5 million), and Yugoslavia under Tito (1.07 million). Other states, including feudal Russia and totalitarian North Korea, are "suspected megamurderers," but precise totals are elusive.

In all, wrote Rummel as the Cold War was thawing, "during the first eighty-eight years of this [the twentieth] century, almost 170 million men, women, and children have been shot, beaten, tortured, knifed, burned, starved, frozen, crushed, or worked to death; buried alive, drowned, hung, bombed, or killed in any other of the myriad ways governments have inflicted death on unarmed, helpless citizens and foreigners. The dead could conceivably be nearly 360 million people. It is as though our species has been devastated by a modern Black Plague. And indeed it has, but a plague of Power, not germs."[15]

The source of this plague—government—is the very institution that we are told now to turn to, to trust, to embrace as the palladium of our "security." Are we being churlish to hesitate before jumping into its open arms?

Lest one leap to the conclusion that this unimaginable epidemic of "death by government" is somehow a product exclusively of totalitarian, communist, and fascist regimes, and that democratic states are immune to the temptation to abuse power, Rummel adds that "democide by democracies" includes "the large-scale massacres of Filipinos during the bloody U.S. colonization of the Philippines at the beginning of this [the twentieth] century, deaths in British concentration camps in South Africa during the Boer War, civilian deaths due to starvation during the British blockade of Germany in and after World War I, the rape and murder of helpless Chinese in and around Peking in 1900, the atrocities committed by Americans in Vietnam, the murder of helpless Algerians during the Algerian War by the French, and the unnatural deaths of German prisoners of war in French and U.S. POW camps after World War II."[16]

Assessing Rummel's findings, Robert Higgs, author of *Crisis and Leviathan*, was forced to rethink the very first sentence of that book: "We must have government." For as Higgs muses, "Can we really imagine that, absent governments to organize and goad them, the world's people would have been so obtuse and antisocial that they would have ended up slaughtering more than 210 million of one another in the twentieth century before coming to their senses? Such a vision of haphazard violence boggles the mind. Even though my own opinion of mankind is, I confess, substantially lower than the average opinion, I still have trouble imagining that without government people would have done even worse than they did with government."[17]

If the crisis of war spells boom for government spending, it marks a bust for civil liberties.

Most of our wars have been accompanied by crackdowns, sometimes massive and sometimes measured, on liberties at home.

Worries about Jeffersonian radicals as well as French influence in the new republic (which was so different from the vision promulgated in a later *New Republic*!) spurred Congress and the John Adams administration to enactment of the infamous Alien and Sedition Acts of 1798, along with the Enemy Alien Act of that same year.

Although the Alien and Sedition Acts have become bywords of censorship and petty tyranny, Georgetown University law professor David Cole notes that it was the Enemy Alien Act whose spirit pervaded the wide-scale lockups of non-U.S. citizens in the three years (and counting) following the World Trade Center massacre. The Act of 1798 permitted the president, upon a declaration of war, to "lock up, deport, or otherwise restrict the liberty of any person over fourteen years of age who is a citizen of the country with which we are at war."[18]

Certainly the case can be made that the U.S. government ought to be able to monitor or even detain foreign nationals who might be in a position to do harm to the host country. But the condition necessary for such a lockup—the declaration of war—is an anachronism today on the order of the periwig or the ferule. Article 1, Section 8 of the U.S. Constitution, which vests in Congress the power to declare war, is no more honored than is the Sixth Commandment at the corner of Hollywood and Vine.

Consider what happened when Congressman Ron Paul (R-TX), intrepid champion of constitutional liberties, made so bold as to move, during debate on H.J. Res. 114, "Authorization for Use of Military Force Against Iraq," that the House vote up or down on a declaration of war against Iraq.

Henry Hyde, the hoary House lifer, scoffed at Paul's naïveté. "There are things in the Constitution that have been overtaken by events, by time. Declaration of war is one of them. There are things no longer relevant to a modern society. Why declare war if you don't have to? We are saying to the President, use your judgment. So, to demand that we declare war is to strengthen something to death. You have got a hammerlock on this situation, and it is not called for. Inappropriate, anachronistic, it isn't done anymore."[19]

Inappropriate. Anachronistic. These are the carefully chosen words of the chairman of the House International Relations Committee (and former chairman of the Judiciary Committee) to describe the Constitution of the United States.

To a limited extent, war critics were jailed during the War Between the States. President Abraham Lincoln suspended *habeas corpus*; ordered the closing of numerous opposition newspapers; oversaw the jailing and exile of Ohio Democratic Congressman Clement Vallandigham, a critic of conscription and defender of freedom of the press; and otherwise restricted liberties in unprecedented ways.

But it was Woodrow Wilson who set the standard for being contemptuous of American liberties; in a very real sense, his administration revoked the right the to dissent. As historian Walter

Karp wrote of the war, "While American troops learned to survive in the trenches, Americans at home learned to live with repression and its odious creatures—with the government spy and the government burglar, with the neighborhood stool pigeon and the official vigilante, with the local tyranny of federal prosecutors and the lawlessness of bigoted judges, with the midnight police raid and the dragnet arrest."[20]

"Americans rotted in prison for advocating heavier taxation rather than the issuance of war bonds, for stating that conscription was unconstitutional, for saying that sinking armed merchantmen had not been illegal, for criticizing the Red Cross and the YMCA. A woman who wrote to her newspaper that 'I am for the people and the government is for the profiteers,' was tried, convicted, and sentenced to ten years in prison,"[21] writes Walter Karp. So you see: the Bush-Ashcroft terror-mongering and the statist measures it has engendered are not really the low points of civil liberty in the United States. We have quite a ways to go before reaching the depths of the Wilsonian nadir. But we are on our way.

Wilson's government prosecuted over 2,000 dissenters, not for passing secrets to the Hun or sabotaging war industries but simply for exercising their First Amendment rights—their obligation, really, in times of peril—to speak on public matters. In the nightmare of World War I, it became a crime to speak "any disloyal, profane, scurrilous, or abusive language...as regards the form of government of the United States, or the Constitution, or the flag."[22]

Harvard law professor Zechariah Chafee wrote: "One by one the right of freedom of speech, the right of assembly, the right to petition, the right to protection against unreasonable searches and seizures, the right against arbitrary arrest, the right to a fair trial . . . the principle that guilt is personal, the principle that punishment should bear some proportion to the offense, had been sacrificed and ignored."[23]

The most famous of the jailed war critics was Eugene V. Debs, perennial Socialist candidate for president and head of the Railway Union. In a 1918 speech in Canton, Ohio, Debs orated, "The master class has always declared the wars; the subject class has always fought the battles." He went on to make the still-pertinent point that while "it is extremely dangerous to exercise the Constitutional right of free speech in a country fighting to make democracy safe in the world," he nevertheless "would a thousand times rather be a free soul in jail than to be a sycophant and coward in the streets."[24]

Acting as a kind of anti-Santa Claus, Wilson granted Debs his wish. The free soul went to jail. He was convicted of violating the Espionage and Sedition Acts and sentenced to ten years in prison. From his federal prison cell in Atlanta, Debs ran for president on the Socialist Party ticket and won close to one million votes, which is more votes than the party had ever achieved before or since. Contrasted with the petty and tyrannical Wilson, Debs cut a profile in nobility, winning praise from the curmudgeonly H.L. Mencken, who noted that despite Debs's "naïve belief in the Marxian rumble-bumble," he was "fair, polite, independent, brave, honest, and a gentleman."[25]

Wilson resisted pleas from many quarters, Republican as well as Socialist, to pardon Debs for his "crime" of free speech. The *New York Times*, never particularly friendly to the cause of liberty, sneered of the prisoner, "He is where he belongs. He should stay there."[26] It was left to the genial Warren G. Harding to pardon Debs.

Wilson and his ferociously anti-libertarian attorney general, A. Mitchell Palmer, lobbied Congress for a peacetime sedition bill after the war had ended, the better to make sure that the likes of Debs (and pacifists and anarchists and communists and critics of the income tax, the Federal Reserve, Prohibition, and other Wilsonian brainchildren) might never again breathe free air.

Karp writes: "Wilson even took time out from his messianic labors in Paris to urge passage of a peacetime federal sedition law, 'unprecedented legislation,' as Harvard's Professor Chafee put it at the time, 'whose enforcement will let loose a horde of spies and informers, official and unofficial, swarming into our private life, stirring up suspicion without end.'"[27]

Wilson forgot, if indeed the Princeton professor ever knew, Thomas Jefferson's declaration that "our first and fundamental maxim should be never to entangle ourselves in the broils of Europe."[28] As Jefferson wrote to James Monroe in 1823 with heartbreaking prescience,

I have ever deemed it fundamental for the United States never to take active part in the quarrels of Europe. Their political interests are entirely distinct from ours. Their mutual jealousies, their balance of power, their complicated alliances, their forms and principles of government are all foreign to us. They are nations of eternal war. All their energies are expended in the destruction of the labor, property, and lives of their people. On our part never had a people so favorable a chance of trying the opposite system of peace and fraternity with mankind and the direction of all our means and faculties to the purposes of improvement instead of destruction.[29]

What might have been, had we not been dragged kicking and screaming into the war that was supposed to not only "make the world safe for democracy" but also "end all wars." As they say in Brooklyn, you should live so long.

Congress, jolted back to its collective senses after the madhouse of wartime, said no to Woodrow Wilson's peacetime sedition law. Wilson pouted, went on his 10,000 mile whistestop train tour to rally support for his League of Nations, and was felled by a stroke before he might further shred the First Amendment.

Franklin D. Roosevelt was less heavy-handed in stifling opposition during the Second World War. The only notable prosecution of war critics centered on a ragtag band of pro-Nazis and neutralists who went free after a mistrial. The great blot on the Rooseveltian escutcheon was the internment of 110,000 Japanese-Americans in government detention camps. Supposed defenders of the freedoms of movement and speech, notably the American Civil Liberties Union, were disgracefully circumspect on the matter of the Japanese internment, leaving it to a handful of constitutionalist conservatives, for instance Ohio Republican Senator Robert Taft, to register opposition to this grossly un-American act.

Smearing skeptics of war is an old and dishonorable practice, and one that the Roosevelt administration practiced with consummate skill. Harold Ickes, the hatchetman of the Franklin D. Roosevelt administration, once called the antiwar aviator Charles Lindbergh a "Nazi fellow traveler" for giving speeches urging U.S. nonintervention in the war, but then Ickes, as playwright Clare Booth Luce once cracked, had "the soul of a meat axe and the mind of a commissar."[30]

The abuses of domestic intelligence during the Cold War and Vietnam have been exposed along with their chief perpetrator, former Federal Bureau of Investigation director J. Edgar Hoover. The FBI, as veteran civil libertarian Nat Hentoff writes, "monitored, infiltrated, manipulated, and secretly fomented divisions within civil rights, antiwar, black, and other entirely lawful organization who were using the First Amendment to disagree with government policies."[31]

Although COINTELPRO, the Counterintelligence Program of the Federal Bureau of Investigation, began as a typical Cold War effort to monitor the activities of foreign intelligence services, it mutated into one of the most egregious violations of the Bill of Rights ever undertaken by the U.S. government. Between 1956 and its dissolution in 1971, COINTELPRO spied on thousands of American citizens, planted lies and rumors within lawful American civic organizations, disgorged disinformation, and, perhaps most famously, harassed and slandered Rev. Martin Luther King, Jr. It made promiscuous use of agents, provocateurs, and snitches, and spread more sex gossip than a columnist for the *Star*. The antiwar and civil rights movements were its primary targets; COINTELPRO was fed by, and reflected, the paranoid obsessions of FBI director J. Edgar Hoover, who hated Rev. King with an almost blinding intensity.

Even after King won the Nobel Peace Prize in 1964 he remained Hoover's quarry. Just prior to the Nobel ceremony, writes Timothy Lynch, bureau agents "threatened to give the news media evidence of King's adulterous affairs if he did not commit suicide."[32]

To the extent that homeland security legislation has placed the territorial United States within the CIA's ambit once more, the Department of Homeland Security's Office of Intelligence, nestled within the Directorate of Information Analysis and Infrastructure Protection, will be where the shady action is. This Directorate is compiling databases on every American citizen: Santa may know who's been naughty and nice, but the Directorate of Information Analysis and Infrastructure Protection knows who's been delinquent with VISA card payments, who's been traveling to Florida, and who's been making those late-night calls to Nebraska. You, dear reader, are on file.

In the past decade, many Bush II partisans were seized by an intense hatred of Bill Clinton and all his works. In a strange inversion, many Democrats harbor an equally fierce antipathy toward George W. Bush. These hostilities exceed the usual political biases; each side seems convinced that the other is, if not the devil incarnate, then an oily and mendacious facsimile thereof.

The irony is that both men, Clinton and Bush, displayed a contempt for civil liberties that was almost Hooverian (J. Edgar, not poor Herbert) in its scope. The Clinton administration, which had been knocked back on its heels almost from the start, with its missteps on health care, gays in the military, gun control, and other hot-button issues, was rescued by the madman Timothy McVeigh's April 19, 1995 bombing of the Murrah Federal Office Building in Oklahoma City. This was treated as an act of war by domestic dissidents: Crisis, predictably, fed leviathan.

The McVeigh bombing was a pot of gold for the cynical Clinton. Christopher Hitchens recounts how the oleaginous Clinton spokesman George Stephanopoulos told him, over drinks, that British Prime Minister Tony Blair was "doing brilliantly" during the hoopla over Princess Diana's death. "This is his Oklahoma City,"[33] burbled Stephanopolous in one of the more repulsive remarks of his career. Clinton, lower lip a-quiver, grasped his Oklahoma City moment like a drowning man grabbing a life raft. He skillfully exploited the horror of the attack, smearing the right-wing populist movement, including those "militias," which leftist Alexander Cockburn had sympathetically depicted as rural and working-class men taking up arms in defense of the Bill of Rights. Though McVeigh had been barred from the Michigan Militia, which found him wacky and suspected him of being an agent provocateur, his crime was pinned on "right-wing dissent" generally, a broad brush stroke that took in everything from the Republican radio talk-show host Rush Limbaugh to survivalists in the Pacific Northwest. The legislative fruit of the McVeigh Moment was the Antiterrorism and Effective Death Penalty Act of 1996, which defined terrorism loosely enough so as to criminalize "material support to groups designated by the secretary of state as foreign terrorist organizations, even when the support takes the form of humanitarian aid or activities that promote a peaceful resolution of conflict."

According to civil liberties lawyer Nancy Chang, the combined Bush and Clinton "antiterrorism" laws "portend a return of the politically motivated spying on peaceful social movements that marked J. Edgar Hoover's troubled tenure as FBI director, and they will cause many who disagree with government policies to engage in self-censorship."[34]

So much of contemporary politics is merely a question of personality conflicts that one is tempted to take the side of those politicos who run afoul of the mainstream media and are reduced to caricatures. Attorney General John Ashcroft, for instance, was so demonized by his critics that anyone with an ounce of compassion must have been tempted to be sympathetic toward him. Throughout George W. Bush's first term, Ashcroft's grim countenance stared back at us from the covers of left-wing paperbacks; his fundamentalist religious convictions were mocked by sophisticated reporters; even his 2004 surgery for pancreatitis was the subject of sport. As a Republican Senator from Missouri, Ashcroft had compiled a respectable record as a advocate of fiscal responsibility and limited government; indeed, no less a civil libertarian than the redoubtable Nat Hentoff of the *Village Voice* viewed him as a promising candidate for attorney general.

But men must be judged by their acts, and in the years since September 11, 2001 Ashcroft has deserved every brickbat tossed in his direction. Those phantoms of lost liberty were sent to the spirit world by none other than John Ashcroft and George W. Bush.

In a perhaps panic-induced *volte-face*, Ashcroft announced that he was altering the historic mission of the Department of Justice. Henceforth, it was to concentrate on the detection and prevention of terrorism. This "wartime reorganization,"[35] as Ashcroft termed it, extended the DOJ's ambit overseas as it takes a lead role in the international effort against terrorism.

President Bush is often mocked for his admitted lack of interest in the printed word, and never has his aversion to those dreaded rectangles called "books" caused him more grief than when he signed off on the acronym for the Uniting and Strengthening America by Providing Appropriate Tools Required to Intercept and Obstruct Terrorism Act of 2001, or the USA-PATRIOT Act.

The title of this Act represented a hybrid of packaged jingoism. The House had fastened on the bill the PATRIOT moniker, with its cynical implication that opponents were unpatriotic. Not to be outdone, the Senate tagged it the USA Act—and who could criticize such a bill without taking on the dear old red, white, and blue in the process? The bill's married name is a bit unwieldy, but then we live in an age of hyphenated surnames.

The Orwellian flavor of the title of this 342-page act raised enough red flags to bring the Daytona 500 to a crashing halt. The law just sounded wicked, as if it had been drafted by a scowling and cynical legislative technician for Big Brother. In *1984*, George Orwell had his totalitarian state first take control of the language: War was Peace, Freedom was Slavery, Ignorance was Strength. Thought criminals were executed in the Ministry of Love; Winston Smith's squalid tenement was named Victory Mansions.

An Orwellian could have told George W. Bush that only the most blatant and unsubtle lover of Big Brother would title legislation restricting traditional liberties and empowering the national police the USA-PATRIOT Act. A president, or a congressional leadership, that regarded books as anything more than the vaguely troubling vaporings of eggheads would have opted for a less obvious title.

As it was, the USA-PATRIOT Act rang so many alarm bells that it became the focus of one of the great lopsided civil liberties debates of our time.

The USA-PATRIOT Act was conceived in the hectic days following 9/11, though various features had been elements of the FBI and Department of Justice wish list for years. As James Bovard writes, House Judiciary Committee Chairman James Sensenbrenner (R-WI) called it a "Magna Carta for federal agents."[36]

The House Judiciary Committee held hearings on September 24, 2001, on a rudimentary USA-PATRIOT Act that bore the clunky title of the "Antiterrorism Act of 2001." A week later, on October 2, Judiciary Committee Chairman James Sensenbrenner (R-WI) introduced a more onerous White House-written substitute.

Ron Paul, the Texas Republican who is as true a friend as liberty has ever had in Congress, was one of three Republicans to vote against the bill on final passage. He concurred with Frank, saying, "It's my understanding the bill wasn't printed before the vote—at least I couldn't get it. They played all kinds of games, kept the House in session all night, and it was a very complicated bill. Maybe a handful of staffers actually read it, but the bill definitely was not available to members before the vote."

Paul explained his vote to *Insight*: "The insult is to call this a 'patriot bill' and suggest I'm not patriotic because I insisted upon finding out what is in it and voting no. I thought it was undermining the Constitution, so I didn't vote for it—and therefore I'm somehow not a patriot. That's insulting."

Added Paul, "This is a very bad bill and I think the people who voted for it knew it and that's why they said, 'Well, we know it's bad, but we need it under these conditions.'"[37]

"These conditions," it seems, provide cover for any number of assaults on constitutional liberties.

The USA-PATRIOT Act breezed through the House of Representatives by a landslide vote of 356 to 66.

The act passed the U.S. Senate by a Soviet-style vote of 98 to 1, the lone dissenter being Wisconsin Democrat Russell Feingold. In the mold of a previous Wisconsin progressive, Senator Robert La Follette, who stood against Woodrow Wilson's wars at home and abroad, Feingold scolded his cowardly colleagues, "Preserving our freedom is one of the main reasons that we are now engaged in this new war on terrorism. We will lose that war without firing a shot if we sacrifice the liberties of the American people."[38]

Senator Feingold achieved a kind of plangent eloquence in his dissent:

> If we lived in a country that allowed the police to search your home at any time for any reason; if we lived in a country that allowed the government to open your mail; eavesdrop on your phone conversations, or intercept your e mail communications; if we lived in a country that allowed the government to hold people in jail indefinitely based on what they write or think, or based on mere suspicion that they are up to no good, then the government would no doubt discover and arrest more terrorists. But that probably would not be a country in which we would want to live. And that would not be a country for which we could, in good conscience, ask our young people to fight and die. In short, that would not be America.[39]

Feingold was the lone senator to call "Halt!" to this epochal legislation that passed through Congress as swiftly, stealthily, and quietly as a thief in the night.

On October 26, 2001, five days before Halloween, President Bush signed the USA-PATRIOT Act into law. The surveillance powers of the federal government had been swollen, the personal liberties and right to privacy of U.S. citizens had shrunk, and members of Congress could boast that they were tough on terrorism.

The frenzied and thoughtless action surrounding passage of the USA-PATRIOT Act called to mind the words of Calvin Hoover, who wrote in *The Economy, Liberty, and the State* that during a crisis, "when critical extensions of governmental power are likely to occur . . . there is little opportunity for a meaningful vote on whether or not, as a matter of principle, the powers of the state should be extended. Instead, there is likely to be an insistent demand for emergency actions of some sort and relatively little consideration of what the permanent effect will be."[40]

Probably not a single legislator had read the entire USA-PATRIOT Act before voting on it. No conference committee was appointed to reconcile the House and Senate versions. No committee report was issued. No dissent from a committee report was published. The Supreme Soviet couldn't have done a better job of rushing the bill to law.

But almost immediately afterward, it became the object of furious denunciations by civil libertarians of right and left.

In hurrying through the USA-PATRIOT Act, Congress "abdicated its responsibility to ensure that civil liberties infringements are justified by compelling national security interests,"[41] in the words of attorney Nancy Chang of the Center for Constitutional Rights

The Act, as James Bovard has said, "treats every citizen like a suspected terrorist and every federal agent like a proven angel."[42]

"Sunset" provisions were written into certain of its domestic spying authorizations—over the objections of the would-be J. Edgar Hoovers of the Bush 43 administration. As of this writing, the Bill of Rights does not contain a sunset provision.

The Department of Justice has acted as if the Act is not only permanent but a kind of sacred text, beyond the criticism of mere mortals. The DOJ essentially disregarded House Judiciary Committee Chairman James Sensenbrenner's (R-WI) July 2002 request for answers to a variety of questions raised within the first six months of the USA-PATRIOT Act's implementation.

According to the Bush administration and the Department of Justice, the Act merely plugged a few loopholes through which terrorists might escape. It "improved law enforcement's ability to obtain stored voice mail and records from communications and computer-service providers." It contained provisions "to combat money laundering." It "expanded information-sharing among law enforcement authorities at different levels of government."[43] These sound unobjectionable. Who but a bearded fanatic in the service of shadowy Muslim terrorists could be anything more than mildly annoyed by such a law?

So what does the Act really do? How is it a threat to the Bill of Rights?

The Fourth Amendment to the U.S. Constitution reads, "The right of the people to be secure in their persons, houses, papers, and effects, against unreasonable searches and seizures, shall not be violated; and no warrants shall issue, but upon probable cause, supported by oath or affirmation, and particularly describing the place to be searched, and the persons or things to be seized."

Section 213 of the act's Title II more or less repeals the Fourth Amendment in permitting the Department of Justice to perform "sneak and peek searches" of a suspect's e-mail, home, office, library, and Internet records. Before Section 213, government officials, armed with a warrant, had to inform the person whose property was about to be searched of the impending search. No more.

This was no mere pettifogging requirement; as the American Civil Liberties Union notes, the subject of the search might "point out irregularities in the warrant, such as the fact that the police may be at the wrong address or that the warrant is limited to a search of a stolen car, so the police have no authority to be looking into dresser drawers."

Once upon a time conservatives believed in the sanctity of the home; they even called a man's home his castle. That castle lies in ruins today, at least in the estimation of the terror-warriors. Rep. Paul wonders what will happen "if the person is home, doesn't know that law enforcement is coming to search his home, hasn't a clue as to who's coming in unannounced...and he shoots them."[44] It could—it will—happen.

"Sneak and peek" searches are done without the suspect's knowledge—even after the searches have been performed. Nothing in the act requires the subject of a "sneak and peek" search to be a terrorism suspect. This would seem to run afoul of Supreme Court decisions holding that police may not conduct searches of or seizures in a dwelling without a prior announcement.

Former Rep. Bob Barr, a sharp critic of the Act, says, "The Fourth Amendment is a nuisance to the administration, but the amendment protects citizens and legal immigrants from the government's monitoring them whenever it wants, without good cause—and if that happens, it's the end of personal liberty."

To the Bush administration's claim that it will use these powers cautiously, Barr scoffed to the *Washington Times*, "We can't say we'll let government have these unconstitutional powers in the PATRIOT Act because they will never use them. Besides, who knows how many times the government has used them? They're secret searches."[45]

Section 218 of the USA-PATRIOT ACT further eviscerates the Fourth Amendment by amending the Foreign Intelligence Surveillance Act to permit wiretapping of American citizens if a panel of eleven federal judges (who are appointed by the Supreme Court's Chief Justice) agree that a "significant purpose" of the wiretapping is to glean information about "foreign intelligence."[46] This represents a real slackening of the standard that the federal government must meet before wiretapping its subjects...er, citizens. Section 207 increases the duration of the wiretap warrants from 90 to 120 days.

The fact that panels of judges determine whether or not a wiretap order should be approved gives only the illusion of a check upon the police power. Between 1996 and 2000, federal and state officials requested 6,207 wiretaps. According to John W. Whitehead and Steven H. Auden, a grand total of three—that's right, three of 6,207—were denied.[47]

Sections 201 and 202 of the Act also expand the federal government's ability to conduct wiretap surveillance of U.S. citizens. These effectively gut the Wiretap Act of 1968, which was meant as a bolster of the Fourth Amendment. That Amendment is rapidly heading toward a state of ineffectuality currently experienced by Amendments Nine and Ten.

Section 209, meanwhile, reverses the intent of the Wiretap Act of 1968 by permitting the federal government to tap voice-mail systems. Under Sections 209 and 210, Internet service providers must permit the FBI to spy on users' electronic mail, without the user's knowledge. (As if filling in the surveillance gaps left by the USA-PATRIOT Act, the Homeland Security Act, in Section 225, which is grandly titled the Cyber Security Enhancement Act of 2002, includes language "permitting Internet service providers voluntarily to provide government agents with access to the contents of their customers' private communications without those persons' consent based on a 'good faith' belief that an emergency justifies the release of that information."[48] Do you really think that your Internet service provider has guts enough to refuse to "voluntarily" spill your beans to the federal government?)[49]

And those warrantless searches are increasingly conducted by federal agents bearing arms. Just as the right of the people to keep and bear arms is being steadily eroded, so is the privilege of arms bearing being expanded for agents of the federal government. The Homeland Security Act continued that disturbing trend by empowering the attorney general to authorize federal agency inspectors general and their subordinates to carry weapons.

Even the venerable privacy of attorney-client conversations has been breached. Radical New York City lawyer Lynne Stewart's conversations with Sheik Abdel Rahman, convicted for his role in the 1993 bombing of the World Trade Center, were taped by the FBI and used as evidence against her in a 2004 trial for aiding and abetting terrorism. This followed an October 30, 2001 order by Attorney General Ashcroft that ostensibly private conversations between prisoners and attorneys in federal prisons were to be monitored. This rule was not limited to terrorism suspects; rather, it includes inmates who are believed to be conversing with their attorneys "to further or facilitate acts of violence."[50]

"Acts of violence" is so broad, so ill defined, that once more we are in the realm of the incredible shrinking liberties. The Sixth Amendment, which guarantees the accused a right to counsel, is inoperative, apparently, in the Age of Terror.

Section 203 of the USA-PATRIOT Act gives the Central Intelligence Agency a role in domestic intelligence gathering; in other words, the CIA is empowered, as it was in the 1950s and 1960s, to spy on American citizens who dare to exercise their First Amendment rights.

The agency, never known for its scrupulous respect for civil liberties, is among the agencies with whom domestic police are permitted to share information, including the contents of intercepted Internet and telephone messages. In turn, the CIA may pass along this information to foreign intelligence services. As Kelly Patricia O'Meara put it in a hard-hitting investigative piece for *Insight*, this creates, in effect, "an international political secret police."[51]

The state's reach into banking, business, educational, and financial records is extended in unprecedented ways by Titles III and V. Medical, dental, financial, credit, educational, even veterinary—veterinary?—records are fair game in the War on Terror. The USA-PATRIOT Act required banks—under the dubiously named Bank Secrecy Act—to report cash transactions exceeding $10,000. And the paperwork mountain grows.

Section 358 of the Act relaxes the Right to Financial Privacy Act of 1978 by giving federal authorities access to previously private banking and financial information if the authorities merely claim that "financial analysis"[52] of such information is related to intelligence investigations. Once again, the standards have been loosened so as to permit the state virtually unrestricted access to private records.

Under Section 215, the FBI is empowered to force librarians to reveal the borrowing habits of patrons on request. This information is provided without the patron's knowledge. Woe betide the library user who checks out a book on terrorism. As one librarian asked the *Washington Post*, "This law is dangerous . . . I read murder mysteries—does that make me a murderer? I read spy stories—does that mean I'm a spy?"[53]

The very idea that the reading habits of American citizens are a proper subject of interest for the federal government would shock and appall our Founders. The awareness that one's borrowing habits may be reviewed by federal agents surely has a sobering, if not chilling, effect on certain patrons. As Emily Sheketoff, executive director of the American Library Association, asks, "If you live in Detroit, and have olive skin, are you going to go into the library and check out a book on the *Koran*?"[54]

Not only libraries are fair game for FBI agents under the USA-PATRIOT Act; so are bookstores, ostensibly private businesses, which under Section 215 may be forced to turn over information about purchases and even inquiries. Only a president who is proud of his aversion to books could fail to understand the "chilling effect," to use the legal cliché, that such governmental powers may have on reading habits.

Section 215 also "stifles the First Amendment rights of businesses," according to conservative legal scholars John W. Whitehead and Steven H. Aden of the Rutherford Institute in their study "A Constitutional Analysis of the USA-PATRIOT Act." Section 215 enables the Attorney General to order the seizure of business records, including computer systems, from any business as long as the seizure is part of "an investigation to protect against international terrorism or clandestine intelligence activities." Owners and employees of the business are prohibited from revealing that such an investigation is taking place. They are "gagged from disclosing that they have been the subject of an FBI search and seizure, presumably including disclosures to the media."[55]

The Rutherford Institute of Whitehead and Aden is located—poignantly—in Charlottesville, Virginia, home of the author of the Declaration of Independence. The authors give the Bush administration the benefit of every doubt yet still conclude that the "unintended consequences" of the USA-PATRIOT Act "threaten the fundamental constitutional rights of people who have absolutely no involvement with terrorism."[56]

And what, you may ask with Clintonian casuistry, is terrorism?

"Domestic terrorism," a new crime under the USA-PATRIOT Act, would seem to be easily defined as the commission of a violent act against civilians for political purposes. Timothy McVeigh was one such terrorist; the abolitionist John Brown, who slaughtered settlers in pre-Civil War "Bleeding Kansas" in his righteous cause, was probably another.

But Section 802 of our Orwellian Act casts its net far and wide and defines terrorism as "acts dangerous to human life that are a violation of the criminal laws . . . [if they] . . . appear to be intended . . . to influence the policy of a government by intimidation or coercion . . . [and] . . . occur primarily within the territorial jurisdiction of the United States."[57]

As lawyer and legal analyst Elaine Cassel has observed, "this definition is so broad that practically any act of civil disobedience could be construed to violate the law."[58] A mass e-mailing that floods the server of a member of Congress might qualify as terrorism.

It is not an exaggeration to say that mass protests and acts of civil disobedience of the sort that opposed the Vietnam War or legalized abortion could be fit under this rubric. But then any political movement not consisting solely of the most quiescent and law-abiding pacifists could very well find itself a candidate for a stint behind John Ashcroft's metal of honor.

As James Bovard writes, "It could take only a few scuffles at a rally to transform a protest group into a terrorist entity."[59] Imagine, say, the crowds of two and a quarter centuries ago protesting the Stamp Tax: They would jostle, hoot, whistle, launch the occasional rotting scarlet missile at a redcoat, all for the sake of "influenc[ing] the policy of a government by intimidation or coercion." In other words, the nation's Founders, long respected as true Patriots, were domestic terrorists under the USA-PATRIOT Act.

The term "McCarthyite" is thrown around rather too freely—after all, Tailgunner Joe, for all his boorishness, was for the most part on-target in his suspicions of the foreign loyalties of several diplomats, as the recently opened Soviet archives have shown. Nevertheless, the term is useful in suggesting the noxious practice of casting guilt by association. And in this the USA-PATRIOT Act is classically McCarthyite.

It is a sign of hope, an inspiriting cry from the heartland, that by the fall of 2004, more than 330 towns, cities, and counties had expressed their official worry or outright condemnation of the USA-PATRIOT Act.

Unfortunately, even raising these questions makes one a virtual al Qaeda secret agent, according to President Bush's former Attorney General. In his extraordinary appearance before the Senate Judiciary Committee on December 6, 2001, in a statement that will live in infamy—or at least it will live in infamy if our republic survives, and somehow finds its way back to its constitutional moorings—John Ashcroft scowled, "To those who scare peace-loving people with phantoms of lost liberty, my message is this: Your tactics only aid terrorists, for they erode our national unity and diminish our resolve. They give ammunition to America's enemies and pause to America's friends."[60]

I doubt if a more shameful and deeply un-American statement has ever been uttered by a U.S. Attorney General—a position that in recent years has been occupied by such characters as Bobby Kennedy, Ed Meese, and Janet Reno, a troika not noted for their slavish devotion to constitutional liberties. Even in this less than Jeffersonian company, Ashcroft stands out for his contempt for basic American liberties.

The Bush administration's suspension of the great writ of *habeas corpus* is exceeded in our history only by the Lincoln administration's suspension of that most basic right—the right to a hearing before an impartial judge, and the right not to be detained without charges—during the Civil War. Unlike in previous wars, U.S. citizens—with a couple of notable exceptions—have not been thrown into indeterminate detention; rather, it has been immigrants who have been detained for unconscionably long periods of time without ever being charged with a crime. Over 600 detainees from forty-four countries filled the makeshift prison at Guantanamo, Cuba; they were charged with no crime but held nonetheless, without access to lawyers or family members.

In previous wars, including the first Gulf War, such persons were entitled to a military review process. But in the amorphous War on Terror, President Bush asserts that such prisoners may be held indefinitely, without any legal recourse whatsoever. Although these matters lie outside the scope of this book, they ought to be the concern of every American who prides herself on our nation's heritage of liberty.

Habeas corpus is a cornerstone of American liberties; indeed, of the heritage of Western jurisprudence. So when Yaser Hamdi, a U.S. citizen who appears to have joined the Taliban, is captured in Afghanistan and then detained for two years without being charged with a crime, we ought to be concerned. Before the Justice Department, heeding a ruling of the U.S. Supreme Court, released Hamdi in the fall of 2004, he had not been permitted even a visit with his lawyer. No charges. No visitors. No trial. Just a cell. This has precedent only in the Civil War.

Similarly disturbing is the case of Jose Padilla, a U.S. citizen who was accused of—but never charged with—planning a "dirty bomb" attack on an American target. Though never charged with a crime, Padilla has been held incommunicado for over two years.

Will such extraordinary violations of the Constitution cease during peacetime? Heritage Foundation senior legal research fellow Paul

Rosenzweig says, "When crisis passes, we return to balance." He further argues that the "Bush administration's push on the pendulum this time around is pretty modest," offering as evidence its failure to herd Muslim-Americans into concentration camps, as President Franklin D. Roosevelt did with Japanese-Americans during the Second World War.

But Professor of Law Stephen J. Schulhofer of New York University, author of the Century Foundation report "The Enemy Within: Intelligence Gathering, Law Enforcement, and Civil Liberties in the Wake of September 11," points out that the Bush administration has repeated countless times that the War on Terror is open-ended and may well last for all our lifetimes. Are we to suspend *habeas corpus* for the next several generations?

Professor Robert Higgs, author of *Crisis and Leviathan*, adds, "As long as you attack people who are marginal, like immigrants, Muslims, and people with unpopular political views, the government has a good chance of getting away with its suppression of liberty no matter how draconian. It is when [government] abuses its power and uses it against people who have the ability to fight back through official channels and the political process that something is likely to happen."[61]

Conservative scholars Whitehead and Aden of the Rutherford Institute warn, "Americans should not labor under the misconception that freedoms forsaken today might somehow be regained tomorrow."[62] The USA-PATRIOT Act, the Homeland Security Act, and the panoply of new laws restricting freedoms in the name of anti-terrorism ought to scare anyone who cherishes the historic liberties of our country. "If the American people accept a form of police statism in the name of a promise of personal security," write Whitehead and Aden, "that would be the greatest defeat imaginable."[63]

Not all Americans are ready to concede defeat. A remnant, at least, remembers the principles upon which this country was founded. It was founded by patriots who "revolted against much more mild oppression"[65] than is contained in the USA-PATRIOT Act, as Rep. Ron Paul says.

Then again, American masochists may find no better way to torture themselves than by reading the writings of the Founders. The "wise and frugal" government they envisioned is so far removed from what we live under today that it is as if some imp of the perverse decided to play the cruel joke of inverting almost every hope they harbored in our earliest years. Take Thomas Jefferson's succinct formulation of the true American political ideals. We are, wrote Jefferson in 1800, shortly before his first election to the presidency, "friends to the freedom of religion, freedom of the press, trial by jury, and to economical government; opposed to standing armies, paper systems, war, and all connection, other than commerce, with any foreign nation."[65]

If a formulation more antithetical to the Bush administration exists, I have yet to discover it.

Notes

1.   Thomas Jefferson Letter to Edward Carrington, May 27, 1788, in *The Political Writings of Thomas Jefferson*, edited by Edward Dumbauld (Indianapolis: Bobbs Merrill, 1955), p. 138.
2.   Ron Paul, "The Homeland Security Monster," www.antiwar.com, November 19, 2002.
3.   Robert Higgs, *Crisis and Leviathan: Critical Episodes in the Growth of American Government* (New York: Oxford University Press, 1987), p. vii.
4.   Ibid., p. ix.
5.   Ibid., p. x.
6.   Ibid., p. 123.
7.   Walter Karp, *The Politics of War* (New York: Harper, 1979), p. 221.
8.   Robert Higgs, *Crisis and Leviathan*, p. 156.
9.   Ibid., p. 261.
10.   Quoted in ibid., p. 159.
11.   Timothy Lynch, "Breaking the Vicious Cycle: Preserving Our Liberties While Fighting Terrorism," Cato Policy Analysis No. 443, June 26, 2002, p. 3.
12.   Doug Bandow, "Tax-and-Spend Politics, Bush-Style," *Chronicles* (April 2004), p. 18.
13.   Ibid., p. 17.
14.   R.J. Rummel, *Death By Government* (New Brunswick, NJ: Transaction 1994), p. xvi.
15.   Ibid., p. 9.
16.   Ibid., pp. 14–16.
17.   Robert Higgs, "Government Protects Us?" *Independent Review*, Volume VII, Number 2 (Fall 2002), pp. 310–11.
18.   David Cole, "The Course of Least Resistance: Repeating History in the War on Terrorism," in *Lost Liberties: Ashcroft and the Assault on Personal Freedom*, edited by Cynthia Brown (New York: New Press, 2003), p. 21.
19.   Quoted in Steven Yates, "An Evening With Dr. Ron Paul," www.lewrockwell.com, February 11, 2004.
20.   Walter Karp, *The Politics of War*, p. 325.
21.   Ibid., p. 326.
22.   David Cole, "The Course of Least Resistance: Repeating History in the War on Terrorism," p. 15.
23.   Walter Karp, *The Politics of War*, p. 326.
24.   Quoted in Bill Kauffman, "A President, His Paperboy & the Socialist, *American Enterprise* (January/February 2002), p. 52.

25.   H.L. Mencken, *A Carnival of Buncombe* (Chicago: University of Chicago Press, 1984/1956), p. 47.
26.   Bill Kauffman, "A President, His Paperboy & the Socialist," p. 52.
27.   Walter Karp, *The Politics of War*, p. 326.
28.   Thomas Jefferson to James Monroe, October 24, 1823, *The Political Writings of Thomas Jefferson*, p. 74.
29.   Thomas Jefferson to James Monroe, June 11, 1823, in ibid., pp. 73–74.
30.   Quoted in Bill Kauffman, *America First! Its History, Culture, and Politics* (Amherst, NY: Prometheus, 1995), p. 75.
31.   Mike Lynch, "Secret Agent Scam," *Reason*, www.reason.com, June 6, 2002.
32.   Timothy Lynch, "Breaking the Vicious Cycle: Preserving Our Liberties While Fighting Terrorism," Cato Policy Analysis No. 443, June 26, 2002, p. 5.
33.   "The Year in Review," *American Enterprise* (January/February 1998), p. 29.
34.   Nancy Chang, "How Democracy Dies: The War on our Civil Liberties," in *Lost Liberties*, p. 41.
35.   John W. Whitehead and Steven H. Aden, "A Constitutional Analysis of the USA PATRIOT Act and the Justice Department's Anti-Terrorism Initiatives," *American Law Review* (Vol. 51: 1081–1133, 2002), www.ratical.org, p. 8.
36.   James Bovard, *Terrorism and Tyranny*, p. 65.
37.   Kelly Patricia O'Meara, "Police State," *Insight on the News*, www.insightmag.com, December 3, 2001.
38.   Quoted in Nancy Chang, "How Democracy Dies: The War on our Civil Liberties," p. 34.
39.   Quoted in Timothy Lynch, "Breaking the Vicious Cycle: Preserving Our Liberties While Fighting Terrorism," p. 7.
40.   Robert Higgs, *Crisis and Leviathan*, p. 17.
41.   Nancy Chang, "How Democracy Dies: The War on our Civil Liberties," p. 33.
42.   James Bovard, *Terrorism and Tyranny*, p. 2.
43.   George W. Bush, "Securing the Homeland: Strengthening the Nation," pp. 4–5.
44.   Kelly Patricia O'Meara, "Police State," *Insight*.
45.   Ralph Z. Hallow, "Patriot Act Divides Bush Loyalists," *Washington Times*, www.washingtontimes.com, April 5, 2004.
46.   John W. Whitehead and Steven H. Aden, "A Constitutional Analysis of the USA PATRIOT Act and the Justice Department's Anti-Terrorism Initiatives," p. 26.
47.   Ibid., p. 31.
48.   Reg Whitaker, "After 9/11: A Surveillance State?" *Lost Liberties*, p. 62.
49.   Privacy of the mail, including e-mail, had once been sacrosanct in our constitutional republic. Justice Oliver Wendell Holmes, in his 1921 opinion defending the private nature of the mail (*Milwaukee Social Democratic Publishing Co. v. Burleson*), wrote, "The use of the mails is almost as much a part of free speech as the right to use our tongues." Quoted in James Bovard, *Terrorism and Tyranny*, p. 134.
50.   John W. Whitehead and Steven H. Aden, "A Constitutional Analysis of the USA PATRIOT Act and the Justice Department's Anti-Terrorism Initiatives," p. 40.
51.   Kelly Patricia O'Meara, "Police State," *Insight*.
52.   John W. Whitehead and Steven H. Aden, "A Constitutional Analysis of the USA PATRIOT Act and the Justice Department's Anti-Terrorism Initiatives," p. 57.
53.   Quoted in Elaine Cassel, "The Other War: The Bush Administration and the End of Civil Liberties" www.counterpunch.com, April 26, 2003.
54.   Timothy Egan, "Sensing the Eyes of Big Brother, and Shoving Back," *New York Times*, August 8, 2004, p. A16.
55.   John W. Whitehead and Steven H. Aden, "A Constitutional Analysis of the USA PATRIOT Act and the Justice Department's Anti-Terrorism Initiatives," p. 22.

56.   Ibid., p. 5.
57.   Nancy Chang, "How Democracy Dies: The War on our Civil Liberties," p. 40.
58.   Elaine Cassel, "The Other War: The Bush Administration and the End of Civil Liberties."
59.   James Bovard, *Terrorism and Tyranny*, p. 3.
60.   Quoted in Aryeh Neier, "Introduction," *Lost Liberties*, p. 8.
61.   Christian Bourge, "Report: Anti-Terror Powers Curtail Rights," UPI, www.upi.com, November 23, 2002.
62.   John W. Whitehead and Steven H. Aden, "A Constitutional Analysis of the USA PATRIOT Act and the Justice Department's Anti-Terrorism Initiatives," p. 6.
63.   Ibid., p. 59.
64.   Kelly Patricia O'Meara, "Police State," *Insight*.
65.   Thomas Jefferson to Gideon Granger, August 13, 1800, *The Political Writings of Thomas Jefferson*, p. 96.

6

Mr. Orwell—and Stephen King —Call Your Offices

Once upon a time in America, Republican presidents frowned on totalitarian schemes to control the citizenry. Ronald Reagan, for instance. Now, Reagan may not have been the most pure classical liberal who ever lived, but he had a prudent fear of overweening government. Martin Anderson, President Reagan's chief domestic and economic policy advisor, tells of a signal moment in the Reagan presidency—a moment in which Reagan revealed himself as a man with a healthy suspicion of Big Brother.

The date was July 16, 1981, in the heady early months of the Reagan presidency. The president had survived the assassination attempt by John Hinckley and had seen his landmark 1981 budget and tax package adopted, albeit in modified form. He was riding high; he was buoyant; he was still in command of his faculties.

Reagan and his Cabinet were presented that July afternoon with an immigration reform proposal that included as its most controversial feature "that every person in the United States be required to have a counterfeit-proof identification card issued by the federal government."

Martin Anderson, who cut his philosophical eyeteeth on the writings of the libertarian novelist Ayn Rand, was appalled. As he explained in his memoir, *Revolution* (1988), "Such a card is an indispensable tool of a totalitarian state, for before a government can really begin to control your life it must know who you are and where you are, and it must be able to demand proof of your existence whenever it encounters you—applying for work, moving to another address, walking down the street. Without a national identification system, it is very difficult for a small number of people to control a large society. With one, it is much easier."[1]

153

The Trojan Horse inside which the national ID card was smuggled in 1981 was, as is the case today, immigration. The card was sold as a quick and painless fix for the problem of illegal aliens. Attorney General William French Smith recited the usual arguments in its favor. It would enable government officials to determine who was in the country lawfully and who was here illegally. It would never be abused; after all, the Social Security card is a de facto national ID, and that is never put to mischievous use, is it? And the topper: The only folks who would object to showing their ID card on demand to the proper authorities are those who have something to hide. It was a smooth performance by the patrician attorney general, Anderson conceded. When Smith finished, no one in the Cabinet registered any objection to what would have been one of the most extraordinary developments in the history of American governance. Finally, Anderson, though not a member of the Cabinet, waved his hand and attracted Reagan's attention.

"Mr. President," Anderson began, "one of my concerns about the national identity card is that the Office of Management and Budget has estimated that it could cost several billion dollars to produce a counterfeit-proof social security card for everyone. I would like to suggest another way that I think is a lot better. It's a lot cheaper. It can't be counterfeited. It's very lightweight, and impossible to lose. It's even waterproof. All we have to do is tattoo an identification number on the inside of everybody's arm."[2]

There were gasps, glares, and withering glances directed at Anderson for his sarcasm. James Watt, the embattled secretary of the interior, mused aloud about the Mark of the Beast. Satanic stigmata, images of Nazi concentration camps: Anderson had flushed out the national ID card. Attorney General Smith tried to regroup, but when Reagan joked, "Maybe we should just brand all the babies,"[3] he knew the game was up. American would remain cardless. For another quarter-century, at least.

Alas, though George W. Bush is familiar with the Mark of the Beast and the significance of the Book of Revelation to the Christian Right, he seems far less sensitive to such matters than Reagan. One wonders if he would even catch the mockery in Martin Anderson's voice; indeed, if a cheeky Anderson somehow made it into Bush's circle of advisors and threw out a similar suggestion, he would quite likely be lauded for his sagacious assessment of the terrorist threat.

Among the most bizarre ironies in the Age of Anti-Terrorism is that if the fates had somehow cut the deck differently, this "cheeky Anderson" in the Bush Cabinet might very well have been none other than John Ashcroft.

Upon being nominated for U.S. attorney general, Ashcroft was vilified by the usual suspects of interest-group liberalism—People for the American Way, Americans for Democratic Action, the National Organization for Women—yet he found supporters among the strongest civil libertarians on the left. Nat Hentoff, the long-time champion of the Bill of Rights at the *Village Voice*, viewed Ashcroft as a U.S. senator who had been unusually sensitive to privacy issues. And Wisconsin Democrat Russell Feingold, who would go on to cast the only vote in the Senate against the USA-PATRIOT Act, actually voted for Ashcroft's confirmation, in part because he saw him as a potential across-the-aisle ally on civil liberties.

Life, alas, is full of surprises, often unpleasant ones. And few political surprises have been less pleasant than the rigidly anti-liberty stance of Attorney General Ashcroft and his successor, Alberto Gonzales. The horrors—potential, realized, petty, unpetty, and always expensive—discussed in this chapter occurred on their watch. For shame.

Ashcroft, betraying his previous pro-privacy inclinations, did not do a Martin Anderson and squash the revived proposals for a national ID card. These calls came largely from a gaggle of liberals, fair-weather friends of civil liberties, who jumped on the National ID card bandwagon after the attacks of September 11. The bumptious TV celebrity and sometime lawyer Alan Dershowitz was among the most prominent turncoats to the cause of liberty.

America, in contrast to so much of the Old World from which our ancestors fled, has never been a land in which one had to carry "papers" or identification to produce at a police officer's whim.

Although some proponents of a national ID claim that it will be "voluntary," it will soon be required to transact so many mundane activities, from cashing a check to boarding a bus to entering a government building, that it will become, de facto, mandatory. Perhaps hermits will be permitted to opt out of the system. Or perhaps not. The Unabomber, after all, lived as a hermit, and his example doubtless will be adduced to argue for its universality. The right to be left alone will be left in the dust.

Unmentioned in the forthcoming great debate over national ID cards will be their utter uselessness. Terrorists will be able to forge such cards, buy them on the black market, or enlist U.S. citizens or legal residents to do their dirty work. We will not be made safer, but we will be substantially less free.

Homeland security horror stories range from the nightmarish to the blackly comical: from *Night of the Living Dead* to *Evil Dead 2*, you might say. The term "homeland security" is so elastic, so nebulous, so protean that it can be stretched, shrunk, or shaped into any object that fits one's purposes. Seldom, though, has it been used as imaginatively as in Philadelphia, which by cruel coincidence was the birthplace of that Constitution rendered so impuissant in recent years.

It seems that the management of the Eagles, that always disappointing band of football players with whom Philly fans have carried on a generations-long hate-hate relationship, moved into the new Lincoln Financial Field in the fall of 2003. The stadium, like most pro football stadia in this age of sporting extortion, was constructed thanks to a $200 million taxpayer subsidy. Yet Eagles ownership, far from expressing gratitude to its taxpaying benefactors, handed down one of the most outrageous decrees in the history or sport: to wit, no food purchased outside the stadium may be brought within.

Given that the consumption of Philly cheese steaks and hoagies are as close to a birthright as exists in the City of Brotherly Love, the ban provoked an uproar. A gustatory ritual long shared by fathers and sons was to be ended. And making matters worse was the reason given by team officials: homeland security. As a team official announced, "You're putting the fans' lives at danger" in permitting the infiltration of non-Lincoln Financial hoagies.

The Eagles claimed that they were simply following suggestions from the Department of Homeland Security. It seems that the risk assessors of the homeland security complex had determined that bombs could be packaged inside hoagie wrappers. Jeff Taylor of *Reason* magazine pointed out, "Sandwich-makers noted that for years they had wrapped their torpedoes of death in clear plastic for easy inspection."[4] But no matter: homeland security trumps all. And if, in this case, it ensures a captive market for the barely edible and astronomically priced food served inside Lincoln Financial Field, well, that's the price of defeating terrorism.

As if facilitating the banning of hoagies isn't enough for the DHS, the department set a new distance record for mission creep when it launched "Operation Predator." The predator in question was not Osama bin Laden or any other terrorist with the blood of infidels on his mind. Rather, it was the creeps who access child pornography over the Internet.

Just how arresting these perverts has anything whatsoever to do with "homeland security" or the War on Terror is a matter that begs conjecture. Perhaps the DHS is simply hedging against that day when the War on Terror, having outlived its usefulness, is declared over. Best not to be the bureaucratic equivalent of the March of Dimes, which virtually collapsed once Dr. Salk invented the vaccine for polio. The DHS, it seems, is trying out new missions.

Acts of tyranny, both petty and serious, are to be expected when government officials use language as sloppily as do George W. Bush and his mandarins. Take their use of the word "freedom," which has, subtly and insidiously, replaced the more precise "liberty," with its specific and evocative attachments to the American Revolution and American history.

Liberty implies restrictions on state authority and the protection of historically grounded personal rights. "Freedom," by contrast, is an airier, more nebulous term. We are forever told that our cause is "freedom." U.S. soldiers occupying Iraq are said to be fighting for our "freedom," though the various Iraqi governments have never so much as whispered a threat against the territorial United States or its citizens. On the afternoon of September 11, 2001, the shaken President Bush announced that "Freedom, itself, was attacked this morning by a faceless coward, and freedom will be defended."[5] We might forgive him this confused jumble, given the circumstances, but "freedom" was not attacked, unless jetliners, the Pentagon, and the World Trade Center are its tropes. The attackers were not faceless, and though their acts were profoundly evil, they were not cowards. Mad, yes; cowards, no. (This commonsensical observation got ABC talk show host Bill Maher fired from his job at *Politically Incorrect*. Apparently there is such a thing as being too politically incorrect, as such candid souls as Maher, baseball relief pitcher John Rocker, and a legion of others have discovered.)

Osama bin Laden was quite clear about his objectives in masterminding the wicked deeds of 9/11. On numerous occasions in the months following, he made clear his policy objectives: (1) the U.S.

must withdraw military forces from Saudi Arabia; (2) the U.S. must cease supporting the Israelis in their conflict with the Palestinians; and (3) the U.S. must end sanctions against Saddam Hussein's Iraqi regime. These U.S. policies, whatever their wisdom or lack thereof, have nothing to do with "freedom" and everything to do with power politics, realpolitik, the "special relationship" between the U.S. and Israel, the alliance of the U.S. and the Saudi royal family, and many other considerations. Yet to the publicists for the war on terror, they were subsumed under the protean word "Freedom."

Kris Kristofferson once wrote, and Janis Joplin once sang, that freedom's just another word for nothing left to lose. But to the Bush administration, freedom was just another word for plenty more to spend.

This is the language of Orwell, of public manipulation.

Just as defense secretary and technocrat par excellence Robert McNamara is said to have remarked that we had to destroy a certain Vietnam village in order to save it, so is it necessary to repeal the most basic constitutional protections in order to preserve the Constitution—or so we are told by that most insidious of Washington creatures, the bipartisan commission.

The Continuity of Government Commission, in its report of June 2003, urged the adoption of a constitutional amendment providing for the abolition of the Founders' handiwork in the event of a terrorist attack.

"In the event of a disaster that debilitated Congress, the vacuum could be filled by unilateral executive action—perhaps a benign form of martial law," wrote the impeccably establishment authors of the report, who had the vestigial decency to add, "The country might get by, but at a terrible cost to our democratic institutions."[6]

But not to worry: the Continuity of Government Commission, with its delicious acronym COG, had a solution: a constitutional amendment providing for the appointment—not election, but appointment— of Congress in the event of a catastrophic attack.[7]

Let us back up just a bit. The COG was a joint project of the American Enterprise Institute and the Brookings Institution, the two oldest establishment think tanks in Washington. AEI is Republican in coloration, generally moderate in politics except for foreign policy, where it is unrelievedly hawkish and expansionist. Brookings, long considered the Democratic Party's cabinet-in-exile, shades to the liberal side of our narrow spectrum, though it, too, is moderately hawkish and interventionist in foreign policy. The only difference is that it tends to be multilateralist whereas AEI is more willing to support unilateral military actions.

In any event, the two think tanks joined heads, or should I say armor, in the fall of 2002. With lavish subsidies from the Carnegie Corporation and the Hewlett Packard, and MacArthur foundations, they set out to solve the most pressing policy issue of our time. No, not the achievement of peace and harmony in the world, or the establishment of market-based economies in nations recovering from decades under command economies, but rather how "to ensure the continuity of our governmental institutions in the event of a catastrophic attack."[10]

To solve this wildly speculative question, COG appointed honorary co-chairs Jimmy Carter and Gerald Ford, in themselves advertisements for the advisability of governmental inaction. As honorary co-chairs, Carter and Ford did none of the work of the commission but gave it the presidential seal of approval. The chairmen of COG were Democratic lobbyist Lloyd Cutler and former U.S. Senator Alan Simpson (R-WY), he of the cowboy wit and Washington connections. Membership on the commission was dominated by lobbyists, including GOP fixer Kenneth Duberstein, former House Minority Leader Robert Michel (R-IL), former Speaker of the House Newt Gingrich (R-GA), and former Speaker of the House Thomas Foley (D-WA). Other members included such functionaries and time-servers as Clinton White House Chief of Staff Leon Panetta, Clinton Secretary of Health and Human Services Donna Shalala, former Congresswoman Lynn Martin (R-IL), and NAACP President Kweisi Mfume.

COG first took aim at the U.S. Congress, specifically the House of Representatives, the people's body. It sought to devise ways in which "Congress could function if a large number of members were killed or incapacitated."[8] Now, this might seem a science fictionish scenario, but then that's all part of the ambiance of homeland security: think the unthinkable, proclaim it from the very rooftops, in order to frighten Americans into giving up their liberties.

"It was, of course, the attacks of September 11th that prodded us to consider how an attack on our leaders and institutions might debilitate our country just at the very time strong leadership and legitimate institutions were most needed,"[9] declared co-chairmen Cutler and Simpson in the introduction to COG's first report, "Preserving

Our Institutions: The Continuity of Congress." Note the emphasis on "strong leadership," which is a phrase notably absent from our nation's founding documents and their supporting literature of liberty.

The Commission sketched a variety of fancifully horrific vignettes. What if al Qaeda had crashed planes into the Capitol the week before 9/11, on September 6, 2001, when Mexican President Vicente Fox was addressing a joint session of Congress? What if an infectious agent, say smallpox, were loosed on the Congress? What if terrorists detonated a nuclear device on Pennsylvania Avenue on Inauguration Day, killing everyone between the Capitol and the White House? What if enemy aliens aimed their photon torpedoes at AEI and Brookings?

Oops—that last possibility was not discussed. But you get the idea. COG raised any number of nightmares that might descend upon our poor quavering vulnerable seat of the nation. Once the reader accepts the premise, she is hooked into a series of repressive, antidemocratic measures to cope with a horror that probably—almost certainly—will never happen.

The sheer flimsiness of this enterprise is revealed by its inspiration: an op-ed piece, of all ephemeral things, by the ubiquitous self-promoter Norman Ornstein, senior counselor at the American Enterprise Institute. Ornstein, trained as a political scientist but scorned by the rest of his fraternity as a lightweight, has the most highly developed publicity-gathering sense this side of Paris Hilton. He has built a career by penning fatuous or clichéd articles parroting the conventional wisdom in a key pleasing to the powers-that-be.

Like any of Washington's op-ed machines, Ornstein is always looking for new (but safe and noncontroversial) topics. So within two weeks of 9/11, he had jotted off a little piece for the Capitol Hill newspaper *Roll Call* warning of the dangers to the Capitol and the Congress posed by terrorists.

This hit a nerve, of course. Many of the folks who read *Roll Call* live on Capitol Hill and do not wish to be vaporized into Nagasaki-land. Many have a sense of loyalty to the institution of Congress, too, and they worry about its "integrity," a quality not always in obvious evidence within the marbled halls. Could this "integrity" survive a dirty bomb? Smallpox? Senator Chuck Schumer? Norm Ornstein said it could—if the right plans were made.

The heart of the COG report on "Preserving Our Institutions: The Congress" is a proposal to turn the institution of Congress, in particular the House of Representatives, upside down; to cut out its heart; to ruin, not preserve, its essential nature.

The "Central Recommendation" of the COG Report on Congress reads: "A constitutional amendment to give Congress the power to provide by legislation for the appointment of temporary replacements to fill vacant seats in the House of Representatives after a catastrophic attack and to temporarily fill seats in the House of Representatives and Senate that are held by incapacitated members."[10]

This is not an amendment that merely corrects an oversight in the U.S. Constitution or addresses some problem unforeseen at the time of its drafting. Article 1, Section 2, Clause 4, reads that "when vacancies happen in the representation from any state, the executive authority thereof shall issue writs of election to fill such vacancies." In other words, when a member dies, resigns, or otherwise leaves office, the governor of his or her state calls a special election, the winner of which assumes the vacant office. As the COG report's authors concede, "no House vacancy has ever been filled by any other method since the adoption of the Constitution in 1789."[11] In other words, every person who has ever sat in the U.S. House of Representatives has been elected to that office by the voters of his or her district. Period.

(The U.S. Senate is different. Under the Seventeenth Amendment, which provided for direct election of senators, governors fill inter-election vacancies by appointment. But then the Senate has never been the people's house; until the adoption of the Seventeenth Amendment, the election of U.S. senators was the job of the state legislatures.)

COG offers two possible means by which governors might fill House vacancies: by appointing anyone they wish to appoint, or by appointing someone from a list provided earlier by the dead or incapacitated House member. (With no doubt unintentional humor, the report's authors note that "Many members have stayed in their elected positions for months or longer, while comatose or clearly unable to perform their duties."[12] Who ever doubted it?) Here the plot of this fantasy gets bogged down in speculative minutiae: the redoubtable Norman Ornstein, the op-ed writer who got this whole mad ball rolling, has offered an amendment of Tolstoyan length and Jamesian complexity in which members of the House and Senate would be required to "designate in advance not fewer than 3 nor more than 7 emergency interim successors to the member's powers and duties."[13] The governors—denominated the "Executive Authority of each State" in the jailboots and clanking door phraseology of homeland security—would appoint new House members from those lists.

The appointed Congress would serve for 120 days, at which time a nationwide special election would refill the House. Appointed members would be eligible to run. Any laws passed by the "temporary" appointed Congress would be permanent. There would be no sunset clause for the damage done by the unelected Congress.

COG is not insensible of the revolutionary nature of its proposal. It detects an "understandable sensitivity to the status of the House as an elected body."[14] But in its *Omega Man* scenario, Washington is reduced to rubble by al Qaeda and the special elections currently mandated by the Constitution would take at least three months to complete. "Three months is too long to continue without a functioning Congress,"[15] intone the report's authors in best grave Washington-speak. In fact, the early republic got along quite well with Congress in adjournment for many more months at a time than three, but apparently the experiences of the pre-9/11 America are irrelevant in our age of empire.

Article I, Section 5, Clause 1 of the Constitution states that "a majority of each [chamber of Congress] shall constitute a quorum to do business." Anyone who has ever visited the House or Senate chambers knows that a majority of members are seldom, if ever, present. The business gets done. But even in the event of a terrorist attack and consequent widescale murder of the Capitol's denizens, a quorum could still be assembled. Charles Rice, the distinguished professor emeritus at Notre Dame Law School, in his "Statement of Opposition to the Continuity of Government Commission's Proposal," noted that it is a "fair conclusion that each House has the inherent power to exclude deceased or incapacitated members in calculating the number necessary for a quorum."[16]

The COG report expressed horror at the prospect that as few as five surviving House members might constitute a quorum and thus start passing laws, willy-nilly, that a full House would never pass. (Such as, say, the USA-PATRIOT Act?) It worried that "a Congress of greatly reduced size would act and that the vast majority of Americans could view this Congress as illegitimate."[17]

The fear is bizarre. For one thing, any bills passed by a mini-House of seven survivors would still need to be passed by the Senate and signed into law by the president. And due to the Seventeenth Amendment, the Senate would never be at less than full strength, for governors may appoint successors to deceased or incapacitated members almost immediately.

Charles Rice has sounded the alarm signal under the aegis of the Committee to Preserve an Elected Congress—and if the very title of that organization doesn't send chills down your spine you are numbed to the severity of the current threat to our liberties and our system of government.

Rice turns the tables on COG, writing of that mythical five-person Congress:

> Suppose, as the COGC report conjectures, 'only five House members survive' an attack. And suppose those five members proceeded to act as the House. The republic would survive quite well. The COGC states that such a small membership could 'call into question the legitimacy of its actions.' But numerous laws have been enacted, often by voice vote, with very few House members present, including, for example, the Wartime Emergency Supplemental Appropriations of 2003, the legitimacy of which has not been called into question. Also, a House of five elected members would have more 'legitimacy,' as the living continuation of the only directly elected entity in our government, than would a House composed of those five elected members and 430 appointed members.

Rice calls the COG amendment "unnecessary as well as dangerous to the integrity of our representative government." Powerfully, he notes, "Without a single exception, every person who has ever served as a member of the House of Representatives has been elected to that office by the people of his district. This is a nonnegotiable point."

This is a nonnegotiable point. Period.

Rice helpfully suggests options in the extremely unlikely event that we are faced with a five-person House of Representatives. For instance, although COG makes much of the fact that the average length of a House vacancy since 1985 has been 126.4 days, this is largely due to local conditions and the lack of urgency attending the filling of such vacancies. The figure could be cut by two-thirds in the event of an emergency. Moreover, Congress could enact "standby legislation"[18] which would provide temporary funding of government services and authorize the president to take appropriate, constitutional actions in the event of catastrophe. Such legislation would have sunset provisions and expire with the election of the new Congress.

"The commission's primary objective," states COG, "is that appointments be made swiftly, legitimately, and decisively."[19] Note the absence of the word "democratically" or a phrase such as "in accordance with American traditions." COG regards such attachments to the old, pre-9/11 America as hopeless sentimentality, libertarian impracticability, and dangerously old-fashioned nonsense. While it concludes, in its report on Congress, that the adoption of a COG amendment would serve "as a warning to those who would seek to topple the United States that our institutions are stronger than those who would try to destroy them,"[20] it would in reality undermine our institutions and make a travesty of them. Thanks to the homeland security mindset, we have come to the point where we need organizations with such names as the Coalition to Preserve an Elected Congress. What, one wonders, would Mr. Jefferson say?

(Or what would he say to the prospect of deploying the armed forces at polling places on Election Day, as former Maryland Governor Parris Glendening considered. "This is an image one would normally associate with a banana republic," wrote Gene Healy of the Cato Institute, "not a free, democratic one."[21])

The COG-Ornstein amendment proposals, however silly or whimsical they might seem, are no mites in the congressional slush pile. They have received congressional hearings and serious consideration; much of the Establishment has lined up behind them. In an earlier age of paranoia, the first years of the Cold War, similar proposals received respectful hearings in the Senate—perhaps because the Senate would be largely unaffected by the amendment, since governors already fill vacancies in that body by appointment.

Three times the Senate passed constitutional amendments granting state governors the power to appoint members of the House in the event of a catastrophe, which in that period was supposed to be a nuclear exchange with the Soviet Union. In 1954, the Senate-passed measure kicked in when at least 145 House seats were vacant; in 1955 and 1960, Senate-passed amendments required that a majority of House seats be vacant before governors gained the power to circumvent elections and appoint members. (The COG report recommends that the trigger for the emergency provisions for congressional appointments be set at "between 15 and 50 percent"[22] of seats vacant. Why COG set the bar at the extraordinarily low figure of 15 percent, or a mere 65 of 435 House seats, was never explained.)

In all three cases, the House ignored the Senate's action. After all, members of the House took a certain pride in their status as the people's tribunes, however inexact or flawed their tribuneship might be. They were not about to let the haughty Senate subvert the very nature of their body. They had pride. They were also perhaps mindful of the adage that when it is not necessary to amend the Constitution, it is necessary not to amend the Constitution.

The U.S. Capitol was not destroyed in a nuclear exchange with the Soviets. In fact, the Soviet Union dissolved. The Senate's panicky action on those revolutionary amendments began to look silly in retrospect. After all, as Congressman Ron Paul has pointed out, "During the Civil War, D.C. neighbor Virginia was actively involved in hostilities against the United States—yet President Abraham Lincoln never suggested that non-elected persons serve in the House." The hysteria generated after September 11, 2001, had the unfortunate effect of reviving some of the most anti-democratic, anti liberty measures ever seriously considered by the U.S. Congress.

We are likely in for a protracted battle over COG-like amendments, which have proliferated in the Congress like poison mushrooms. Constitutional alternatives have been proposed, such as the Continuity of Representation Act, which passed the House in May 2004. This act required "the holding of special elections within 45 days after the Speaker or acting Speaker declares 100 or more members of the House have been killed."[23] Thus the vacancies would be filled swiftly, decisively—and democratically. For we must never allow the homeland securiat to induce us to forget the essential point made about the House of Representatives in *Federalist 52*: that it "should have an immediate dependence on, and an intimate sympathy with, the people. Frequent elections are unquestionably the only policy by which this dependence and sympathy can be effectually secured."[24]

Elections must not only be frequent; they must also be regular. This has never been a problem under our system of constitutional government. Even during the bleakest days of the Civil War, Abraham Lincoln never thought about, much less suggested, cancelling an election. But George W. Bush, to paraphrase Lloyd Bentsen's immortal putdown of Dan Quayle, is no Abraham Lincoln.

In the July 19, 2004 issue of *Newsweek*, investigative reporter Michael Isikoff broke one of the most bizarre and chilling political stories of the whole mad Era of Terrorism. "American counterterrorism officials," reported Isikoff, "are reviewing a proposal that could allow for the postponement of the November presidential election in the event of [a terrorist] attack."

Isikoff disclosed that the prospect of another al Qaeda attack somewhere, sometime, via some method, was the inspiration for this
breathtakingly revolutionary threat by the Bush administration. More
specifically, the germ of election postponement was traced back to
the Department of Homeland Security. It seems that Secretary Ridge
had asked the Office of Legal Counsel within the U.S. Department
of Justice "to analyze what legal steps would be needed to permit
the postponement of the election were an attack to take place."

Ridge forwarded a letter from one DeForest B. Soaries, Jr., a minister and failed politician who had traded in God's work for that of
the...well, never mind. Soaries, pastor of the First Baptist Church of
Lincoln Gardens in Somerset, New Jersey, had lost a race for Congress in 2002. He was appointed chairman of the U.S. Election Assistance Commission. (Before 9/11, our elections ran quite without
assistance from this federal entity.)

Chairman Soaries expressed alarm in his letter to Secretary Ridge
that "the federal government has no agency that has the statutory
authority to cancel and reschedule a federal election." This is quite
true. The federal government also has no agency that has the statutory authority to declare martial law and imprison any citizen who
expresses dissident political opinions. In fact, the federal government lacks agencies empowered to commit all sorts of violations of
basic American liberties, but in the past, the absence of such agencies had not been seen as a pressing problem.

Yet 9/11 changed everything, as we have been told ad infinitum.
Soaries, like any turf-coveting bureaucrat, urged Ridge to convince
Congress to pass legislation—"emergency legislation"[25]—giving the
power to cancel federal elections to the heretofore unknown U.S.
Election Assistance Commission.

Soaries defended his extraordinary reach for power with this
classic example of circumlocutory bilge: "Look at the possibilities. If the federal government were to cancel an election or suspend an election, it has tremendous political implications. If the
federal government chose not to suspend an election it has political implications. Who makes the call, under what circumstances is
the call made, what are the constitutional implications? I think we
have to err on the side of transparency to protect the voting rights
of the country."

Just how canceling a presidential election is acting to "protect"
the voting rights of "the country" (does he mean American citizens?)

Mr. Soaries never deigns to tell us. In fact, as columnist Justin Raimondo of antiwar.com writes, "His proposal amounts to a usurpation of power: in effect, a coup."[26] Hard to believe that we are seriously considering coup-like measures in the United States of the twenty-first century.

On July 22, 2004, the House of Representatives voted 419-2 to affirm that no agency or individual has the authority to postpone a national election. Soaries was grounded. But he—and those who give petty bureaucrats like him their marching orders—had shown their hand. Their trial balloon had been shot down. But the wonder is that it had been launched at all.

Not that our constitutional protections are all that robust in the absence of martial law or election cancellation. In March 2003, Justice Antonin Scalia told a Cleveland audience, "The Constitution just sets minimums. Most of the rights that you enjoy go way beyond what the Constitution requires." In fact, the Constitution strictly limits the powers of the federal government, not the rights of citizens, whose plenteousness is described by Amendments IX and X:

ARTICLE IX: The enumeration in the Constitution, of certain rights, shall not be construed to deny or disparage others retained by the people.

ARTICLE X: The powers not delegated to the United States by the Constitution, nor prohibited by it to the States, are reserved to the States respectively, or to the people.

Nevertheless, Scalia warned the Ohioans that in time of war, "the protections will be ratcheted right down to the constitutional minimum. I won't let it go beyond the constitutional minimum."[27] Now that's reassuring.

Among the constitutional rights slipping from our fingers is the right to trial by jury, which the Supreme Court in *Ex Parte Milligan* (1866) declared "one of the most valuable in a free country" and one that is "preserved to every one accused of crime who is not attached to the army, or navy, or militia in actual service."[28]

The "military order" issued by President Bush in November 2001 that provided for the trial of suspected terrorists before military tribunals instead of civilian courts was a clear violation of *Ex Parte Milligan* and the Sixth Amendment, which reads, "In all criminal prosecutions, the accused shall enjoy the right to a speedy and public trial, by an impartial jury."

Ah, you say, but that applies only to furtive Middle Eastern types: foreigners not born to American rights.

Not so fast. For the rights of even the most red-blooded Americans are not secure in a paranoid age.

The king of all Orwellian schemes hatched in the hectic days after 9/11 was the Department of Defense's Total Information Awareness Project (TIA), overseen by disgraced Admiral John Poindexter. This was the kind of quasi-totalitarian scheme that would have been laughed out of the political arena during sane times—but with every replay of the collapse of the Twin Towers, the sanity level in the body politic took a dip.

The TIA was sold by its proud architects as a kind of Big Brother program twenty years too late and perhaps far too ambitious for *1984*. It called for the creation of an enormous database—think those humongous light-blinking, smoke-belching, paper-excreting computers of bad 1950s science-fiction movies—which included information on every American's financial and credit lives, travel and health records, marriages and divorces and real-estate transactions, telephone and Internet activities.... In short, on everything that every American does outside of quiet contemplation.

William Safire, the former Nixon speechwriter and later token conservative at the *New York Times*, was among the first to sound the warning of alarm over the TIA. He wrote on November 14, 2002, that should the Total Information Awareness program be enacted:

> Every purchase you make with a credit card, every magazine subscription you buy and medical prescription you fill, every Web site you visit and e-mail you send or receive, every academic grade you receive, every bank deposit you make, every trip you book and every event you attend—all these transactions and communications will go into what the Defense Department describes as "a virtual, centralized grand database."[29]

As if this weren't enough, Safire added, the database would also include the many strands of information about citizens that governments at all levels have already collected: passport applications, marriage and divorce records, drivers' licenses, pistol permits . . . the whole shooting match.

The computer mavens of the TIA program would then sift through this avalanche of information looking for links, connections, hints, red flags, and an ocean full of red herrings that might tip them off to suspicious activity. According to the project's website, "The goal of the Total Information Awareness (TIA) program is to revolutionize the ability of the United States to detect, classify, and identify foreign terrorists—and decipher their plans—and thereby enable the U.S. to take timely action to defeat terrorist acts."[30]

But liberty won a victory here. Or did it? TIA was officially terminated in September 2003. But the termination seems to have been for public consumption—to alleviate the fears of all you nervous Nellies out there who don't want the federal government having "Financial, Education, Travel, Medical, Veterinary, Country Entry, Place/Event Entry, Transportation, Housing...[and] Communications" information about you or identifying you by your "Face, Finger Prints, Gait, [and] Iris"[31] biometrics. Work on TIA programs continues elsewhere within the Department of Defense. And TIA by any other name smells just as rotten.

The TIA's tone-deafness to traditional American liberties was astonishing. Just as bizarre was the Bush administration's choice to direct the project: Admiral John Poindexter.

Poindexter, as Safire conceded, had a reputation for brilliance: possessor of a doctorate in physics, he had graduated at the top of his class at the Naval Academy and later scraped and clawed his way to the top of the military bureaucracy, emerging as President Reagan's national security advisor and successor to the suicidal Robert "Bud" MacFarlane. Despite his name, with its timeless connotations of excessive dweebiness, Poindexter reveled in cloak and dagger nonsense. He was a central figure in the Iran-Contra scandal that almost brought down the Reagan presidency.

Poindexter is also a convicted felon, five times over. He lied to Congress in sworn testimony, though this conviction was overturned by a federal appeals court on one of those technicalities that conservatives usually see as evidence of the "softness" of the system. It seems that the fact that he had been promised immunity for his testimony excused his mendacity. Which does not change the fact that he is a convicted liar.

The Bush family, as observers have often noted, prize loyalty in the way that the Kennedys do: that is, they reward those whose loyalty to the advancement of various Bush interests overrides any concerns of ethics, honesty, or fair dealing. So from the pit of disgrace Admiral Poindexter was rescued and in January 2002 he was installed as director of the new Information Awareness Office in the Defense Department's Defense Advanced Research Projects Agency (DARPA).

The name Poindexter may lack the panache of, say, James Bond, but the admiral was to oversee an array of top-secret, Art Bell-ish projects that are either the key to a secure future or a "supersnoop's dream,"[32] as William Safire says. Indeed, the menacing nature of Poindexter's portfolio even roused the establishment media from its post-9/11 slumber. The *Washington Post*, usually so solicitous of the bureaucracy, opined that "anyone who deliberately set out to invent a government program with the specific aim of terrifying the Orwell-reading public could hardly have improved on the Information Awareness Office."[33] The Office's slogan—*scientia est potentia*, or "Knowledge Is Power"—might have adorned the office wall of the Cigarette-Smoking Man in *The X-Files*.

Poindexter spoke in an unnerving patois that combined the language of the bureaucrat, the spy, and the creepy voyeur. "We must become much more efficient and more clever in the ways we find new sources of data, mine information from the new and old, generate information, make it available for analysis, convert it to knowledge, and create actionable options," he declared in a speech after assuming his position. And yet he seemed to understand, if vaguely, that the public might not be ready for a Poindextrian surveillance state: "We can develop the best technology in the world," he lamented, "and unless there is public acceptance and understanding of the necessity, it will never be implemented."

TIA, unlike most elements of the Bush administration's War on Terror, was swamped—though not drowned—in criticism. It brushed dangerously close to breaching the wall of recently enacted privacy statutes, among them the Privacy Act of 1974, the Right to Financial Privacy Act, the Fair Credit Reporting Act, and the Electronic Communications Privacy Act. Former senator Gary Hart, who had served with fellow grey eminence Warren Rudman on the U.S. Commission on National Security, called TIA "a huge waste of money" in service of "an Orwellian concept."[34]

The nightmarish vision of TIA consisted of an enormous database on every freeborn American citizen. If you are what you buy, sell, call, type, contract, take pills for, and fly to, well, then the database contained you. Everything but your dreams would be part of this database, and you can bet that DARPA is working on that as we sleep.

"We're just as concerned as the next person with protecting privacy," Poindexter unctuously averred to the *Washington Post*, though columnist Jacob Sullum added the tart postscript—"Maybe, if the next person happens to be J. Edgar Hoover."[35] And like Hoover, the TIA mandarins are unlikely to lose much sleep over the occasional mangling of a few archaic constitutional amendments.

The TIA got off to a rotten start, aesthetically speaking. Its obtuse image-makers chose as its logo an all-seeing eye, a creepy cross between Masonic imagery and something out of a paranoid science fiction movie about evil aliens enslaving earthlings. (The all-seeing-eye logo was later removed during an image makeover.) Speculative talk of the TIA's biosurveillance and biorecognition projects excited and horrified the great mass who were to be surveilled and recognized, but as privacy expert and Emeritus Professor Reg Whitaker of Canada's York University writes, "It is possible to become overalarmed about the Orwellian prospect, especially if one accepts too readily the techno-hype behind it. The intentions may be alarming, but the means of delivering Total Information Awareness are as yet more suspect than enthusiasts like Admiral Poindexter believe."[36]

That's a relief, but it hasn't stopped the flow of tax dollars to TIA-like projects or the scramble for TIA-cut pork chops by the hungry multitude of defense and security contractors.

The TIA's successors are developing methods by which the police and the military can identify persons by their walk, their talk, their irises, their facial features, and even, incredibly, their usual smell. (Who would have thought that flatulence could become a subversive act?) As James Bovard, scourge of would-be police statists, wrote, "The Pentagon issued a request for proposals to develop an 'odor recognition' surveillance system that would help the feds identify people by their sweat or urine—potentially creating a wealth of new job opportunities for deviants."[37]

And others are not quite as sanguine as Professor Whitaker that the TIA's ambition overreaches its capabilities. At the least, it will cast suspicion upon utterly innocent Americans and give them, if not all of us, a taste of life under the total state. "How many innocent people are going to get falsely pinged?" a prominent computer scientist asked the *Washington Post.* "How many terrorists are going to slip through?"[38]

John Poindexter's luck finally ran out. With his almost preternaturally tin ear for inappropriate and ghoulish schemes, he advanced a betting pool whereby defense employees could place wagers on the likeliest targets for terrorist attacks. Surely the Pentagon lunchroom was abuzz: "I'll put a hundred bucks on sarin gas at Disneyworld! I'll raise you two hundred and take a dirty bomb in Times Square! I'll throw in five hundred on two planes crashing into the...ah, never mind."

The Poindexter plan was scuttled not by a John Ashcroft lecture on the immorality of gambling but by monumentally bad press. Poindexter himself rolled snake eyes: he had become a liability and in July 2003 he was deposed, taking retirement in the lush groves of the military-industrial complex. He had best not take any clients in Costa Rica, however, for he is banned from that Central American land for his alleged role in the sale of narcotics to fund the "contras" of Nicaragua in their civil war against the Sandinista government in the 1980s.

Despite the sinister intentions of Poindexter, private firms may very well benefit from limited use of biometrics. Your friendly neighborhood veterinarian might implant a chip in your dog that will help you find Fido when he wanders off. Voice prints and retinal, iris, or face scans can ensure that trespassers don't invade sancta, whether religious, communal, or even commercial. The increased use of biometrics is perhaps inevitable in the private sector. But as technology analyst Wayne Crews says, "No one wants to be treated like a human bar code by the authorities or monitored around the clock by the Homeland Security Department."[39] And that is precisely the threat posed by governmental use of biometrics. For a citizen can opt out of biometrically inclined credit cards or stores. At last check, she cannot announce her secession from the United States of America.

Again, hearken to the words of Justice Louis Brandeis in his eloquent 1928 dissent in *Olmsted v. United States*: the Founders, wrote Brandeis, "conferred, as against the government, the right to be let alone—the most comprehensive of rights and the right most valued by civilized man."[40]

The biometric state confers no such right. It thus stands as a digitized enemy of civilization.

Just as DARPA gave birth, in best Rosemary's Baby fashion, to TIA, so must we expect HSARPA to bear its own brutish offspring. HSARPA is the Homeland Security Advanced Research Projects Agency, created in Section 307 of the Homeland Security Act of 2002.

HSARPA promises to be yet another ATM for the military-industrial complex. In Fiscal Year 2003, its very first year of operation, the agency was showered with $500 million in taxpayer funds, a number that is growing like Topsy as the homeland security establishment bulks up. Empowered to distribute grants to "businesses, federally funded research and development centers, and universities," the primary goal of the HSARPA is "to promote revolutionary changes in technologies that would promote homeland security."[44]

The phraseology fascinates. "Revolutionary changes": These are not usually thought to be desirable in a constitutional republic whose system of checks and balances and federalism discourage "revolution." But we are at war, as our warmakers never tire of reminding us, and as the grim parade of dead bodies, American and Middle Eastern, remind us every night on the television. The big question, it would seem, is whether our venerable Bill of Rights is also in for "revolutionary changes" as a result of the technologies HSARPA is charged with developing. That such a revolution would be at antipodes from the Revolution which established this nation in 1776 seems not to have occurred to the architects of the Homeland Security Act.

Secretary Ridge singled out HSARPA for special mention in lobbying for his fiscal year 2005 budget request. He noted that HSARPA "has already engaged hundreds of private companies and universities in developing new cutting-edge technologies,"[42] which is another way of saying it has expanded the frontiers of corporate welfare.

The Homeland Security Advanced Research Projects Agency sits within the Science and Technology Directorate. (How the fingers of any red-blooded American resist typing the totalitarian-sounding word "directorate.") Since September 2003, the director of the HSARPA has been Dr. David Bolka, whose resume hits all the stops (the U.S. Navy, Lucent Technologies, and Bell Laboratories) on the military-industrial complex highway.

HSARPA is the unlovely begotten child of the unholy alliance of the military and Big Science. In his extraordinary Farewell Address, President Dwight Eisenhower cautioned his heedless countrymen against the "danger that public policy could itself become the captive of a scientific technological elite." He warned against Big Science falling into bed with Big Government: "The prospect of domination of this nation's scholars by federal employment, project allocations, and the power of money is ever present—and is gravely to be regarded."[43]

HSARPA is what happens when you ignore Ike's wise advice. And like the pod people in the science fiction classic, *Invasion of the Body Snatchers*, it just keeps on coming. In 2003–4, HSARPA's parent department awarded 100 students DHS Scholarships and Fellowships; another 100 students were dubbed scholars and fellows of the DHS in the 2004–5 school year. These subsidized scholars have been reduced to the status of bought-and-paid-for researchers for Ike's military-industrial complex. From cradle to grave, or rather from sheepskin to pension, they may travel on the king's shilling. Perhaps they will spend a year or two at one of the DHS's University Centers of Excellence, located in the home district of whichever congresspeople happen to be holding the purse strings at the moment. Then it's off to a rewarding career with Haliburton or some other DHS subsidiary. Of such stuff are homeland security heroes made.

During the 2002 DHS debate, alarms were sounded, vainly, that one byproduct of the department would be the funneling of money to the school that retiring Senator Phil Gramm (R-TX) hoped to lead, Texas A&M. (Presumably the money was not to be spent on bonfire control.) Well, the naysayers, as is their wont, were right on the money. Gramm didn't get the job, but Texas A&M got the loot. And Tom Ridge says the DHS doesn't "do politics"![44]

On April 27, 2004, the Department of Homeland Security issued a press release announcing that "Texas A&M University and the University of Minnesota have been chosen to lead two new Homeland Security Centers of Excellence on agro-security. The Department anticipates providing Texas A&M University, the University of Minnesota and their partners with a total of $33 million over the course of the next three years to address security in two key agricultural sectors—foreign animal diseases and food security."[45]

"Chosen" doesn't quite capture the nature of these awards: The process was as noncompetitive as a Montessori school game of kickball. The Homeland Security Act, Section 308, had directed: "Establish a coordinated, university-based system to enhance the nation's homeland security." The pols took it from there.

Language itself is one of the first casualties of war. In naming these grantees "Centers of Excellence," the Department of Homeland Security and its semanticists committed a masterstroke. For who can possibly oppose a Center of Excellence? Would not the gainsayer thus mark himself as a partisan of lousiness, or at the very best mediocrity?

Texas A&M got the lion's share of the $33 million: $18 million for the study of animal and zoonotic (that is, transmissible from animal to human) diseases. Mr. Gramm got his grant, even though he had by that time retired from the Senate. The Texas A&M Center of Excellence is also called the National Center for Foreign Animal and Zoonotic Disease Defense. By inserting the word "national," its creators assert its perpetual right to a claim on the national treasury. And the word "defense" has long been a key to the exchequer: Witness those impeccable Cold War babies of almost half a century ago, the National System of Interstate and Defense Highways and the National Defense Education Act. Their sponsors sold these costly and perhaps unconstitutional programs by associating the formerly peaceful activities of road building and education with "defense." In 2004, a similar linkage was made to all sorts of pacific studies, including that of animal disease.

The University of Minnesota took its $15 million down payment and created a Center for Post-Harvest Food Protection and Defense. Note, again, the canny insertion of the d-word. It's the closest thing to a guarantee of eternal life this side of getting bitten by a vampire.

Not only does the homeland-security complex swallow education, it gorges itself on previously private companies as well. Penrose Albright, assistant secretary of the Science and Technology Directorate within the DHS, has actually bragged, "There are companies that didn't used to work [for the government] who now do work for Homeland Security. Part of my job is to marshal that huge enterprise for addressing the problems of homeland security."[46] That is to say, part of Penrose Albright's job is to corrupt private enterprise, to tether ever more private firms to the federal government, to slip the poisoned teat of state subsidy into so many private mouths. And this in a Republican administration!

For the most part, Democrats and Republicans alike in Congress have rolled over and played dead when presented with anti-terrorism proposals from the Bush administration. Who wants to be seen as an enabler of bin Laden? But with the Terrorism Information and Prevention System (TIPS), conceived in the dank bowels of the U.S. Department of Justice in the summer of 2002, the Bush team overreached.

When word of TIPS leaked, even the most timorous civil libertarians found their voice. The plan, as the Department of Justice website proclaimed, was to launch "a nationwide program giving millions of American truckers, letter carriers, train conductors, ship captains, utility employees, and others a formal way to report suspicious terrorist activity"[47] directly to the Justice Department. "Our interest in establishing the Operation TIPS program," said DOJ mouthpiece Barbara Comstock, "is to allow American workers to share information they receive in the regular course of their jobs in public places and areas."[48]

In other words, TIPS would set Americans to spying on other Americans in a vast snoop system rivaling that of Cuba, the erstwhile Soviet Union, and other totalitarian states. The friendly neighborhood mailman, the cheery meter-reader, the solicitous cable guy, the salt-of-the-earth truck driver, even the noble UPS delivery person: All were to be part of this spy network. These "volunteer voyeurs," as legal analyst Gene Healy dubbed them, didn't need a warrant, as TIPS constituted an "end-run around the Fourth Amendment."[49]

From a pilot program in ten cities in August 2002, TIPS was slated to expand to include four percent of the population, or 11 million snitches. Rep. Ron Paul called it a sinister program "to use millions of Americans to spy on their neighbors, an idea appropriate for a totalitarian society"[50] but not for the United States of America.

Just what constituted "suspicious" activity was not clearly defined: Reading the works of F.A. Hayek? Underlining passages from *1984*? Decorating the bathroom with anti-Bush posters? Failing to stand while the national anthem blared from the TV set before a baseball game? Why not? After all, the DOJ envisioned the TIPS snitches as having limitless portfolios. If something didn't seem right, they were to report it to the authorities. The DOJ, wrote Robert A. Levy of the Cato Institute in the *Los Angeles Times*, would be buried under "an avalanche of worthless tips."[51] You might find American liberties at the bottom of that avalanche, too.

Unlike the USA-PATRIOT Act, which rolled over a frightened Congress in blitzkrieg fashion, TIPS was stopped—rather like the tank in Tiannenman Square. One after another, members of Congress of both parties stood to denounce the almost unprecedented federal spy program. I say almost unprecendented because only once before in American history, during the harshest repressions of Woodrow Wilson's administration during the First World War, had American citizens been recruited wholesale to spy on other American citizens.

Historian Walter Karp writes, "By August 1917 Attorney General Thomas Gregory boasted that he had 'several hundred thousand private citizens' working for him, 'most of them as members of patriotic bodies...keeping an eye on disloyal individuals and making reports of disloyal utterances, and seeing that the people of the country are not deceived.'"[52] So at least the Ashcroft-Castro snoop tradition has a pedigree.

Wilson's 250,000-member American Protective League, its volunteers decked out in ridiculous tin badges and with the identification cards so fetishized by petty tyrants everywhere, "harassed labor organizers; intimidated and arrested opponents of the draft; and spied on Mexican-American leaders in Los Angeles, pacifist groups, and anti-war religious sects,"[53] as Gene Healy has written. It cast a wide net (six million investigations) but came up with a pathetic catch: a single German spy.

But the American Protective League looked like the ACLU when compared to Bush's would-be 11-million-strong army of home invaders.

No crime need to have been alleged; under TIPS, private citizens were to report any kind of information they chose to report—whether it concerned a fellow American's religion, political persuasion, sexual activities, or even his taste in home furnishings or football teams—to a voracious federal government. TIPS was quite possibly the single most totalitarian measure ever proposed by a prominent American politician, let alone a president of the United States.

And for once, the side of Messrs. Jefferson, Madison, and Mason won. Outrage was so widespread, so ardent, so impassioned, that the administration backed down.

Operations TIPS was foiled—for the nonce—by outgoing Texas Republican Rep. Dick Armey, who amended the Homeland Security Act as such: "Any and all activities of the federal government to implement the proposed component program of the Citizens Corps known as Operation TIPS are hereby prohibited."[54]

TIPS was part of the ominously named Citizens Corps, which the DHS describes as "a variety of programs to engage ordinary Americans in specific homeland security efforts in their own communities."[55] This is an uncomfortable echo of World War I and George Creel's army of civilian bully-boy propagandists. The Snitch Corps might be just as accurate a name.

The Citizens Corps is as yet somewhat inchoate, as its spiritual core (TIPS) has been removed—or so it seems to have been. Its other components include a Medical Reserve Corps, which is an effort that duplicates the far more efficient paramedical services offered by volunteer fire departments across the country; and a Volunteers in Police Service, whose acronym of VIPS is uncomfortably close to the ill-fated TIPS. VIPS, with its patronizing echo of Very Important Persons, would augment police forces with civilian volunteers who would be subordinate to those forces. Neighborhood Watches are a much more effective means of private citizens organizing to police their neighborhoods.

Since the DHS sees its mission as overarching, the citizenry must be enlisted in the crusade. "The Department faces challenges of monumental scale and complexity, but it has no higher purpose than to ensure the security of our people and way of life,"[56] says a typical DHS publication. The people will—they must—help carry out this almost megalomaniacal goal. Spy on the neighbors, send reports to the DHS, march and drill and act in paramilitary ways: This is the role assigned to American citizens. Exercising the right to dissent, even the right to be left alone, is shrinking as an option.

Warns Jerry Berman of the Center for Democracy and Technology: "We have to be very wary. Because of this crisis people are saying, 'Give us security,' and no one wants to leave any stone unturned. So there's a tendency to want to collect, wiretap, share, gather, all this information. But in the past, when our FBI or any intelligence agency has been panicked by a Red Scare or war into that kind of mentality, they've gone overboard and they've ended up not hitting their target in terms of national security, but violating the privacy of Americans."[57]

The line between public and private databases has eroded to the point where the latter often act, de facto, as the former. Take ChoicePoint, Inc., recently rated one of the top 100 fastest-growing technology companies in the United States, with 2003 revenues of almost $800 million. Significantly, almost half of that ($340 million) accrued to the Business and Government Services department.

ChoicePoint, according to a profile by Shane Harris in GovExec.com, owns some 19 billion records on American citizens. These bits of information include criminal, medical, credit, financial, and academic records—many of which are illegal for the U.S. government to collect. Thus, as Harris writes, "an unusual alliance has grown" between the government and companies like ChoicePoint, which conducts background checks on airline screeners for the Transportation Security Administration, identities for the Homeland Security Department, and a variety of tasks for the Department of Defense, the Internal Revenue Service, and other fundaments of the American welfare and warfare states.

ChoicePoint has made some serious mistakes. In 1998, it falsely identified 8,000 persons as felons; they were then purged from the voting rolls of the Sunshine State. In retrospect, Albert Gore wishes they hadn't been. A woman named Mary Boris was awarded $447,000 by a jury (later reduced to $100,000 by a judge) after ChoicePoint incorrectly identified her as a potential arsonist.

The CEO of ChoicePoint, Derek Smith, says that his company is helping "to create a safer, more secure society." You will note that he did not say "freer." In fact, Smith unapologetically refutes Justice Brandeis's assertion that an American has a basic right to be let alone.

"It is the anonymous person, or small group of people, who represent the greatest risks—economic, physical, or emotional—facing us today," says Smith. You have no right to be left alone. You have no right to anonymity. You are a number, and you will be bent, folded, spindled, and mutilated whenever They feel like it.

Predictably, CEO Smith has joined with journalist-attorney Stephen Brill to launch Verified Identity Card Inc., which Brill regards as the forerunner to a "voluntary nationally accepted identification card." Brill's resolve to push this quasi-totalitarian scheme was stiffened, he says, when Clinton national security advisor Sandy Berger, a partner in the ID card scheme, "waited in line behind a deli employee bearing the sandwiches Berger and Brill were about to eat." The indignity of it all! That Sandy Berger should have to wait in line behind a mere deliveryman! ID cards for everyone![58]

Sometimes the most vexing violations of liberty are those that seem, to outsiders, to be routine—just another cost of doing business, or living a life, in a state at perpetual war with a fuzzily defined enemy. Take, for example, the Catholic population of one small community in extreme northwestern Maine. For generations, these Americans have simply walked across the border to avail themselves of medical care, shopping needs, and church services. In this particular region, such services are located exclusively on the Canadian side of the border.

This had never posed a problem before. The U.S. citizens had obtained a form from the INS that amounted to a "cross at will" pass, enabling them to go back and forth whenever they wished. Well, as the cliché goes, September 11 changed everything. Among the things it changed was U.S. border policy. The "Form 1 program" under which the Maine citizens had been able to pass freely to and from Canada was revoked. (Significantly, the Canadian government did not alter its policy.) The Americans had to cross the border at a specified gate, which was locked on evenings and weekends. As a result, Catholics in this small settlement were effectively forbidden to attend Mass.

Northwestern Maine Catholics who took seriously their weekly obligation had two choices: either take a series of backroads through the Maine woods for over 100 miles to reach a different border crossing that was manned on Sundays, or cross illegally. Overwhelmingly, they chose the latter. And they were caught and fined—all for the crime of trying to attend the church which they and their ancestors had always attended.[59]

A small problem? A minor nuisance? A matter to be shrugged off? Or is this a touching instance of the ways in which post-9/11 America is becoming less and less American?

The economist Charlotte Twight has argued that the various components of the USA-PATRIOT Act and the Homeland Security Act, if integrated, add up to a "virtual surveillance state."[60] Just as the barrier between private and governmental databases is being razed, so is the barrier between our private and public selves. To be a citizen is to be one of the surveilled; it is to be a subject, docile in the face of the state's total information awareness. It is to be, sadly, less than an American.

Nothing sends Americans running to the comfort of the Nanny State quite like the fear of Something Awful.

The fear-stokers of the Department of Homeland Security came up with a crudely effective barometer of terror called the color-coded threat level. It is as if we are, henceforth, to live our lives always under the blinking shadow of a traffic signal. Red is the direst of the color codes: It means that a "severe" threat of terrorist attack exists. We have yet to scale the heights of terror to Red as of this writing, though several times the DHS has advanced the threat level from yellow, the color in the middle (which means "elevated") to orange, or "high." The two lowest threat levels, blue and green, remain unused, since they indicate an easing of the terrorist threat and might be taken as a sign that the Department of Homeland Security budget could safely be trimmed.

Even the selection of the colors has attracted criticism. In hospitals, "code blue" means the highest form of emergency, while to the

DHS it means—or would mean if ever we achieved that stress-free state—that vigilance may be relaxed. Moreover, the department attaches to each threat level no set of instructions or advice; just what we are to do with these vague threats is a mystery.

Threat levels rise and fall with no apparent pattern. As Cato Institute defense analyst Charles V. Pena noted, a 2002 FBI warning that al Qaeda was planning an attack on U.S. passenger trains carried with it no corresponding color change. The FBI did add, helpfully, that al Qaeda would be "possibly using operatives who have a Western appearance."[61] That certainly narrows down the range of suspects. For a few weeks, Amtrak was a rolling stock of paranoia. Nevertheless, one Bush administration flack hectored skittish Americans to "continue to ride our nation's rails,"[62] threat be damned. Nothing can stand in the way of Amtrak and eternal profitlessness!

The U.S. invasion of Iraq, which the Pentagon labeled, á la Orwell, Operation Iraqi Freedom, was accompanied by an orange risk threat that bore the name Operation Liberty Shield. The level has also been raised to orange during Muslim holidays and September 11 anniversaries. During the 9/11 alert of 2002, Attorney General Ashcroft informed Americans that the heightened level was the result of threats against targets in South Asia and the Middle East. "We have no specific threat to America,"[63] said President Bush. But it seems that Michael Jackson's treacly pop anthem had come true: We are the World.

As Senior Editor Brian Doherty of *Reason* magazine cogently argues, "the system applies a national standard to what are surely (if they are worth anything) more localized expectations of threats, and muddles every sort of threat into one."[64]

For instance, Senator Susan Collins (R-ME) has said that "the City of Portland spends an additional $5,000 each week in the extra police costs alone whenever the National Terrorism Alert increases to Code Orange."[65]

Thus a rumor of sabotage against, say, the Golden Gate Bridge causes the threat level to be bumped up a color or two, panicking the more credulous residents of Portland, Maine, and depleting their city coffers. The color shift tells us only that somewhere in this vast land a more or less credible threat has been detected; we are all to be made uneasy, our daily lives unsettled, until the threat indicator drops to a more relaxed color. We never knew what hit us—or, more accurately, what did not hit us. But we do know, or we are supposed to believe, that intrepid government officials, selflessly burning the midnight oil and taking risks beyond our imaginings, have kept us from meeting a terrible end. We are grateful to them; we are grateful to Washington; our protector, the state, has come through again. We rest a mite easier, though tomorrow we may once again be thrown into a state of agitation when the color, and our mood, darkens. The one constant is fear. Is this, we wonder at odd and lucid moments, any way to live? Is this America?

The "most visible achievement" of the DHS, as Brian Doherty of *Reason* has written, "has been a kind of public relations campaign calculated to produce a sense of inchoate uneasiness, followed immediately by the equally vague sense that Something is Being Done."[66] What is being done is probably less helpful to the average toiler in the next edition of the World Trade Center than are the more than 1,000 "high-rise kits"[67]—that is, parachutes— that skyscraper workers have bought from one New York company.

Secretary Ridge, his successor, Michael Chertoff, and the Department have committed enough p.r. blunders to rank with James Watt and Earl Butz in the ranks of Cabinet klutzes, but the gravity of his portfolio is such that Ridge has paid no real political price. One of Ridge's most egregious mistakes was his infamous February 2003 advice to Americans that they stock up on duct tape and plastic sheets and wrap their houses in huge prophylactic sheaths to guard against chemical or biological warfare. While a boon for owners of Home Depot stock, the advice was so outlandish as to actually earn Ridge and the DHS hoots of ridicule.

The Department also created a website, www.ready.gov, which offers this piece of Solomonic wisdom: "During a nuclear incident, it is important to avoid radioactive material if possible." Having mastered Survival 101, the web-hopping American citizen is next advised to "Consider if you can get out of the area."

No such equivocation is evident in ready.gov's advice in the event of a chemical attack: "Take immediate action to get away."

Biological attacks can have subtler indicators, as the DHS website helpfully reminds us. Nevertheless, the operative counsel—run like hell!—remains the same: "If you become aware of an unusual and suspicious substance nearby, quickly get away."

Biological attacks do offer opportunities for budding sleuths to do some detective work. Ready.gov urges vigilant citizens with the observational powers of Sherlock Holmes to:

- "Watch for signs such as many people suffering from watery eyes, choking, having trouble breathing or losing consciousness."

Yes, that would be unsettling. Ready.gov further recommends:

- "If a family member becomes sick, it is important to be suspicious."

Creatures of the land, air, and sea also merit watching:

- "Many sick or dead birds, fish or small animals are also cause for suspicion."[68]

Armed with such Solomonic wisdom, the intrepid American is ready for anything.

Yet as Brian Doherty has pointed out, "even the most imaginatively fearful can't help but notice that if our nation is indeed crawling with al Qaeda sleeper agents with the desire and ability to pull off murderous assaults on our way of life, they are sleeping suspiciously soundly."[69]

Where—not to put too fine a point on it, or to tempt fate—are the new 9/11s?

When President Truman was casting about for ways to galvanize the war-weary citizenry in support of the Cold War against the Soviet Union, Senator Arthur Vandenberg (R-MI) famously urged him to "scare the hell" out of the American people. Which he did. And Congress, in turn, passed the Marshall Plan, ratified NATO, and endorsed the separate elements of the Truman Doctrine with overwhelming votes.

Yet Give 'em Hell Harry was the mildest milquetoast compared to the Give 'em Weaponized Anthrax men and women of the Bush war cabinet.

How scared should we be of the terrorist threat?

To put things in perspective, as James Bovard has done in *Terrorism and Tyranny*, the State Department reported that a grand total of 7,745 people were killed by international terrorism between 1980 and 2000. (The State Department defined terrorism as "the use or threat of the use of force for political purposes in violation of domestic or international law."[70]) That's roughly 387 people a year, or fewer persons than are killed annually by carbon monoxide poisoning. Admittedly, that number spiked upward by about 3,000 in

2001, but even with the horrific events of 9/11 and the later hysteria over anthrax, the number of people who die every year of terrorism is dwarfed by those who die in automobile accidents (44,000)—or even boating accidents (800).

In any comparative discussion of those killed tragically or in gross violation of the norms of civilization, one runs the risk of insensitivity. So let me emphasize that even a single death at the hands of a terrorist is a tragedy, an outrage, and that the perpetrator ought to be punished to the fullest extent of the law and our moral code. But as these numbers suggest, terrorism is a minor, almost insignificant factor in the contemporary causes of death, and for the U.S. government to swell its budget, distort its role, curtail the liberties of its citizens, and invite the hatred of the Muslim world in an ill-defined—perhaps undefinable—"war on terrorism" is sheer madness.

"If we try to protect everything, we will in fact protect nothing,"[71] said Rep. Chris Cox (R-CA), chairman of the House Select Committee on Homeland Security.

The exploitation of the 9/11 tragedy has been itself a travesty. Cynical men in the federal government seized on this horrific but isolated incident to fan irrational fears of ridiculously magnified dangers. It was as if America had been reduced to a playpen crammed with 270 million cowering babies.

For a month, six months, a year, two years—even now—yellow journalists, fed by the eager publicity machine of "homeland security," have scared the bejeesus out of us with highly conjectural tales of biological agents gone wild. Plagues, killer bacteria, viruses, and poisons are the death masks worn by our grim future. The sky is falling, the earth is swallowing us up, the very air we breathe and water we drink has become suspect. We are frightened, as a nation, as never before—not even during a real world war, sixty years ago.

If only we could collectively sit back, gather our wits (and scatter our half-wits), and take stock.

We live with risk every day. Some risks are worth worrying over, or taking preventive action against. For instance, the average American faces a one in four chance that he will die of heart disease and a one in seven chance that she will die of cancer. The wise person without a death wish will exercise, not smoke, and have her blood pressure monitored. The risk of dying of such diseases is real; precautions are prudent.

At the other end of the risk spectrum, an American has a one in 240,000 chance of dying of the plague and a one in 730,000 chance of dying of anthrax. He or she is far more likely to die in a snowmobile accident (lifetime odds of 94,000 to one), while scuba diving (41,000 to one), or in a flood (89,000 to one).[72] Yet the Department of Homeland Security and its bioterrorism division are on the bureaucratic equivalent of steroids, while plans for a Department of Snowmobile Safety or an Anti-Scuba Diving Agency have yet to really gather momentum.

These sobering figures are from the Harvard Center for Risk Analysis, whose phone number, alas, does not seem to be in the Rolodex at Fox News. The acting director of that Center, George Gray, and its director of risk communication, David Ropeik, have supplied the antidote to overdoses of hysteria with their 2002 compendium, *Risk: A Practical Guide for Deciding What's Really Safe and What's Really Dangerous in the World Around You.*

"Fortunately," write Gray and Ropeik, "carrying out an attack with biological agents which kills large numbers of people is difficult."[73] To say the least. Even the most determined homicidal nutcases have failed at bioterror. Aum Shinrikyo, a Japanese cult, tried anthrax, botulinum toxin, sarin (a nerve gas), and other bioweapons, without crippling Japan. Their most successful attack, the unleashing of sarin in the Tokyo subway in 1995, killed twelve and injured 3,800 riders.

According to the Centers for Disease Control, six pathogenic microbes—anthrax, smallpox, plague, tularemia, botulism, and viral hemorrhagic fever—are at present the bioterrors from which we have the most to fear. Yet as Gray and Ropeik write,

Distributing these pathogens in a way that exposes large numbers of people is not simple. You don't just brew up some deadly germs in a lab and go somewhere and shake them out of a jar. For most biological weapons to reach more than just a few people, they have to be dispersed in the air. To accomplish that, the agent has to be dried, then ground up or 'milled' into tiny particles that can remain airborne for days, and in some cases further treated to control clumping. These steps take time, money, special equipment, and expertise. They also require sophisticated protective clothing, filters, and containment equipment if the people who want to use them as weapons don't want to become their own first victims.[74]

Anthrax, the disease of sheep and cattle, of the baa-baa black sheep set, took center stage as the national nightmare in the autumn of 2001, when five people died and seventeen fell ill after a sicko mailed anthrax spore-laced letters to a bizarre combination of people in the U.S. government and in the Florida offices of the tabloid the *National Enquirer*. This was, to be sure, a horrific event for the tiny number of persons affected, though we ought not to lose sight of the fact that most survived, as indeed anthrax is very much survivable if one begins antibiotic treatments early enough.

And let us remember that fewer people died in this media-hyped anthrax scare than die in automobile accidents in a typical American day. As with many of the bogeymen of bioterrorism, mass death caused by an anthrax attack is highly improbable. We may as well implement a crash program to defend against a rogue meteor: the risk of a widespread anthrax outbreak is barely more likely.

The threat of smallpox is in many ways more immediate than that of anthrax. Most of us over the age of 40 remember the smallpox vaccines we received in elementary school until 1972. Word that those vaccines had worn off, and would need to be supplemented by booster shots in the event of a recrudescence of this awful disease, bothered even the most stoic among us. After all, wasn't the eradication of smallpox one of the great success stories of modern medicine? No case had been reported worldwide since isolated incidents in 1977 and 1978, and the last appearance of smallpox in the United States was in 1949. Of all the matters that weigh on a worrywart's mind, smallpox had virtually disappeared.

But then came the scare. Smallpox, we were told, could be weaponized; it could be spread by suicidal terrorists. If men and women could be found willing to strap explosives to their torsos and blow themselves up, surely there were madmen out there who would gladly undergo the disfigurement, pain, and torture of a smallpox infection for the sake of mass murder. Or at least we assume there are such madmen: To date, we have no evidence that smallpox is part of the terror arsenal.

Smallpox is a legitimately frightening disease. Some strains are invariably lethal; as Gray and Ropeik note, the disease may have killed "500 million in the twentieth century alone, perhaps twice as many casualties as in all that century's wars."[75] Although vaccination is effective, no cure exists for the unlucky soul who gets smallpox, and perhaps one-third of those afflicted will die. The rest bear indelible scars.

The early symptoms are so ordinary—headache, fever, fatigue—as to scare your typical hypochondriac half to death. And that may be what is most worrisome about smallpox: it, unlike many of the more fanciful bioterrors—is not unthinkable. It once killed with grim efficiency, and with the right set of circumstances it could again claim lives. But the vaccination is 100 percent effective, and any outbreak would be confined to a relatively short period of time. As long as we maintain a basic standard of vigilance, smallpox is not a realistic threat to claim large numbers of lives.

One little-noticed aspect of the bioterror scare is the expulsion of the principle of voluntarism from vaccination. While the vast majority of medical professionals and the preponderance of research attest to the efficacy of vaccination, a small percentage of Americans resist the practice on medical, religious, or personal grounds. And that is their right. Yet Section 304 of the Homeland Security Act, which bears the curiously bland title "Conduct of Certain Public Health-Related Activities," authorizes the Secretary of Health and Human Services, upon the determination that an "actual or potential bioterrorist incident" involving smallpox is occurring or has occurred, to order the "administration of a covered countermeasure to a category or categories of individuals." That "covered countermeasure" is a smallpox vaccine.

Although Section 304 is primarily concerned with protecting the U.S. government, its officials, and pharmaceutical companies from lawsuits filed by the small number of people whose health may be impaired by such a vaccination, "allowing government officials to force people to receive potentially dangerous vaccines based on hypothetical risks" is a "blatant violation of liberty," as Rep. Ron Paul declared. Paul raises the specter of "federal agents"[76] running riot over the countryside, sticking Americans with needles based on mere rumors of smallpox. He may sound alarmist, but then the most pertinacious defenders of liberty have often sounded that way.

Parenthetically, the protection of pharmaceutical companies has been a persistent theme in homeland security legislation, or so say Democratic critics. The legislation creating the DHS gave liability protection to pharmaceutical companies for drugs that might be produced or deployed in a response to bioterrorism.

Sen. Barbara Boxer (D-CA) charged that "a big campaign contributor of the Republican Party was awarded phenomenally." That contributor, Eli Lilly, was said by Sen. Thomas Daschle (D-SD) to have produced "mercury-based vaccine preservatives that actually have caused autism in children,"[77] a matter which some would dispute.

Whatever the link between autism and Eli Lilly's thimerosal, Eli Lilly did contribute more to congressional candidates in 2002 ($1.6 million) than any other drug company. And 79 percent of its contributions were to Republicans, which explains why Democrats, also usually in hock to corporate lobbies, felt fee to take off after the pharmaceutical giant.[78]

Senator Bill Frist (R-TN) defended the provision, saying that "the pharmaceutical companies . . . are the only ones who can make the smallpox vaccine, the frontline for that weapon of mass destruction. . . . Why would they stand out totally exposed for making a medicine that is lifesaving, yes, but . . . one lawsuit can wipe out their whole development process, their whole manufacturing process."[79]

Perhaps sensing that smallpox wasn't scary enough, Sen. Frist also raised the prospect of an Ebola vaccine never making it into circulation if liability protections were not in place. Once you start scare mongering, the sky-that-is-falling is the limit.

The Homeland Security Act includes "no personal, religious, or medical exemptions"[80] from mandatory smallpox vaccines, according to the medical dissidents of the Connecticut Vaccine Information Alliance and Parents Requesting Open Vaccine Education. While the vast majority of us are convinced of the effectiveness of the practice of vaccination, which has saved countless lives over the decades, we ought not to let fear-mongering over the remote prospect of killer-disease epidemics blind us to our heritage of liberty.

Believe it or not, smallpox killed more people in the twentieth century than the plague—or The Plague—has in its various outbreaks throughout recorded history, most notoriously the Black Death of the fourteenth century, in which 25 million people perished in Europe alone.

Contrary to popular belief, the plague, a bacterial disease most often transmitted by rats via fleas, has not been eradicated. Perhaps 3,000 cases are reported each year, of which a dozen occur in the United States. Although no vaccine exists, antiobiotics are an effective treatment if begun early enough, before the onset of shock and delirium. Absent such treatment, more than half of cases of the plague end in death.

Just how deadly a weaponized form of the plague would be is problematic. The Japanese used plague in the form of infected fleas dropped from airplanes against China in the Second World War, with a casualty total in the tens of thousands. More likely, however, it would be "released in an aerosolized form that can be inhaled."

The plague is "much less transmissible than smallpox,"[81] but its enshrinement in (fact-based) myth as the deadliest disease in all of history, the epidemic that almost wiped out Europe, the "red death" described so horrifyingly by Edgar Allen Poe, brings a shiver to even the most imperturbable of people.

So does Ebola, the most feared of the viral hemorrhagic fevers on the CDC list. Subject of horror films and sensationalistic novels, this "monkey virus," whose provenance seems to be Africa, is wrenchingly painful and often fatal. It is transmissible by blood or bodily secretion but not by air, as far as epidemiologists can tell; nor is there a vaccine or effective treatment. As David Ropeik and George Gray summarize, "There is no evidence that these viruses [Ebola and the related Marburg] have been worked on as potential weapons, but they're included on the CDC's list of agents of concern because of their potency and virulence."[82]

In the United States of Amnesia, as Gore Vidal calls our country, we are prone to having no historical memory that stretches back beyond, say, last Tuesday. Bioweapons, bioterror: surely these horrors were born on September 11, 2001. (Even though the terrorists' weapons of choice on that day were prosaic airplanes.)

In fact, bioterror is as old as the smallpox-laced blankets the British and American soldiers gave American Indians in the eighteenth and nineteenth centuries.

For instance, tularemia, a.k.a. "rabbit fever," a slow-developing bacterial disease with a mortality rate among the untreated of 30 percent, was part of the armamentarium of horror of the Soviet Union, Japan, the United States, and probably other military powers of the mid and late twentieth century. The Soviets apparently used it against the Germans, with a terrifying boomerang effect, for the rabbit fever hopped right back into the USSR. Thus it "demonstrates another of the problems of using biological agents as weapons"[83]: To wit, he who unleashes the horror may well have to face it himself.

Another bacterial disease, botulism, has been called "the most potent killer known: one nanogram per kilogram of body weight can be lethal."[84] The disease has been largely wiped out in the United States: there are perhaps twenty-five cases a year, and most are treatable with intensive medical care. If it remains at the margins of public awareness—a kind of "bad mushroom" illness of the sort that everyone has heard about but no one ever contracts—botulism is, perhaps, poised for growth in the terror market.

Tommy Thompson, secretary of health and human services in the administration of the second Bush, has said, "I am more fearful about this than anything else." He was referring not specifically to botulism but more generally to foodborne diseases. Botulism, e-coli, salmonella: we are used to the occasional localized outbreak of these nasty diseases, though they tend to be limited and easily contained. The worst case of purposeful food contamination was the bizarre 1984 episode in which followers of an Oregon guru, Bhagwan Shree Rajneesh, laced a salad bar with salmonella in order to depress turnout by normal people in a local election. No one died, but 751 non-Rajneesh voters got sick.

Bioweapons are effective bogeymen to scare people into supporting ever more massive governmental spending and intrusions, but most dispassionate observers—that is, knowledgeable men and women who aren't trying to sell books or newspapers—doubt their potential for widespread destruction. Airborne contaminants are too dependent upon wind conditions, humidity, sunlight or lack thereof, and a delivery system to pose a credible threat. Contamination of water is even less likely, for "the enormous volume of water that passes through a municipal water system hourly would dilute any agent put into it."[85]

(For folks who need a bit of terror now and then to keep their adrenalin flowing, consider the fact that the *lifetime* odds of dying from the injuries received in a car accident are 1 in 247.[86] Car accidents occur frequently, and the consequences can be very severe. Thus, statistically, the real terrorist is the teenage driver in the souped-up Honda racing down the road alongside us while simultaneously talking on the cell phone and hiking up the volume on the car's stereo. Risk-wise, the teen driver makes bin Laden and all his ilk look like an amateurs.)

Be prepared, as the Boy Scouts say. Yet the preparations implicitly recommended by the hysterical are nigh useless, except as a way to whip up panic.

Duct tape, gas masks, and stockpiles of antibiotics aren't going to save you in the extremely unlikely event of a bio-attack. Unless solid evidence of an imminent attack exists, mass vaccinations are unwise: the chances of a negative reaction outweigh the very improbable chance that one will be exposed to a dangerous biological agent.

In the end, the risk analysts at Harvard offer what is probably the best advice, and it is a simple, commonsensical injunction: "If any outbreak of any disease begins, you can protect yourself simply by not shaking hands, by wearing gloves, or by washing your hands frequently. And a person known to have the disease can limit transmission by wearing a simple paper or cloth mask."[87] Such advice isn't going to make the bioterror lobby rich or fortify the spirits of the Department of Homeland Security, but it should work for the rest of us.

Yet agents and spokesmen of the federal government have wielded the language of fear with a Stephen King-like intensity since 9/11. Not for them the prudent risk analysis of Gray and Ropeik. From the start, the Bush administration promised "an aggressive research and development program" to meet the bioterror threat. "An effective biodefense will require a long-term strategy and significant new investment in the U.S. health care system," according to President Bush's 2002 report "Securing the Homeland: Strengthening the Nation." The President's first post-9/11 budget proposed a 319 percent increase in bioterror spending (from $1.4 billion to $5.9 billion). The needs he outlined were seemingly limitless; they ranged far beyond subsidizing scientific research and included massive spending on "isolation facilities for contagious patients"[88]; antibiotics to treat 20 million people for anthrax, plague, and tularemia; and updating information systems, which is another way of saying that federal dollars will pay for new telephones in hospitals.

The effectively named Project BioShield is growing like Topsy in the fields of bioterror. Described by its supporters as an "initiative that allows the Federal Government to buy critically needed vaccines and medications for biodefense as soon as experts agree that they are safe and effective enough to be added to the Strategic National Stockpile,"[89] Project BioShield's budget swelled from $900 million in fiscal year 2004 to $2.5 billion in fiscal year 2005.

The DHS is expected to purchase up to 75 million anthrax vaccines and possibly even more smallpox vaccines through Project BioShield. Critics point out that it makes more sense to plan for post-exposure treatment, as there would seem to be no way that the citizenry could be vaccinated against every possible contagious disease. But those critics don't control BioShield's purse strings.

Project BioShield is one the several DHS programs suffering from joint custody: though within Homeland Security, it is managed day to day by the notoriously sluggish Department of Health and Human Services.

Rep. David Obey (D-WI) has questioned the effectiveness of dual parentage: Working for both HHS and DHS, he says, "is as if you set up two fire departments in the same town and assigned one to handle arson and another fires caused by accidents."[90]

The bioterror boom had begun even before the Bush administration. In 1998, President Clinton, after reading Richard Preston's page-turning bioterror novel, *The Cobra Event*, gave new stimulus to this dormant field, but it wasn't really until after 9/11 that the skies opened and the heavens rained federal dollars.

Before Clinton picked up his penny-dreadful melodrama, the nation's sole biodefense lab was the U.S. Army Medical Research Institutes of Infectious Diseases. But as of 2004, a "national biodefense campus" is under construction at Fort Dietrick, Maryland. With startup costs conservatively pegged at over $1 billion, this cluster of three laboratories (under the control of the Department of Homeland Security, the U.S. Army, and the National Institutes of Health) joins existing or planned federally subsidized labs at Boston University, the Galveston branch of the University of Texas Medical School, and Rocky Mountain Laboratories in Hamilton, Montana, to create what Rutgers University biochemist Richard H. Ebright calls "an enormous overcapacity" in biodefense research.

The DHS piece of this unholy trinity is the National Biodefense Analysis and Countermeasure Center. A fourth lab is also being considered: Run by the Department of Agriculture, it would study zoonotics, or diseases that spread from animals to humans, those frightful staples of such modern films as *28 Days*. The Department of Agriculture is perhaps not the snuggest fit on this campus: its Plum Island Animal Disease Center is famed for its hoof-and-mouth disease research, while its Animal and Plant Health Inspection Service keeps tabs on the nasty glassy-winged sharpshooter, an insect that carries Pierce's Disease, which wreaks havoc in the vineyards of California. These DOA duties now lie within the DHS, which is rather more interested in glassy-eyed Muslim sharpshooters than the California insect.

In any event, the proposal for the Fort Dietrick campus struck many researchers as so profligate and unwise an expenditure of $1 billion that several spoke out in opposition.

"Influenza kills annually about 50,000 people in this country, but we don't put our money into that," observed Milton Leitenberg of the University of Maryland's Center for International and Security Studies. "We sink it into bioterrorism. We're putting billions of dollars into a putative threat of disputed relevance at a time when there's a shortage of flu vaccine and measles vaccine."

"Bioterrorism is hollowing out public health from within," complained Dr. David Ozonoff, professor of environmental health at Boston University, to the *Baltimore Sun*. "It's much more likely that bird flu will kill millions of people than anthrax."[91] The great bioterror scare of our age, the anthrax-laced letters sent to various media and political personalities in late 2001, killed a grand total of five people.

The leftist journalist Doug Ireland wrote that with the DHS legislation, "Bush completes the militarization of the nation's already strained public health service by putting civilian medical research programs from Health and Human Services into the new department. This means every health crisis, from AIDS to the epidemic of drug-resistant strains of tuberculosis, will take second place to Bush's war."[92]

Just how "strained" and effective this system was and is open to debate; Tom DiLorenzo and I have written skeptically of the public-health bureaucracy and its gargantuan nonprofit allies in several previous works. But Ireland's basic point—that putatively civilian medical and scientific programs are being militarized—is indisputable.

Whereas HHS was once responsible for monitoring and subsidizing counters to bio-terror, the DHS has swiped that turf.

In November 2002, the American Public Health Association passed a resolution soundly based in risk analysis. With an affirmative vote of 95 percent, the APHA declared itself "oppose[d to] the subordination of public health to national defense and antiterrorism" in light of "the hypothetical nature of the risks such [bioterror] attacks might pose to public health, as compared to existing and inadequately controlled problems, such as contaminated food and water and breakdown in immunization rates."[93]

The CDC was among those agencies co-opted, if not swallowed, by the DHS whale. Secretary Ridge said that the centers are now possessed of a "dual infrastructure": They remain, in part, the federal government's prime public health bureaucracy, but "they will now be tasked to do research relative to biochem weapons and the impact on human beings as well,"[94] as Ridge told the House Government Reform Committee.

What is the purpose of scaring the American people half to death with lurid stories of killer viruses, rabbit fever, and The Plague—new Black Deaths to snuff out millions of lives, borne this time not by rats but by something even less hygienic: feral terrorists, crazy-ass Middle Easterners who want us all dead, and in the most gruesome, *Night of the Living Dead* way possible?

Well, listen to Homeland Security Chief Tom Ridge as Christmas Day 2003 approached: "Your government will stand at the ready 24 hours a day, seven days a week, to stop terrorism during the holiday season and beyond."[95]

Forget, if you can, that lifeless politically correct locution "the holiday season." (Ridge is taking on bloodthirsty terrorists but he won't even risk offending a hypersensitive humanist at home? He shakes his rhetorical fist in the bearded face of Osama bin Laden but he won't even utter the word "Christmas"? This is a tough guy?)

P.C. etiquette aside, Ridge's 24-7 promise is really a threat to the American people, not any real or chimerical terrorists. What he is really saying is that the U.S. government, fortified by hundreds of billions of new tax dollars and powers undreamt of by even J. Edgar Hoover, stands at the ready to expand, to inflate beyond all proportion, to become bigger, fatter, and more intrusive, and if you don't like that—if you have the effrontery to complain about this selfless act of protection—then you are not only a coddler of terrorists, an un-American mesmerized by what Attorney General John Ashcroft so chillingly called "phantoms of lost liberties," but you are an ingrate as well!

Rep. John Tierney (D-MA) has made the valid point that "we can't have everybody taking the worst-case scenario and doing our planning on that, because . . . we don't have those kind of resources."[96] But when confronted with a terrifying array of horrific potential epidemics, each promising an unusually painful method of death, who dares pick and choose which studies, which antidotes, should be funded? Why not just fund them all?

That, it appears, is precisely what we will do.

Notes

1.   Martin Anderson, *Revolution* (Orlando, FL: Harcourt Brace Jovanovich, 1988), pp. 273–4.

2.   Ibid., p. 276.
3.   Ibid., p. 277.
4.   Jeff Taylor, "Meal Ticket," *Reason*, www.reason.com, July 22, 2003.
5.   James Bovard, *Terrorism and Tyranny*, p. 317.
6.   "Preserving Our Institutions: The Congress," Continuity of Government Commission, May 2003, p. 4.
7.   "About the Commission," Continuity of Government Commission, www.continuityofgovernment.org, February 10, 2004.
8.   Ibid.
9.   "Preserving Our Institutions: The Congress," p. II.
10. Ibid., p. 14.
11. Ibid., p. 21.
12. Ibid., p. 12.
13. Ibid., p. 25.
14. Ibid., p. 15.
15. Ibid., p. 19.
16. "Statement of Opposition to the Continuity of Government Commission's Proposal by Professor Charles E. Rice," Coalition to Preserve an Elected Congress, www.electcongress.org, undated.
17. "Preserving Our Institutions: The Congress," p. 19.
18. "Statement of Opposition to the Continuity of Government Commission's Proposal by Professor Charles E. Rice."
19. "Preserving Our Institutions: The Congress," p. 28.
20. Ibid., p. 31.
21. Gene Healy, "Deployed in the U.S.A.: The Creeping Militarization of the Home Front," p. 11.
22. "Preserving Our Institutions: The Congress," p. 27.
23. Ron Paul, "The House of Representatives Must Be Elected!" www.antiwar.com, June 4, 2004.
24. Alexander Hamilton, James Madison, and John Jay, *The Federalist Papers* (New York: New American, 1961), p. 327.
25. Michael Isikoff, "Exclusive: Election Day Worries," *Newsweek*, www.msnbc.msn.com, July 19, 2004.
26. Justin Raimondo, "A Scheme to Cancel the Elections?" www.antiwar.com, July 12, 2004.
27. "War Means Rights May Be Scaled Back," *The Guardian*, www.guardian.co.uk, March 19, 2003.
28. Quoted in Timothy Lynch, "National ID Cards and Military Tribunals," *Cato Handbook for Congress* (Washington, D.C.: Cato Institute, 2003), p. 128.
29. William Safire, "You Are a Suspect," *New York Times*, November 14, 2002, editorial page.
30. Quoted in Jacob Sullum, "Poindexter's Laboratory," *Reason*, www.reason.com, November 15, 2002.
31. Gene Healy, "Deployed in the U.S.A.: The Creeping Militarization of the Home Front," p. 8.
32. William Safire, "You Are a Suspect," *New York Times*.
33. Reg Whitaker, "After 9/11: A Surveillance State?" p. 67.
34. Jacob Sullum, "Poindexter's Laboratory," *Reason*.
35. Jacob Sullum, "Poindexter's Laboratory," *Reason*.
36. Reg Whitaker, "After 9/11: A Surveillance State?" p. 68.
37. James Bovard, *Terrorism and Tyranny*, p. 157.
38. Jacob Sullum, "Poindexter's Laboratory," *Reason*.

39.   Clyde Wayne Crews, Jr., "Put Controls on Emerging `Surveillance State,'" www.cato.org, June 23, 2003.
40.   Quoted in Senator Bill Nelson, "Grave Questions of Invasion of Privacy," www.salon.com, November 26, 2002.
41.   "Homeland Security Act of 2002," H.R. 5005, Section 307, p. 35.
42.   "Budget in Brief," U.S. Department of Homeland Security, Fiscal Year 2005, p. 2.
43.   Quoted in Bill Kauffman, "Lunar Skeptics," *American Enterprise*, December 2004, p. 45.
44.   "Bush Using Incumbency to Full Advantage," Associated Press, October 25, 2004.
45.   "Homeland Security Selects Texas A&M University and University of Minnesota to Lead New Centers of Excellence on Agro-Security," U.S. Department of Homeland Security, press release, April 27, 2004.
46.   Pam Zubeck, "The Big Business of Protection Against Terror," *Colorado Springs Gazette*.
47.   James Bovard, *Terrorism and Tyranny*, p. 154.
48.   Robert A. Levy, "United We Stand, But We'll Snoop Divided," www.cato.org, July 25, 2002.
49.   Gene Healy, "Volunteer Voyeurs?" www.cato.org, July 29, 2002.
50.   Ron Paul, "Department of Homeland Security—Who Needs It?" www.antiwar.com, July 25, 2002.
51.   Robert A. Levy, "United We Stand, But We'll Snoop Divided."
52.   Walter Karp, *The Politics of War*, p. 328.
53.   Gene Healy, "Deployed in the U.S.A.: The Creeping Militarization of the Home Front," p. 9.
54.   "Homeland Security Act of 2002," Section 770.
55.   "DHS Organization," U.S. Department of Homeland Security, www.dhs.gov, p. 1.
56.   Ibid., p. 2.
57.   "Unparalleled Access to Private Information," www.abcnews.com, March 17, 2004.
58.   Shane Harris, "Watching People on Behalf of Uncle Sam," www.govexec.com, March 16, 2004.
59.   Hearing of the Senate Governmental Affairs Committee, February 9, 2004, p. 22.
60.   Charlotte Twight, "Homeland Insecurity: Big Brother is Watching You," www.cato.org, December 6, 2002.
61.   Charles V. Pena, "Homeland Security Alert System: Why Bother?" www.cato.org, October 31, 2002.
62.   Charles V. Pena, "Homeland Security: Follow the Bouncing Ball," www.cato.org, May 6, 2003.
63.   Charles V. Pena, "Homeland Security Alert System: Why Bother?"
64.   Brian Doherty, "Life During Wartime," *Reason*, www.reason.com, December 31, 2003.
65.   Hearing of the Senate Governmental Affairs Committee, February 9, 2004, p. 9.
66.   Brian Doherty, "Life During Wartime," *Reason*.
67.   Pam Zubeck, "The Big Business of Protection Against Terror," *Colorado Springs Gazette*.
68.   "The Department of Homeland Security for Dummies," Citizens for Legitimate Government, www.legitgov.com, March 19, 2004.
69.   Brian Doherty, "Life During Wartime," *Reason*.
70.   James Bovard, *Terrorism and Tyranny*, p. 7.
71.   Jordan Carleo-Evangelist, "No Town Left Behind in Terror Funding Flow."
72.   David Ropeik and George Gray, *Risk: A Practical Guide for Deciding What's Really Safe and What's Really Dangerous in the World Around You* (Boston: Houghton Mifflin, 2002), pp. 423–28.

73.   Ibid., p. 186.
74.   Ibid., pp. 186–87.
75.   Ibid., p. 189.
76.   Ron Paul, "Oppose the New Homeland Security Bureaucracy!" www.antiwar.com, November 15, 2002.
77.   "Securing the Homeland," www.pbs.org/newshour, November 15, 2002.
78.   "Department of Excess Profit Security," Ouch!, www.ouch.org/pipermail/ouch/2002.
79.   "Securing the Homeland," www.pbs.org/newshour.
80.   Jennifer Van Bergen, "Homeland Security Act: The Rise of the American Police State."
81.   David Ropeik and George Gray, *Risk: A Practical Guide for Deciding What's Really Safe and What's Really Dangerous in the World Around You*, p. 190.
82.   Ibid., p. 191.
83.   Ibid., p. 190.
84.   Ibid., p. 191.
85.   Ibid., pp. 192–93.
86.   Richard Morin, "Unconventional Wisdom: New Facts and Hot Stats from the Social Sciences," Washington Post, January 16, 2005, p. B5.
87.   David Ropeik and George Gray, *Risk: A Practical Guide for Deciding What's Really Safe and What's Really Dangerous in the World Around You*, p. 193.
88.   George W. Bush, "Securing the Homeland: Strengthening the Nation," pp. 12–13.
89.   "Department of Homeland Security," Office of Management and Budget, Fiscal Year 2005, p. 12.
90.   Guy Gugliotta, "Unintended Tasks Face New Security Agency," *Washington Post*, June 10, 2002, p. A1.
91.   Scott Shane, "U.S. Biodefense Campus Set for Fort Dietrick; 3 Agencies Gain `Synergy,' Security; Critics See Waste," *Baltimore Sun*, February 11, 2004, p. 1A.
92.   Doug Ireland, "Homeland Insecurity," *In These Times*, July 22, 2002, p. 9.
93.   Janlori Goldman, "Balancing in a Crisis? Bioterrorism, Public Health, and Privacy," *Lost Liberties*, p. 169.
94.   Hearing of the House Government Reform Committee, June 20, 2002, p. 42.
95.   Quoted in Robert Crook, "Robert's VIrtual Soapbox (not on the South Beach Diet)," www.blogs.salon.com, December 21, 2003.
96.   Hearing of the House Government Reform Committee, June 20, 2002, p. 32.

7

Is Big Government Back in the Saddle?

Although the Bush administration has emphasized its rhetorical commitment to traditional marriage, Bush policies have thrown together some awfully strange bedfellows. Libertarians and constitutional-minded conservatives have made common cause with the civil liberties movement of the left in protest against excesses in the War on Terror.

The "imperial presidency," once a concern of conservatives appalled by the domestic empire-building of Presidents Roosevelt, Truman, and Johnson, is now equally reviled on the left. Nancy Change, the leftist senior litigation attorney at the Center for Constitutional Rights, rails against the post 9/11 "radical shift of power to the executive branch that has placed the Bill of Rights—with its First Amendment guarantees of freedom of speech, political association, religion, and the press, its Fourth Amendment protections against unreasonable searches and seizures, its Fifth Amendment guarantees of due process and equal protection, and its Sixth Amendment guarantees to criminal defendants of a fair and speedy trial and the right to confront adverse witnesses—in danger of becoming yet another casualty of the 'war on terrorism.'"[1]

As the indefatigable James Bovard has so mordantly written, "The terrorists' success supposedly proved that the federal government needed more power over Americans and practically everyone else in the world."[2]

The War on Terror and the Bush administration's prosecution thereof have been simply disastrous for the Republican Party, at least from a perspective that cherishes limited government. Old-timers and antiquarians—say, those whose historical memories stretch back beyond 9/11/01—will recall that Republican politicos once made fine speeches insisting upon the primacy of individual rights, free markets, and a government strictly limited to its constitutional functions. Sure, the GOP was awash in hypocrisy—at many points in our history, the Democrats have actually been the party of governmental restraint—but still, since the era of the New Deal the Republicans have incorporated personal liberty and attacks on Big Government as tried-and-true themes.

No longer.

The age of Republicans as at least fitful foes of the overweening state died somewhere between George W. Bush's lips and the teleprompter. Under the spur of homeland security, the party has jettisoned its commitment to a limited government; indeed, partisans now attack those who doubt the need for an ever larger and more intrusive state.[3]

Even those think tanks aligned with the Republican Party have adopted an essentially LBJ-ish orientation: They favor greater spending on the military, on foreign wars, and on domestic policy initiatives, though when possible they insert words like "Opportunity" and "Faith" into their Big Government programs on the homefront. Or—excuse me—in the homeland.

Take the Heritage Foundation. Born in 1973 as the flagship think tank of the "New Right," which was once the bug-eyed bogeyman to all good liberals everywhere, Heritage was a fairly reliable voice for deregulation and decreased spending on domestic programs. They were largely co-opted by the Reagan administration and have been ever since ensconced firmly in the GOP's right pocket, but Heritage finally abandoned any vestigial interest in restricting leviathan under the administration of George W. Bush.

The Heritage Foundation's research papers in the age of Bush II read like those ground out by, say, the establishment liberal Brookings Institute during the heyday of Cold War liberalism. Spend, spend, spend. Regulate, regulate, regulate.

Typical of this new mindset among Republican think tanks was Heritage Executive Memorandum #897, "Harmonizing House and Senate Appropriations for Homeland Security," an August 20, 2003 paper by James Jay Carafano, whose verbose tagline informs us not only that he is a Ph.D. but that he is Senior Research Fellow for National Security and Homeland Security in the Kathryn and Shelby Cullom Davis Institute for International Studies at the Heritage Foundation.

Mr. Carafano, Ph.D., is pleased that "federal homeland security spending increased by some 240 percent after the September 11 attacks," but he worries that Congress—that parsimonious, penny-pinching old Congress that we all know so well—"must ensure that key initiatives are not shortchanged."[4] (Walter Mondale never said it better.)

The Heritage fellow demands that the House and Senate conferees "Increase spending on Coast Guard modernization,"[5] a phrasing borrowed from the neoliberals of the 1980s, who tried to sell the same old New Deal-Great Society programs by adding the word "modernization"—as though buying new stuff and using trendy M.B.A. jargon revitalizes tired old warhorses.

"Give the TSA time," pleads the Heritage fellow—no more bureaucracy-bashing at the think tank of a secure homeland! And to think that even the most timid Republicans once made fun of the federal transportation complex.

Carafano insists that Congress must "Support robust research and development," which Heritage used to call pork in more innocent times. "[T]he DHS will have to create new research and development (R&D) capabilities."[6] This, too, is straight out of the neoliberal playbook. Gary Hart, Michael Dukakis, Bruce Babbitt: They said it first, and better. Federal R&D is nothing more nor less than federal subsidization of universities, business, and middle-class engineers. But then Republicans seem not to have any philosophical objection to federal subsidies in the New Age.

Finally, Carafano implores Congress to "express its intent that the DHS create national standards for emergency preparedness."[7] Again, this is so contrary to what once was the standard "conservative" view that one feels as though the political universe has flipflopped. The Right, or at least the Beltway Right, wants "national standards." No more local diversity, variety, experimentation in those laboratories of democracy which we once held states and localities to be. No, now Washington calls the tune. It pays the piper, after all, and will pay him ever more handsomely if the Republicans and their think tanks get their way.

The Heritage Beltway Right has gone over almost completely to the statist side. "Major investment is necessary" declares a Heritage Backgrounder on the DHS, using the language of welfare-state Democrats. They are also obsessive executive-branch expanders. Countless are the complaints about congressional "micro-managing,"[8] which is just another word for the legislative branch carrying out its constitutionally prescribed duties.

As the presidential campaign of 2004 got into full swing, former President Ronald Reagan died after his tragically long struggle with Alzheimer's Disease. Reagan was eulogized in the usual flowery language, but despite President Bush's effort to don his mantle, it didn't quite come off. Yes, there is an enormous gap in articulateness between the Great Communicator and the cringe-inducing orator that is Bush. But the real problem was that the Republican oratory for which Ronald Reagan was known, with its emphasis on liberty, freedom, and hopefulness, is absent from the Party of Homeland Security. Reagan's oft-quoted remark that government is the problem, not the solution, would get him booted out of the Bush ranks faster than Michael Moore at a Young Republicans' keg party. Government, in the middle years of the first decade of the twenty-first century, is the solution—or so insist the new breed of Republicans. Ronald Reagan—and especially his soaring oratory of liberty—would have no place in the party of George W. Bush.

Dissent, which our forbears regarded as an obligation, as a civic duty, as a civic pleasure, even, is becoming a "privilege" to be revoked at the whim of Attorney General Gonzales or George Bush. The word "liberty" disappears, replaced by the more nebulous "freedom," which is what our soldiers are always said to be defending whenever they are scattered to the four corners of the globe. C'mon, Washington could deploy half a million troops to Antarctica to wipe out the penguin population and the flacks and publicists of the system would trumpet the servicemen and women as heroes "defending our freedom." Dissent, complain, even clear your throat at the wrong time and you would be a penguin-lover who is abusing the "privilege" of "freedom." The patriot can only sit back, chuckle grimly—and redouble his or her efforts on behalf of real American liberty.

The typical American, upon hearing the phrase "war on terror," thinks of a focused military effort to wipe out al Qaeda and those responsible for the 9/11 attacks. Although such a war may have collateral effects upon the politics of the Middle East, these are not essential to its successful prosecution. Get the bastards who sponsored the hijackers of 9/11, eradicate their funding sources, and then let us to return the U.S. to being a "normal country," in the words of Ronald Reagan's National Security Advisor, Jeane Kirkpatrick.

If only that could be. Alas, just as marches inevitably attract nuts and oddballs of all shapes and sizes—and distressingly photogenic, too; they are irresistible to newspaper and network photographers and cameramen—so does a war gather behind it an array of world-changers and Men Who Would Be King, all of them eager to steer the war-hardened ship of state in the direction they prefer. And just as a march takes on a life of its own, its personality drawn from the characters who seize the microphones and chant for the reporters, so does a war often have consequences very different from the stated aims of those who prosecute it. Woodrow Wilson didn't entangle us in the First World War with the ulterior motive of imposing Prohibition from sea to thirsty sea, but that's what happened. Harry Truman didn't foresee the Vietnam debacle when he staked out the U.S. position in the Cold War, but that is where events led.

So, too, with the War on Terror. Or perhaps especially with the War on Terror, since it has been defined so nebulously, so indefinitely. We have been told by Vice President Cheney that this war is a more or less permanent condition; thus the USA-PATRIOT Act and other deformations in the U.S. polity are explicitly not temporary. We are in this for the long haul, or so they say. And over a long haul, anything can happen.

Listen, for instance, to what the most influential liberal supporters of the Terror War and its manifold foreign and domestic features have to say about their goals. Paul Berman, who like so many of the pro-war liberals was a youthful socialist whose political views today are still barely distinguishable from socialism, is regarded as perhaps the leading intellectual light of what we might call the War Liberals. In his widely heralded *Terror and Liberalism* (2003), Berman calls for a "liberal American interventionism," which he sees as the logical extension of the War on Terror. The working-class kids from Akron, the rural boys from Oklahoma, and the kids from the barrios and ghettoes of San Antonio and Detroit who enlisted in the armed forces after 9/11 may have been motivated by a praiseworthy patriotism, or by a desire to avenge the rivers of blood that spilled from the Twin Towers, but what they really signed up for will come as a rude surprise. Berman, who rejoices in "the panorama of the Terror War" as though it were a magic-lantern show, sees it as engendering a "Third Force" role for the U.S. military. This Third Force activism will be "different from the conservatives and the foreign policy cynics who could only think of striking up alliances with friendly tyrants; and different from the anti-imperialists of the left, the left-wing isolationists, who could not imagine any progressive role at all for the United States."

Having caricatured the views of his opponents beyond recognition, Berman turns to the new role of the U.S. military. It is to be a "Third Force devoted to a politics of human rights and especially women's rights, across the Muslim world; a politics of ethnic and religious tolerance; a politics against racism and anti-Semitism, no matter how inconvenient that might seem to the Egyptian media and the House of Saud; a politics against the manias of the ultra-right in Israel, too, no matter how much that might enrage the Likud and its supporters; a politics of secular education, of pluralism, and law across the Muslim world; a politics against obscurantism and superstition; a politics to out-compete the Islamists and Baathi on their left; a politics to fight against poverty and oppression; a politics of authentic solidarity for the Muslim world, instead of the demagogy of cosmic hatreds. A politics, in a word, of liberalism..."[9]

Well. Isn't that ambitious? We can be sure that Mr. Berman won't be shouldering a rifle in forcing these wonderful gifts upon the Islamic people, but as he would no doubt point out, the pen is mightier than the sword anyway. As Ed Crane and William Niskanen of the Cato Institute have observed, "Merely living in a free society appears to be insufficient for neoconservatives."[10]

The sheer bulk of a military-industrial complex large enough to remake the entire Islamic world might brighten the cold hearts of Grumman, Lockheed, and Haliburton, but it would leave us with budgets so elephantine as to make George W. Bush and Lyndon Baines Johnson look like skinflints. The agenda of Berman and the War Liberals, who had influential positions in the campaigns of both Albert Gore in 2000 and John F. Kerry in 2004 and will of course be well represented in the coterie of the Democratic candidate of 2008, is gape inspiring in its breadth. It calls for no less than the eradication of Islam as a religious force. Muslims are to be secularized as thoroughly as, say, European Catholics or Jews. They are to be forced to give up their own religious—and private—schools, and send their children to secular schools (administered perhaps by young Americans?) at which they will be taught that their parents' religious beliefs are "superstition." Western notions of "women's rights" are to be forced upon Muslims, at gunpoint; and though Berman did not enumerate it, one should have no doubt that this Third Force of righteous bomb-dropping liberalism will also introduce Islamic villages to such novel concepts as gay marriage.

The Bush administration's Department of Justice may have useful tips for those mandarins whose charge it will be to enforce Bermanian thought control across the Middle East. At home, conscription will be necessary to fill the foreign legions that will occupy the Middle East until its denizens have been reschooled. We might also conscript an army of bureaucrats to direct the War on [Middle Eastern] Poverty foreseen by Berman. We may expect it to have the same level of success as the War on Poverty begun stateside four decades ago.

Through the wars in Iraq and Afghanistan we can see, dimly and grimly, the outlines of this policy. Consider the bounties delivered— or at least promised—unto Arabia, the Levant, and the entire Middle East courtesy of the U.S. taxpayer: 1,000 newly built schools in Iraq, 14 women's centers in Afghanistan, a major Kabul-Kandahar-Herat Highway in Afghanistan. Western life, Western thought, Western technology, Western ideology: exported not through the natural workings of free trade but at the point of a gun.

"You can put no price on security," says National Security Advisor Condoleezza Rice. Yes you can. The price can be measured in record budget deficits, lost liberties, and a central government that is growing beyond the dreams of the most fervent statist.

Have Americans really signed on to the War on Terror? Are they ready and willing to send the next generation of young people halfway across the globe to fight for the "democratic socialism" of Berman and the Democrats—or for the open-ended "war on evil" of Bush and the Republicans?

I would like to think not.

"When every hometown is secure, the homeland will be secure,"[11] was Secretary Ridge's favorite adage.

It is just as accurate to say that when the Bill of Rights is secure, our liberties are secure. When government is confined to its proper and constricted sphere, our polity is secure. And when the vast pork barrel known as homeland security is finally exposed as the expensive scam that it so manifestly is, our pocketbooks will be pleasingly heavier.

Don't hold your breath waiting for that day. But neither should we despair. America was built on hope, on optimism, on a belief in the capacity of ordinary people to live freely and peaceably with their neighbors, without an intrusive state ordering them hither and thither.

"This is a mission that will never end,"[12] said Secretary of Homeland Security Tom Ridge. That, at least to those of us who still take seriously American liberties, is one hell of a threat. We had best be ready to meet it.

Notes

1.   Nancy Chang, "How Democracy Dies: The War on our Civil Liberties," *Lost Liberties*, p. 35.
2.   James Bovard, *Terrorism and Tyranny*, p. 63.
3.   As James Bovard, "Free-Speech Zone," p. 14, notes the the neoconservative media, from Fox News to the *Weekly Standard,* advance positions precisely opposite those which have been traditionally associated with conservatism. Indeed, some openly embrace a police state. The *New York Sun,* daily organ of neoconservatism in Gotham, urged the New York Police Department to "send two witnesses along for each participant [in a February 2003 antiwar protest], with an eye toward preserving at least the possibility of an eventual treason prosecution." Not to put too fine a point on it, but these people hate liberty.
4.   James Jay Carafano, "Harmonizing House and Senate Appropriations for Homeland Security," Heritage Foundation Executive Memorandum #897, p. 1.
5.   Ibid., p. 2.
6.   Ibid., p. 4.
7.   Ibid., p. 3.
8.   Michael Scardaville, "Emphasize How, Not How Much, In Domestic Preparedness Spending," Heritage Foundation Backgrounder No. 1628, February 27, 2003, pp. 1–2.
9.   Paul Berman, *Terror and Liberalism* (New York: Norton, 2003), pp. 189–90.
10.   Ed Crane and William Niskanen, "Upholding Liberty in America," www.cato.org, June 24, 2003.
11.   Testimony By Governor Tom Ridge, House Select Committee on Homeland Security, July 15, 2002, Federal Document Clearing House, p. 7.
12.   Siobhan Gorman, "Homeland Security Still Seeking to Define, Measure Performance."

Index